*Harold, ya don't know the trouble I'm in.
It's jus awful. I'm warning ya. The 13th year
is scary. I'm stuck here in a dinky ol place
called Haderslev and gotta stay at my
uncle's house fer about 3 months, maybe
longer. It's a torture. It's all gotta do with
that they don't think I know nothing.*

*This is a rotten time and a terrible hardship.
Course it ain't half as bad as in the pioneer
days, but pioneers had exciting hardships
and mine are so grim and dismal.*

*Anyways it's better than going to public
school. My uncle is what ya might call a
gentleman. We didn't have any of them in
Junction and who needed them anyways?*

LARGE COVER PHOTO
Danish Summer School 1933, Junction City, Oregon

Top row, left to right:
Marie Aasted, Elsie Reerslev, Agnes Nielsen, May and Marie Lauridsen, Alfred Larsen, Visti Favrholdt, George Mikkelsen and teacher E.M. Favrholdt

Middle row, left to right:
Esther Nielsen, Helga Reerslev, Xenia and Vita Favrholdt, Dorothea Larsen

Bottom row, left to right:
Otto Larsen, Einar Skovbo, Clarence and Clifford Mortensen, Jim Hansen, Ingvard Skovbo, Marion Jensen

SMALL COVER PHOTO
Realskolen, Kolding, Denmark

Junction City
to Denmark

A BOYHOOD JOURNEY

Visti Favrholdt

DANISH AMERICAN HERITAGE SOCIETY

JUNCTION CITY TO DENMARK

Published by
Danish American Heritage Society
29681 Dane Lane, Junction City, Oregon, U.S.A. 97448

Printed by
Sudden Graphics Ltd.
Richmond, British Columbia, Canada V7A 4V5

ISBN: 0-9652961-0-5

First Printing, June 1996

Printed in Canada

Printed on recycled paper

Thanks to Harold
for keeping all our childhood
correspondence in a shoebox
for more than half a century.

PREFACE

Oregon first captured the attention of American and European explorers during the last decade of the 18th century. They began to trade for furs with the Native American peoples who had lived in the region for thousands of years. The existence of two early non-native settlements, as a direct result of the fur trade, were Fort Astoria and Fort Vancouver. The first Euro-American settlers (Canadians of French, English and Scottish extraction) in Oregon were those who retired from the Hudson's Bay Company and settled in the Willamette Valley near Champoeg.

New England missionaries focused their attention on Oregon in the 1830's, leading to the establishment first, of missions, then farms, in the Willamette Valley near Salem. Non-mission related settlers soon followed. The American population increased significantly as a result of the large wagon train emigrations in the 1840's.

By that time the question of whether Great Britain or the United States was to annex Oregon was no longer postponable. In 1818 Great Britain and the United States had agreed on joint occupancy for the region. Citizens of either country could settle there. In 1846, the dispute with Mexico over Texas was coming to a head and President James K. Polk decided it was time to settle the boundary dispute with Great Britain. The two countries extended the existing boundary along the 49th parallel to the Pacific Ocean.

In order to encourage Americans to move west and fill up the empty country (the Native American population having been decimated by disease), the United States Congress passed the Donation Land Act in 1850. This law (exempting Black Americans, Hawaiians and full-blooded Indians), allowed a married couple to take ownership of 640 acres of land, providing they had lived for four years on the land before 1850. Couples moving to Oregon after that date and until 1858 could claim 320 acres of land. The consequence of the law was that before the Civil War, most of the good land in the Willamette Valley was occupied by Americans of European descent. Another consequence was that Oregon was rather thinly settled. A relatively small number of settlers had claimed a huge percentage of available land. The size of Oregon's population did, however, warrant admission as a state in 1859.

Obviously, many Americans who settled in Oregon were of foreign birth. Some foreign-born immigrants founded 'colonies' just for themselves and their fellow countrymen. Bohemians settled in Scio and Malin. Finns, Norwegians and some Swedes settled in Astoria. Chinese worked the gold fields and founded a short-lived colony in John Day. At the turn of the century Japanese began farming along the Columbia River.

Danish immigrants, after first living elsewhere in the United States and Canada, founded two 'colonies' in Oregon. Both were founded at the turn of the century - Danebo at the west edge of Eugene and another, established in 1902 in and around Junction City, some 15 miles north of Eugene.

Junction City, after existing for a number of years as an unincorporated community, became an incorporated town in 1876. It was a typical pioneer and railroad town with a population of about 800 when the developer and realtor from Withee, Wisconsin, A.C. Nielsen, took an option on 1600 acres and began to advertise land for sale, exclusively to Danish immigrants. The advertisements were placed in Danish language newspapers. Within two years there were about 30 Danish families. Eventually, over 100 families from Denmark moved to the area around Junction City. The majority of them were farmers.Within the city itself, Danes comprised a very small percentage of the residents.

Immigrant Danes of Junction City founded a Lutheran congregation, and soon established Danish Brotherhood and Danish Sisterhood lodges, a Danish language lending library, and other Danish clubs and activities.

The Danish church for the first three decades of its existence called pastors who were born and educated in Denmark. Among them was E. M. Favrholdt who had been a pastor in Danish churches in Manistee, Michigan and Vancouver, British Columbia. In 1930 he accepted a call to Junction City and moved there with his family. These were depression years. The salary was meager. By 1933 Favrholdt decided to apply for a more secure position in Denmark where the churches were administered by the state and salaries paid by the government.

Therein lies the background for the boyhood journey of Pastor Favrholdt's oldest son, Visti, who was thirteen at the time. Visti had grown up in the United States and Canada. He spoke no Danish. All his boyhood friends were as American as Tom Sawyer. To leave everything behind for a new life in Denmark was not only psychologically devastating but put him on the defensive. He idealized Junction City and maintained his emotional connections there by writing letters to his friend, Harold Bruce.

Fifty years later Harold discovered the letters in a shoebox and returned them to Visti. The letters form the core of the book *Junction City to Denmark* and makes it unique - for a number of reasons. Firstly, the move from one country to another is rarely recorded by a teenage boy. Secondly, the letters record so movingly the discontent caused by departure from what was remembered as a boyhood paradise. And thirdly, the letters vividly describe life in Junction City and Denmark during the third and fourth decade of this century from the point of view of a sensitive youngster with sharper than usual powers of observation.

The Danish American Heritage Society is pleased to serve as the publisher of a story which not only has historical significance but also moves one to tears and laughter.

> *Gerald Rasmussen, President*
> *Danish American Heritage Society*
> *Junction City, Oregon*

CHAPTER ONE

Junction City, in the early thirties, was a small, sleepy town located in the Willamette Valley of Oregon. With a population of only a few hundred, it could hardly be called a city. But the forefathers had visions of a major railroad and highway junction at this location, providing prosperity and a great future for all. As it was, the railroad went straight through town and trains seldom stopped there. Likewise, the two-lane concrete highway called Highway 99, coming down from Harrisburg to the north, crossed the tracks at Main Street, creating a junction of sorts, but there was very little out of town traffic - at the very most, maybe five cars an hour. It was in Eugene, fourteen miles farther south down the highway, that the so-called junction took place, whatever it entailed. Junction City was a mere whistle-stop.

As an eleven year old boy, these problems were of no importance to me. It was much more important to practise shooting tin cans off a fence with a slingshot - a finely crafted weapon, created out of a wooden crotch from a tree, preferably an oak tree, complete with two attached heavy duty rubber bands and a leather pouch. Every responsible boy had one, hung around his neck for visual impact or stuck in his pocket for instant use. It was a necessary item in our continuous battle with our enemy, the Moore gang, who lived in the area between the Oregon Electric railroad tracks, a block from our house, and the Southern Pacific railroad tracks over on Front street. The enemy gave us a purpose - a purpose to form the Hornibrook gang, build a wooden clubhouse with a lookout tower, have secret meetings to plan strategy and to rally the forces when danger became apparent. We never encountered the enemy as a gang but the potential was there. There were a few dubious kids around that we had to keep our eye on. The fact that we all attended the same school - the only grade school in the town, didn't stifle our resolve or imagination. We had a job to do - to protect our turf.

For my father, these territorial problems were of no importance. He had more serious things to be concerned about - such as how to feed a family of eight with the Depression going on. He was the Danish Lutheran minister in Junction City, blessed with a hard working wife and six children - three girls and three boys, of whom I was the eldest. He and his blessings needed continuous financial help from the faithful but poor congregation, mainly made up of farmers from the surrounding area, who themselves were in need of help.

We lived in a house at the corner of Seventh Avenue and Ivy street which was known as the parsonage. Next to the house was the church meeting house. Both structures faced Ivy Street which was also Highway 99. The parsonage was an older house, a one storey affair with a large front porch called a veranda and a entrance door that led into what we called the front room, but what others would refer to as 'the parlor.' Unlike the traditional use and purpose of a parlor, being a place to receive guests and conduct polite conversation, this room was our living room, dining room and playroom all in one. The large dining room table was the centerpiece of the house. It was where we were together for meals, where ironing and sewing took place, where homework was done, and where we worked out jigsaw puzzles and listened to stories being told by my father. To the right of the front room was a door that was often closed. It was the door to the study, a small cozy room with bookshelves loaded with books, a desk, a chair, and with a window that looked out on to our garden with fruit trees. It was here in this room that Sunday sermons were prepared.

My father, whom we called Daddy, spent many hours in the quiet study working on his sermons. We had great respect for what he was doing. I knew at the time that the preparation of sermons was serious business, because it helped put bread on the table and save the souls of other people. My mother constantly reminded us to keep as quiet as possible and avoid using the front room, when Daddy was preparing sermons - which was mainly Thursdays, Fridays and Saturdays. We were to behave like angels.

Beyond the front room was my mother's world - the kitchen, where she spent ten hours a day, seven days a week, slaving away, never complaining and always happy. It was here we children could register our complaints, receive comfort and love and be on our way again. Every second day, eight loaves of white bread came out of the wood burning kitchen stove - a total of 1460 loaves a year. I remember thinking at the time, that if my father and mother could only figure out how Jesus managed to feed the five thousand on a couple of loaves of bread, it would save her a lot of work, yet this was only a fraction of what had to be done in the kitchen. We, as my father often pointed out, were bestowed with many blessings. However, I did not feel that there were very many in the kitchen. Only my mother herself, but no blessings in the form of laborsaving devices. There was only the stove, the kitchen sink, a table and the cupboards with food, dishes and cutlery. The house also had three bedrooms and a bathroom off the kitchen. Beyond the kitchen was the outside screen door to the backyard, to the woodshed and grape arbor, to my dog, Blackie and to a tremendous, large woodpile. The woodpile was like a mountain - or so it seemed to me, because it was my job to chop wood daily for the kitchen stove.

Directly across the street from the parsonage was our church. It was a white painted, wooden building, rectangular in shape and with a pitched shingle roof. There were four Gothic-shaped windows on each side, a bell tower in front with a high spire and with entrance doors below. From the outside, the church looked quite modest, almost humble in appearance. But on the inside it was even more so. The entrance area was small with space for only about six people at a time. A second set of doors from the entrance area opened into the church which had a wooden floor, wooden pews and a black belly stove half way down the centre isle to one side. The belly stove featured a six inch, black stove pipe going right up through the roof - at least twenty feet above the floor. To prevent the pipe from collapsing, a few wires, tied to the pipe, criss-crossed the room to the side walls. A simple organ that had seen better days, was situated on a platform to the left of the altar. The altar itself was raised one step above the church floor. It was very plain. There was a white statue of Jesus, a lace covered table with candles, the open Bible and a surrounding railing. Visually, it had a very quieting effect, but mostly for those of the congregation who sat in the pews in front of the belly stove. For others seated at the back, the long black stovepipe seemed to not only distort the view, but became the focal point of the church decor. On cold days the belly stove provided more comfort than anything else.

To the right of the altar, close to the first pew row and elevated six feet above the floor, was the all-overpowering pulpit. It was served by a staircase from behind and its configuration dominated everything, like the bow of a ship. From here every pew could be seen - even the row behind the belly stove. Or perhaps I should say, from every pew one could see the pulpit. However, as a boy, it seemed the other way around. The church door was never locked. As my father said, the church was a place for the tired, the weary and for those in spiritual need - and they were welcome any time.

Although the parsonage, the church and the small one-storey meeting house were located along the main highway and only two blocks from the center of town, it was a quiet neighborhood - particularly in the afternoons with hardly a soul around. On hot summer evenings, looking up and down the street, there would be no one in sight, except an old lady sitting in her rocking chair on her front porch across the street about three houses down towards Main Street. She was always there. Occasionally a car would pass by, but not very often. I figured that a beetle could cross the highway at almost any time and stand a very good chance of reaching the opposite sidewalk without getting squashed.

A couple of times a week, from a house across the street from the church on the north side, the sound of a kid learning to play the trumpet would disturb the serenity of the warm summer evenings. His name was Francis. From what I heard, he was supposed to practise every day. Twice a week was enough. It was always the same tune: *Tell me the tales that to me were so dear- long, long ago, long, long ago.*

As a boy in Junction City, I had lots of time for play and daydreaming. Being part of a large family with Daddy to guide us along and Mom to keep tummies full and clothes clean, we children had little to complain about. But complain we did - about too much homework, about teasing each other, about taking each others toys and so on. Even Daddy complained - about too much noise in the house. The only cool head was Mom. She always managed to solve all complaints, except the noise problem. If we persisted in our complaints or worries, her answer was 'Don't worry, you'll soon be dead.' Although we would never dream of complaining to Daddy, he did on occasion solve a problem by saying, 'In Heaven all is well.' It didn't seem to help us much, but I understood his point. He was implying that angels have no worries. Secretly, I felt they had a lot of worries, for the simple reason that they were perched on fluffy clouds with little harps. That would be okay for a short while, but in the long run it could become extremely boring - especially if it went on forever and ever. Also, not everyone is born musical. I think I had good reason to think the way I did at the time, because all the pictures of angels in our picture books showed them on fluffy clouds with harps. They were also nude and sprouted small wings; wings which, definitely, were far too small to allow them to become airborne.

Daddy was regarded with great respect. He was quite stern, extremely impractical and knew very little of how to bring up children. He left it all to my mother. Only in so-called serious matters would his judgement be called upon - like the time I picked all the apples off the apple tree in the early summer instead of in the late fall. In cases like that my mother would say, 'Wait until your Daddy hears about this!' Just the anticipation of a stern lesson in obedience and the traditional spanking was in itself punishment enough.

His verdict was also required by my mother when it was discovered that we children had gone over to Miller's Funeral Parlor across the street on a number of occasions during a service. By mingling with friends of a deceased who were paying their last respects, we could file passed the open flower-decorated coffin and see what the body looked like. A stern lecture on respect for the dead followed.

Being a preacher involved much more than preparing the weekly sermon. My father also had to conduct baptisms, funeral services and visit the sick and needy. Our church was not the only church in town. There were four others, all with very poor attendance. It was said that if all the people in Junction City went to church, the town would be empty on Sunday mornings. But it was the Depression. Things were not normal.

CHAPTER TWO

My parents came to the United States in 1923 as immigrants from Denmark. My sister, Xenia and I tagged along. I was three at the time and Xenia was one. Our family name was Favrholdt. My father was Danish and my mother was English. They met in England, where he was attending a theological course. Moving back to Denmark, he found work as a newspaper journalist but got in conflict with the editor as to how newspaper articles should be written, and decided to emigrate to the United States. His father, a farmer in Jutland, knew a Danish bishop in Chicago, and so that city became our destination.

Upon arrival my father tried to get work as a journalist but ended up working in a shoe store. Having to kneel in front of customers when fitting shoes, an inspiration gradually took form, resulting in a 'call' to become a church minister - something you feel inside we were later told, and so he took up theological training in his spare time. Eventually, he became officially ordained by the Danish bishop in Chicago.

In Denmark, where the church was under the state and financed by the taxpayers, this brief training for the ministry would not have been considered satisfactory or sufficient for a position as church minister. However, this was the United States - the land of opportunity, and the Danish state had no business meddling in church affairs of another country.

My father's first call was to serve as minister for the Lutheran church in Manistee, Michigan - north of Chicago. After four struggling years at that location with the extremely cold winters, and now with two additional children, we decided to look for greener pastures. It was apparent my father had chosen a poverty-stricken profession. We were poor. On the other hand, being without an abundance of worldly possessions, might enhance our prospects of going to heaven some day. Poverty could be regarded as an advantage and a virtue.

An opening eventually came for my father to serve as minister for the Danish Lutheran church in Vancouver, British Columbia - so the six of us boarded the Empire Builder of the Great Northern for the long train trip to the west coast.

In Vancouver new problems came about. A country-wide recession seemed to be developing into a real depression. And there were problems with the church congregation. Instead of praising the Lord and looking for everlasting life in paradise, some members of the congregation were engaged in social affairs such as ladies aid activities and rummage sales. They even had the gall to request space in the church newsletter to advertise these 'church' activities.

Since the one and only mimeograph machine for the printing of the monthly publication was under the jurisdiction of the church minister, my father turned down their request - stating that the church newsletter was for religious news only. He was obviously too religious for their liking. The consequence of his ruling gradually created a conflict with a divided congregation. It was time to move on.

Again, an opportunity came just at the right time. The Lutheran church congregation in Junction City, Oregon was looking for a new Danish minister. It seemed that the last one they had stole some money that helped close the State bank in town. My father seemed to be the only one around, available and willing to bring comfort to the disillusioned congregation - so all our worldly belongings were packed into a truck. Now a family of seven, we sat on top of the suitcases, baggage and crates and headed for Junction City.

The fact that we now were five children was a natural state of affairs for a preacher's family. I was quite convinced at the time that our family multiplied as a result of prayer. The harder my parents prayed, the more kids they got. I did a lot of thinking and had the answer to most of life's mysteries. What I could not understand is why they prayed so hard to have more kids when we were so poor. On the other hand, each and everyone of us children were glad to be alive.

Soon after our arrival in Junction City, lo and behold, another was born. Whether or not this impressed the church congregation was difficult to say. All they really wanted was a preacher, not a whole army. Oh well, here we were, - and financially at their mercy.

The main meal of the day was at suppertime. Everyone was there and we all sat in our correct places - Daddy at the head of the table, Mom at the opposite end, three boys on the right side and three girls on the left side - everything in perfect balance. We children were as follows: myself, age eleven; Xenia, age nine; Vita, age seven; Benedict, age five; Sonya, age three; and David, age one or less and in a high chair. And about twice a week there would be a guest for supper, completely unannounced, and on very short notice.

During the Depression years in the thirties, there was a great number of unemployed men traveling all over United States in search of work. They rode the rails free of charge, not by permission, but by toleration on the part of the railroads. The freight trains on the Southern Pacific line, passing through our town had their share of passengers, which were called hobos. There could be as many as three or four hundred on one train, many of them sitting at the sliding door openings of the box cars, but most of them on the roof. They looked dirty and tired. Many were unshaven with scruffy-looking clothes. We saw them every day. Freight trains only stopped in Junction City to shunt box cars. Nonstop daytime trains passing through town would slow down to allow hobos to jump off or on the trains. Not many got off in our town. They seemed to know that Junction City was not a place to look for work.

Of those who did, some would find their way to our house. We always knew when there was a knock at the front door, that it must be a 'guest' as my father called them. A guest for supper suddenly meant that my mother had to go into the kitchen and start preparing more food. It was amazing how much these hobos could eat. I had the feeling that she wasn't exactly enthusiastic about the extra work, but for my father it was an opportunity to bestow a blessing on a fellow man, fulfilling a request from God and being a good Samaritan.

He would invite the guest in to his study for pleasant, relaxed conversation, while my mother slaved away in the kitchen, frantically rushing around, trying to scrape together enough ingredients for another mouth to feed. In those days, it was only natural that the husband, being head of the household, entertain a guest while the wife prepared and served the food. I think what bothered my mother most was that it was all on such short notice and there really was very little food to begin with.

However, an arrangement was made to ease the pain. The guest would be invited to chop some firewood at the back of the house as a token of appreciation for the meal he was about to receive. I thought it was a brilliant idea, because it meant that I would not have to do it, at least for that day. There was enough wood to be chopped for the next two years, so any outside help could only help me. Some guests would chop wood for about an hour and others would just look at the woodpile in dismay, overwhelmed by the size of it all and leave for a meal elsewhere.

The guest would be invited to sit next to my father at the head of the supper table. When there was a stranger at the table, we children were very quiet. As my father always said, children should be seen but not heard. The meal started with grace, which we all sang together and which almost always made the guest look most uncomfortable. It was the hymn that starts with 'Praise God, from whom all blessings flow.' The second line was cause for some concern: 'Praise God, his creatures here below.' I was sure this referred to bugs, insects and things because I never regarded myself as a 'creature.' However, the last line 'Praise Father, Son and Holy Ghost' made me somewhat uncomfortable in the presence of a stranger. Out of the corner of my eye I would squint at the guest to see if this 'Ghost' thing bothered him as it did me.

My visual impression of the trio was of a man with his son standing at his side and then this Halloween type ghost in a white sheet with two big black eyes. It never occurred to ask my father for an explanation about it, being that as a preacher, his word was gospel. Also, one did not question religious things. That would be the same as being in doubt. Well, the stranger never batted an eyelash, so I assumed that the white ghost had its rightful place somewhere in heaven.

After the meal, for which the stranger was usually most grateful, my father would ask if he had a place to stay for the night, being that the midnight freight did not slow down going through Junction City. The answer was always no, so he would then say,

"You are most welcome to sleep in our church. It's open all the time and the door is never locked. It's the one just across the street."

The stranger would then be given the privilege of using our bathroom for shave and cleanup. After thanks and handshakes all around, he would cross the street, enter the church and sleep in a pew for the night.

Sunday was an important day. After many days of preparation, Daddy's sermon was ready for the morning service. Following the early family breakfast, my first chore was to go over to the church and light up the belly stove if there was a chill in the air. I was instructed by my father to wake any hobos sleeping in the pews and bring to their attention that there would be a church service and that they were invited to attend. So, with a bucket full of firewood, I would crossed the highway, open the squeaky church door, stand at the back in the church facing the altar, and with as much authority as I could muster, say,

"Excuse me, sirs. It is Sunday today and there will be a church service here at ten o'clock. You are welcome to stay for the service."

There would be rumbling in the pews with sleepy heads popping up all over the place. At times there could be as many as twenty. They sat up rather dazed and somewhat confused, concerning the decision they suddenly had to make so early in the morning. Nobody said anything. I just went to the belly stove, raked out the ashes and prepared the stove for a new fire. By the time I was finished they had all left.

On Sundays we all dressed in our very best, which were the same clothes we wore during the first part of the week, except that they had been cleaned and ironed. We were rather fortunate to have two of everything, which in my case was two shirts, two pairs of pants and one decent pair of shoes. Clothes were always passed down the line to the younger ones as they grew older, so as far as I was concerned, being the eldest, I never got hand-me-downs.

At nine-thirty in the morning Daddy would go over to the church to get everything ready. At ten minutes to ten he would start ringing the church bell, dressed in his long black church gown with the white ruffled, pie-shaped, 'Sir Walter Raleigh' collar. The bell rope, being right in the middle of the small entrance area, made it difficult for people entering the church to get around him. But they managed and Daddy also managed to greet the congregation one by one, shaking their hands and pulling the rope - all at the same time. To me, that showed good coordination of mind and body.

The ringing of the bell was also the signal for the rest of us to leave the house and cross the highway to the church. My mother, the organist, carried her sheet music. I carried the family Bible, Xenia carried David who carried a blanket, Vita carried a Montgomery Ward catalog, Ben carried a Sears, Roebuck & Company catalog, and Sonya carried a crayon book and a box of crayons. We were followed by our dog, Blackie, who waited outside the church door during service. Going down the isle to our pew, which was the front one on the left, I could always feel the eyes of the seated congregation looking at us and probably thinking that we lovely children, being the pastor's family, were exceptionally righteous and certainly a good example to all other children in Junction City. We sat in the pew, side by side according to our age, with the exception of David, who was cared for by Xenia until he became old enough to sit in his proper place at the end of the line by himself.

The platform with the organ was directly in front of our pew, allowing my mother to keep an eye on her flock while she played the hymns. My father, standing at the altar and facing the congregation, also had a good view of his six blessings, and even more so from the pulpit.

Following the opening prayer and after the page number of the first hymn was announced, Sonya opened her crayon book and started coloring, Vita and Ben opened their illustrated catalogs to look at pictures and Xenia and I opened the hymn book we shared between us. David had his security blanket so all was well.

I did a lot of daydreaming during the service and did not follow much of what my father said. However, when he talked about souls being saved, it seemed to me that it would be just as important to save the heart and everything else. I didn't know exactly where the soul was located, but Burton, one of the kids in the Hornibrook gang, said it was located just below the stomach. He said he knew for sure, because his grandfather had an operation done on his soul just before he died. I was more inclined to believe it was just below the heart.

During the singing of the hymns, I was more interested in the squeaky sound of the organ foot pedals, than the hymn itself. I think there was also a leaky valve somewhere because my mother had to pump the two pedals very vigorously with her feet, to keep up the air compression. However, there was one hymn that stirred me. It was 'Onward, Christian Soldiers.' My thoughts immediately went to the Hornibrook gang.

The church was usually only half full on Sundays. These were lean times. There was no choir, no Sunday school, no ushers, no janitor (except me) and no business-minded administration to keep the church buoyant. Things were simply held together by the dwindling congregation on faith alone. I remember thinking, that if the hobos had stayed in church for the service, there would be a full house. But it was understandable that they could not dwell on the prospect of a worry-free life in paradise at some future date, when what they needed was something right now.

Whether or not the sermon would have helped the hobos in any way was doubtful, as a prerequisite for entering heaven was that we were all sinners and had to be saved. For the majority of the hobos, just trying to save their families from poverty and starvation was a full time job.

The closing prayer after the sermon most certainly indicated that the hobos weren't the only ones in dire straits. With bowed heads the congregation silently listened as my father prayed for humanity - for the sick and the homeless, those in hospitals and in old peoples' homes, those who are tired, sad and weary, those who experience loss of loved ones, those who are in sorrow or great despair, victims of earthquakes, floods and other natural disasters, those in insane asylums, the unfortunate in prisons, seamen in storms on the high seas, the unemployed, those who must go hungry, those in far away foreign lands who need help but do not receive it, those who are blind, deaf or handicapped, those in wheelchairs, those with terminal illnesses, those who live in fear and do not know peace, those who are engaged in armed conflict in far away places through no fault of their own, for the Royal family in Denmark, the President and Congress of the United States, those who are separated from their love ones due to circumstances beyond their control, those who are orphans, those who do not know of life hereafter, those who have sinned and need forgiveness, those who are suffering and in great pain. It went on and on. The list was endless. As I sat there listening, it seemed that the whole world around us was in turmoil. Only here in Junction City was all well - and maybe in Harrisburg and Eugene.

Finally, my father came to the end and there was a moment of silence. Maybe he was trying to remember if he missed someone, or maybe it was just so the sheer impact of it all could sink into the humbled congregation, who sat there in stolid silence as lifeless as a picture postcard. In fact, the only sign of activity was that of a fly buzzing away against the window pane where I sat, trying to get out.

Then came the 'Amen.' It was like the sudden closing of a book. Everybody seemed relieved. There was a lot of coughing and some movement but many were still under the humble spell of guilt. After the stirring, emotional prayer, the tin collection plate was passed around from pew to pew, a few coins were collected, a closing hymn followed and then the congregation, which had been getting into a state of depression, suddenly came to life, with everybody getting up and shaking hands with each other. The service was over. My mother closed the organ, we children gathered all our belongings and together we filed out of the church into the bright noon sunlight, feeling very good. Blackie was there, happy and excited, wagging his tail.

Sunday, according to my father, was supposed to be a day of rest. That was one day I did not have to mow the lawn or chop firewood. Actually, it was best if we didn't do anything that could be regarded as labor, and that suited me just fine. After a long lazy afternoon and evening, we all gathered around the dining room table to hear Bible stories by my father, which he read to us from illustrated children books - stories like David and Goliath, the great flood with Noah's Ark full of animals, floating around forty days and nights in continuous rain, Adam eating apples from Eve, five thousand people getting a full meal from a few fish and a couple of loaves of bread, storms on the sea of Galilee with Jesus walking on the water, and Samson's long hair that made him so strong he could destroy a temple. I was determined to grow my hair long for added strength, but somehow I ended up once a month in the barber's chair. And then there was Pilgrim's Progress, a story book with line drawings of a funny little figure called Christian who looked sort of like an ant and, with a pack on his back, had to battle his way along a road fighting tigers, robbers and everything else on his way to the Celestial City. There he would be able to get rid of his backpack, which in the book was described as a burden. With all the difficulties Christian had, it sure looked like he could have used a little help from the Hornibrook gang. So by bedtime I had enough to think about.

On weekdays during the evenings, we would spend a lot of time working on jigsaw puzzles, if there was no school homework to be done. We had no radio. However, we did have an upright piano made in Boston, a gift from the congregation when we lived in Michigan. My mother played piano and Xenia received piano lessons, so there was music in the house. Of all us children, Xenia seemed to have been the most gifted. She was very good at the piano and for that reason received free piano lessons from a music teacher. She was also very temperamental. If she didn't get her way she would go into a tantrum, throw herself on the floor kicking and screaming, looking for pity and hoping my mother, in desperation would say,

"Oh, you poor girl. Why must you suffer so? Have we been unkind to you? Tell us what you want so that we can give it to you and make you happy."

The reality was that it had no effect whatsoever on my mother. But for me it was hard to take. It only happened when Daddy was not home.

"Mom, ain't ya gonna do somethin' to stop all this screaming?" I would say. And she replied in a carefree way,

"Don't worry, she'll get over it and besides, it helps her develop her voice."

Unfortunately, Xenia did suffer from asthma and it was always a concern whether her emotional outbursts would trigger an asthma attack.

During the summer nights I used to sleep outside in what we called the grape arbor. It was next to the woodshed behind our house. The air was warm, the nights were clear, with millions of stars above and there was the sound of crickets all around. Blackie would be curled up next to my bed and in the dark I would lie there looking up at the Milky Way, thinking of the things I did during the day and what I was going to do tomorrow. It was a happy life. Very plain, logical and tranquil. Nothing really to disturb the peace. Nothing that is, except the midnight freight.

Every night about midnight far away somewhere in the distance, a sound seemed to break the stillness of the air. It was a whistle, very faint - probably a dozen miles north of Harrisburg. A period of silence followed and then, still far away, but now quite clear - a sort of forlorn, moaning sound. Again all was quiet. A very distant rhythmic sound gradually seemed to develop out of nothing. It was the faint clickety sound of train wheels on rails. The rhythm gradually became firmly entrenched and bit by bit increased in volume. Again, the whistle - now very clear, and I knew that the midnight freight must be tearing through little Harrisburg, four miles to the north, bearing down on Junction City.

The railroad crossing signals at Main and Front street suddenly started clanging as if in a state of great discovery and nervous excitement. A ground tremor seemed to ripple through the dark, sleepy landscape, as the thundering steam locomotive, pulling a long string of freight cars, suddenly plunged into the city with a great roar. The shrieking whistle, the huffing and puffing, the clickety click of the rails, the clanging of the signals, the noise and the vibration all came together in a deafening crescendo, causing hundred of dogs all over Junction City to howl and wail in distress - including my dog, Blackie.

With everyone wide awake, this was the ultimate calamity. Like a tornado, the midnight freight swept through town and disappeared into the night. All the commotion, infernal noise, tension and excitement seemed to follow the speeding train out of town and dissipate together with the bellowing smoke down the railroad track.

Order and peace returned, except for the dogs, who continued their concert of anguish and distress for a little while longer - obviously, completely overwhelmed by the trauma. The sound of the train gradually died in the night as it raced towards Eugene, its next victim. Eventually, it was so faint I could hardly hear it at all. Silence returned. The night was still. The crickets, sensing that all again was well, resumed their chirping - and I fell asleep in the grape arbor with all the stars above.

CHAPTER THREE

Opal Burgess wasn't your average school teacher. As a boy I thought she was very special. She was brilliant, witty, fairly good looking, had a unpredictable temper and kept everyone in the class wide awake by throwing a piece of chalk at any pupil who didn't pay attention. She taught arithmetic and other subjects in the seventh grade. She must have been about thirty. That might sound like a lot, but it was nothing compared to Old Lady Ballard in the eighth grade who taught geography. It was said she was so old, she actually knew her uncle, Buffalo Bill, while he was still alive.

At Junction City Grade School, Opal Burgess was the most popular teacher as far as the pupils were concerned. I always looked forward to her class and liked her very much. Sometimes I didn't feel good about it, because in the Hornibrook Gang we kids took an oath never ever to have anything to do with females. No one wanted to be a sissy. Of course, all I was doing was looking at her in a harmless, blissful way from my desk near the back of the room, instead of paying attention to what she was writing on the blackboard. This sort of daydreaming was not good. 'Lack of concentration' was one of the remarks that showed up on my report card. My marks were not the best. However, I was pretty good at drawing and gave Opal Burgess one of my masterpieces, a little pencil drawing on a piece of paper showing Columbus's ship, the Santa Maria - hoping that it would help make up for the problem I seemed to be. Inside I knew I was clever, but the school didn't. There was also a number of distractions, like the flowing hair of Ruth Pryor who sat directly in front of me. Her hair filled the whole picture. It was hard to see the blackboard. I had to constantly resist the temptation of wanting to put some of her hair in my inkwell. It was certainly long enough for that purpose. But Opal Burgess had the eyes of an eagle, so that was out of the question.

Like every well balanced, sensible boy with all his marbles in place I hated school. It took too much of my valuable time. However, we did get to know a terrible lot about Oregon, the most important state in the Union, and all about the Lewis & Clark Expedition and the Oregon Trail. The school day started with all pupils and teachers gathered in the assembly room to pledge allegiance to the flag of the United States of America. Up on the stage would be a boy and a girl with the folded flag. After the pledge they would go out in the schoolyard to the flagpole and raise the flag. Then we would sing 'The Star Spangled Banner' and disperse to our classrooms. The assembly room was also used for major announcements, like getting a day off if it snowed outside, the Christmas play and the glee club where, with piano accompaniment, we sang songs like 'A Capital Ship on a Ocean Trip,' 'Dixie,' 'Polly Wolly Doodle,' 'Swanee River' and 'Home on the Range.'

In the classroom, the three R's - reading, 'riting and 'rithmetic plus spelling were the important subjects, but we also had to read piles of stuff about George Washington, the Constitution, Abraham Lincoln, the Civil War and the names of all the generals and battles of that time - and memorize the names of our 48 states. With our history and geography being all about the United States, there were only a few pages available in our school book to cover the rest of the world. We knew the rest of the world was out there, just like the stars above, but with the center of the universe being Oregon, it was of little interest to any one - except maybe to Old Lady Ballard.

Reading and spelling were very important subjects, we were told, but the art of writing was where it became personal. It was called penmanship. We had to spend hours and hours practising writing, using scratchy pen nibs and ink. Each desk had an inkwell in the right top corner. Everyone was forced to use their right hand. Being left-handed, this was very difficult for me. It was all right to throw a baseball with your left hand, but in the classroom there were rules. Every letter in the alphabet had to be a masterpiece, having the right shape, slant, loop, curve and height. This was achieved by scrawling each letter on paper one hundred times, one line after another. We went through the whole alphabet this way with the result that everyone in the class ended up with the same handwriting - like clones. This hundred-time thing was also used as punishment. The morning I momentarily gazed out of the window instead of at the blackboard, lightning struck and a piece of flying chalk just missed me. Immediately, Opal Burgess called me to the front, told me to turn around and stand facing the class and say ten times,

"I will not look out of the window during class hours."

I did what I was told, feeling perfectly awful and exposed, with everyone staring at me. Then after that was over, she added,

"And Visti, you will stay after school and write it one hundred times on the board. And let this be a lesson to the rest of you. Keep your eyes on the blackboard!"

So after school when all the kids had left, there I was at the blackboard, going through punishment. Opal Burgess sat at her desk checking papers and hardly noticing I was there, so it seemed to me. Everything was too quiet - just the sound of the chalk on the board and of kids playing outside in the school play shed. Although I did not feel too good, there was a feeling of excitement in being alone in the same room as Opal Burgess. Finally I got it all on the blackboard - one hundred times!

"Okay, Miss Burgess, I'm finished," I said with a feeling of achievement.

She turned around, got up and looked at the board.

"Very well, that looks good. Now you realize that all this was unnecessary, Visti. You must learn to pay better attention. We won't let it happen again, will we?"

"No, Miss Burgess."

"Okay, you can go now."

As I left the classroom I thought, wasn't it nice that she was sharing this incident with me by saying, 'We won't let this happen again, will we,' instead of saying 'You will not let this happen again, will you.' I thought that was very thoughtful of her. We were in this together. It made me feel real good. As I walked down the school corridor passing by the open door of Old Lady Ballard's classroom, I noticed a kid at her blackboard, writing something about paper airplanes. Daydreaming was regarded as a minor incident. A major incident would require going to the dreaded principal's office and receiving the strap. That would have been a nightmare. But it never happened to me.

To keep everything in high gear, report cards were marked by the teachers and given to the pupils six times during each school season, to take home for their parents' signature. This revealing report about our very existence was frequently questionable and often required confidential consultation between parents and teacher but somehow we got through it all and at the end of the school season we all passed, despite poor grades and disturbing revelations. The long, awaited summer vacation finally came for the teachers, as well as for the pupils - almost three months of carefree, warm, lazy, do-nothing existence - a well-earned paradise for all.

Meanwhile, back at the parsonage, my father and mother continued their daily struggle to put food on the table. For them there was no holiday.

The Willamette Valley, with the Coast Range mountains to the west and the Cascade Range to the east, was a perfect place for summer vacation, if it wasn't for the bean fields. The river flowed northward through the center of the valley, providing a rich agricultural landscape for all the farms surrounding Junction City. It was said in the thirties that the Willamette River was so clear you could read a newspaper under twenty feet of water. We tried. The only problem was that you couldn't read the print at that distance. But it was a perfect place for swimming and the river went right past the bean fields.

Harold Bruce was a very good friend of mine. In fact we were partners. He was one year younger than me. We both belonged to the Hornibrook gang and spent practically all our daylight hours together, loafing around or working on secret plans to develop a better defence system against the Moore gang. His father ran the only one-chair barber shop in town, the place where I had to have my hair cut every month, preventing me from becoming strong like Samson.

Together, during those long, hot summer days we would walk out on Dane Lane to Jimmy Hansen's farm and spend hours in the big hay barn, jumping from the rafter cross beams way up under the roof, to the mountain of soft, loose hay far below. This would be followed by a very, very slow walk by the cherry orchards of the Gripskov farm and then to our favorite swimming hole down by the river, where we sometimes would remain until sundown. We were able to spend countless number of hours doing very little.

Dane Lane, a country road, was about a ten minutes walk out of Junction City, on the east side. It was where most of the Danes lived and where all the farms were. It was there we could see cows being milked, chicks hatched, hear the turkeys gobble, help pick fruit in the orchards and go for hayrides in the fall. It was also here we got most of our food - everything from dairy products to vegetables. I don't know if my father paid for it. Nobody had any money.

The barter system, goods exchanged for goods, was very prevalent in those days. The only thing my father had to barter in exchange for food was his sermons - which were not something the receiver could later use in another exchange. A sermon was there if you thought about it and gone if you thought about something else. And it wouldn't work very well in a grocery store or Bruce's barber shop. After a haircut it would be difficult for my father to say,

"Thanks for the haircut. Now, as payment I will give you a short sermon."

There were complications. First of all, a haircut cost ten cents, so the sermon would have to be very short. One must remember that it took my father three days to prepare a sermon, which made his sermons worth a lot more than ten cents. Secondly, if another customer was waiting in the barber shop to be served, the preaching would delay things. Thirdly, Bruce was not religious. He seldom went to church, because he was too busy working on an old car he wanted to get running. Fourthly, he and his nagging wife lived in an old, leaky shack on the edge of town which she was always complaining about, and a sermon most certainly would not pay for fixing the roof. So, being a preacher in a barter-oriented community wasn't easy. Sometimes I had the feeling that the Favrholdt family was a charity case. I guess it was natural to be as poor as church mice.

If it wasn't for the bean fields, our summer vacation would have lasted right from the last of May to early September - undisturbed. Nobody ever went anywhere in the summer, so there should have been good reason to really enjoy a long, lazy, uninterrupted period of tranquility, but right in the middle of it all when we least wanted it, came the call for bean field pickers. It was an annual event. Lots and lots of kids used to pile into trucks early every morning at assembly points to be driven out to the bean fields down near the river, myself and Harold included. It was not compulsory, but just something everyone did every summer. It had always been this way and always would be - for a period that could last up to six weeks! When we spilled out of the truck it was all there - the weigh scales, the checkers, the empty sacks, the countless number of endless rows of beans and the foreman issuing orders as to what rows were to be picked.

Although the mornings were cool, Harold and I always knew that by early afternoon, we would be feeling like being on a chain gang in a heat wave. One fortunate thing about the rows of beans, was that the vines were about six feet high providing good coverage from the foreman, if not from the sun above. Since bean picking was completely voluntary, it did not matter whether we decided to pick one single bean a day or a million. So, it was understandable that after a little bit of work, Harold and I plus a few other kids, sort of slowed down a bit, hid our sacks under the vines and wandered down to the far end, where there was a peach orchard with juicy ripe peaches just ready for us. And beyond that was the cool, clear river just waiting to cool us off. We felt that a couple of hours to refresh and bring ourselves back to full productive strength was well justified and we only did it on hot sunny days -which seemed to be almost every day.

During the late afternoons we would work real hard in the bean rows to make up for lost time. Five o'clock was the time to report to the weigh scale checker. Payment was one cent per pound of beans, payable once a week. It was embarrassing to discover that girls picked a lot more than boys. Harold and I were of the opinion that they, by nature were more fragile and helpless than boys. They certainly did not have the strength we had. In fact, all the Zane Grey cowboy books Harold read, and he certainly read many, clearly indicated that it was the women, who in a state of continuous distress had to be saved by men. It was never the other way around. Women did not go galloping on horses across the prairies, leaning over and grabbing men in the face of charging buffalo herds. Therefore, it was hard to really understand how they could beat us in the bean fields - even with the small intermission we took daily to give ourselves additional energy.

The long, lazy summer drifted along. Every morning was one day less in the fields and one day closer to school. We couldn't win. Eventually, the day of reckoning came for the beans. With the picking season over, we all gathered at the weigh scale in the evening sun for the last time to hear the final tally for the six-week ordeal. Sure enough, the girls were way ahead with many earning as much as 18 dollars for the six weeks work. Harold and I cleared around 11 dollars each. This was still a lot of money, considering one could buy a horse for 12 dollars. We blamed the low figure on plain poor pickings in the bean rows we worked in, and that seemed to be generally accepted as being plausible. But I think I heard someone at the weigh scales mention something about 'plain poor pickers' as we were getting on the truck heading back to town. The money earned was used for school books ($1.00), clothes ($5.00) and my allowance for a whole year ($5.00). All in all, it could have been better.

Whenever there was a small problem in the family or a questionable event such as the bean field earnings, my mother, being English, used to solve it all by saying,

"Now, I think it's time for a nice cup of tea."

Junction City had a show house on Greenwood street called the Rialto. On Saturday afternoons there were always good films for kids - such as 'Tom Mix,' 'Our Gang' and a weekly serial about fires and fire engines. Admission to the show house was five cents or a sack of tin cans. Nobody had any money so the barter system was used. It was recycling drive and only applied to kids going to matinee shows on Saturdays. The consequence of this was, that it gradually became increasingly difficult to find tin cans anywhere in Junction City. No kid wanted to miss the serial about the fire engines and fires, because each week that particular film series always ended with the fire engines racing to a new disaster - 'to be continued next week' - and we simply could not miss that. The Junction City garbage dump was cleaned right out and we searched for tin cans as far north as Harrisburg and half way down to Eugene. The recycling program was part of a national effort to reuse materials that were in short supply due to the Depression. The sacks of tin cans were piled up on the street in front of the show house on Saturday afternoons - a clear indication of the stamina and dedication of American youths' participation in a worthwhile community effort of recycling.

In reality, the kids didn't give a hoot about recycling. Inside the show house was bedlam, with kids running up and down the isles, jumping over seats, firing paper airplanes and other objects all over the place, thoroughly enjoying an atmosphere of hoopla and confusion. But when the lights went out and the curtain opened, there was total silence and dedication. The serial called 'Our Gang' starring Mickey Rooney always came first to fill part of the bill and build up suspense. For some kids it was okay, but the majority wanted the real stuff. After a few moments of darkness to change reels in the operator room, there it was - another alarm at the fire station with firemen sliding down poles, grabbing their fire helmets and racing through city streets in fire engines with sirens screaming. Not a single second of the film could be missed. Sure enough, the fire engines arrived at a fire that was far bigger and more devastating than any we had previously seen, and we sat on the edge of our seats with our eyes riveted to the screen. Flames and smoke were bellowing out of the windows of a tall office building with frantic people screaming for help. Firemen were rushing around, pulling hoses and cranking up ladders to reach all those in distress, particularly the pretty girl on the seventh floor who was leaning out of the window almost engulfed in smoke and hysterically waving her arms. It didn't matter to us that this seemed to be the same girl that had to be saved in another fire the previous week and the week before that. It was obvious that she was always in a state of continuous distress, which in turn, required continuous help. It was just her bad luck that she always happened to be in buildings that were catching on fire.

Personally, I had a small problem. Just as the firemen turned on the hydrants and directed their hoses towards the blaze, I had to go to the bathroom. It never failed. There was something about water on a screen that made things very urgent and it always seemed to happen at the most critical moment - just when the firemen were saving the girl. So after the show, my friend Harold, usually filled me in with the details of the dramatic rescue that I missed. He had a flair for describing what happened that was almost as realistic as the film itself. The main thing was that the girl had been saved and was ready for more distress the following week. The film always ended with the firemen back at the station suddenly getting another urgent call and the fire alarm clanging away. Truly an emergency! The search for more tin cans continued.

Another feature in Junction City was the library. It was a little wooden shack, five feet wide and twelve feet long, located just behind the church on the Seventh Avenue. It had a door at the one end and a window at the other. There were bookshelves loaded with books along both side walls right down to the far end, where a spectacled elderly lady sat behind a desk. The aisle was a little over two feet wide and two light bulbs lit up the place. The first thing you saw when opening the door was this menacing looking, awful person staring at you from the far end of the 'tunnel.' It was enough to scare anyone away. I never went in there, but Harold, being a bookworm, ventured inside about once a week. Only two people were allowed in the library at any one time due to the restricted aisle space. Sometimes, Harold had to wait outside for his turn to enter. We would sit on the doorstep and wait and wait. It was on one such occasion that I got the brainwave of the century.

"Why don't we," I said, "include the library in the things we are gonna tip over on Halloween night? We gotta dozen outhouses on the list so it's not much more work to tackle the library."

Harold didn't quite see it that way.

"Gee, I dunno. There's lots of Zane Grey books in there that I hain't read an' besides, do ya know what books weigh? It'd take an army to tip this thing over."

"Gosh, we got the whole Hornibrook gang and kin probably get help from Mike Morgan's gang an' maybe even the Rinkydink gang."

"I dunno. It looks too darn heavy to me," said Harold, getting up to look the thing over. We went around to the side of the building, put our shoulders against the wall and pushed as hard as we could, but it didn't budge.

"It's those darn books. There's too many of them."

"I think it's that awful lady in there. She must weigh a ton. And hey, wait a minute, there's two more in there. No wonder, That's the reason."

We decided to return later when the awful lady had gone home and the library was closed. A few days passed and we reckoned that even without the awful lady and customers inside the building, there was no way the Hornibrook gang could tackle the job. We didn't really feel we could trust the other gangs with such an important assignment. They might squeal. We definitely had a problem and it was ours alone.

The solution came in a flash the following Sunday during the sermon in church. In the pulpit my father was preaching about the disciples on the sea of

Galilee who, having fished all night without catching anything, were ready to call it quits, when a voice from the shore told them that their net was on the wrong side of the boat.

'Throw it over the right side and you will catch plenty of fish,' the voice said. That was it. The solution! We would, with discretion and due respect, remove as many books as possible from the library shelves on the one side of the building and put them in the shelves on the other side. The result of this would be that one side of the building would be much lighter than the other, making it much easier to tip over. I could hardly wait to tell Harold.

He thought the idea was great and together we worked out a plan in detail. On the day of Halloween, he would take out as many Zane Grey books he could borrow on his library card. At the same time, and while the lady was serving another customer at her desk, Harold would discreetly and quickly move as many books as possible from the south side bookshelves to the north side bookshelves. He reckoned ten minutes would be enough. He didn't think I should go in, being a preacher's son and scared of the librarian.

Halloween was a major annual event for kids in Junction City - almost more important than Christmas. There were hayrides, jack-o'-lanterns, ghosts, goblins, fireworks and the destruction of outhouses. About half of the houses in Junction City seemed to be without bathrooms, so an outhouse in the rear yard was a necessity. It was also regarded as a good place to sit and meditate. For the Hornibrook gang, Halloween was the night we crossed the railroad tracks into enemy territory to topple all the outhouses we could find. Needless to say, the Moore gang had the same idea.

Our clubhouse, in our back yard next to the parsonage and right at the sidewalk, was the biggest eyesore in town. It had a twenty-seven foot wooden lookout tower that resembled an oil derrick. We were continuously adding more height to the tower and hoped to reach one hundred feet. But in spite of numerous complaints, with reference to the tower of Babel, my father accepted it as part of the landscape. It was vital that the clubhouse and tower be protected from possible destruction on Halloween. Unfortunately, this year it was my turn to guard the place. My father and mother were usually in the house to back me up if there was trouble. The Hornibrook gang's secret plan for Halloween night was of no interest to my father, nor did he know about it. He just hoped that the night would pass peacefully without incident.

At eight o'clock in the evening on Halloween we had a meeting in the clubhouse. Everybody was there - Hornibrook, Burton, Jimmy Hansen, the two Skovbo kids, Donald Dill, Pete, Harold, myself and Freddie with his dog, Jiggs. Everything looked good for the night's rampage. Harold reported that the library was now light on the south side and heavy on the north side. He had no trouble carrying out his mission earlier in the day. Undetected, he managed to move an awful lot of books, while another customer conveniently blocked the view. He was sure the librarian didn't see a thing. So we decided that the list for the night ahead was twelve outhouses, the Moore gang's clubhouse and the library. He and the others left together as it was getting dark. They had a job to do.

We had a ball game at the baseball diamond the following afternoon. I had noticed that morning much to my surprise, that the library was still standing and I wanted to know the reason why. Hornibrook and Harold were sitting at the sideline waiting for their turn to bat. They didn't seem happy.

"Looks like things didn't work out," I suggested.

"Yer not kidding," Harold said, "Can ya believe it, the light was on in that darn library right up to midnight."

"Ya mean it was open that late?"

"Yer darn tootin.' She was inside!"

"Something's fishy here," I pondered, "Nobody ever goes to a library on Halloween night. D'ya think somebody squealed?"

"I dunno," Hornibrook chipped in, "but she looked awfully busy when we sneaked up and looked in the window."

"Doin' what?"

"I dunno. She was down on her knees doin' something with the books."

It was Hornibrook's turn to bat. He got up and went to the plate. One thing I suddenly knew for sure. That awful woman obviously found out that there was something wrong with her library.

"Boy, are ya ever in trouble, Harold. She must've found out what ya did."

"Me in trouble? It was yer idea."

"Yeah, but yer were the one in the library. I've never been near the place."

We sat in silence, thinking. Hornibrook bunted the ball and made it to first.

"How 'bout the books ya borrowed? Ya gotta go in there sooner or later and give 'em back."

"So what?"

"Well, she'll see ya and think, that's the kid who was in here Halloween day and messed up all my books, and then ya'll be in trouble."

"I'll say it was the preacher's son who started it all."

"No ya won't. You know ya can't do that when we're pardners."

Hornibrook stole a base and made it to second. We did some more thinking.

"Somehow ya gotta get the books back when they're due . Let's see, - that's two weeks from now. What are we worryin' about? We'll think of somethin' when the time comes."

"Sure," Harold replied. "We'll figure out something."

It was his turn to go to the plate. I lay on my back looking up at the blue sky and tried to do some figuring.

It is surprising how slowly time passes by when you are bored or forced to do unpleasant things and how quickly it goes when there is something you like to do. Likewise, it's a mystery why things that taste good are bad for you, and things that taste bad are good for you. Cod liver oil, our daily remedy, was one example. School hours seemed to last forever. Free time passed far too quickly. Spinach tasted awful. Candy tasted good. Sermons in church lasted forever. Films at the show house were far too short. Obedience was boring and predictable. Disobedience was exciting and a challenge - and it just so happened, that I found myself suddenly faced with such a challenge and a tough one at that.

It was determined by democratic vote, that I should return the Zane Grey books to the library! All members of the Hornibrook gang were of the very definite opinion that, since I thought of the idea in the first place - and in church of all places - I was responsible for getting the books back. I would simply walk in the library and return them on behalf of Harold Bruce who, due to unknown circumstances, could not deliver the books himself. A relatively simple matter. Nothing to it. Nobody would ever be suspicious of a poor preacher's son. The imaginary halo over my head was my protection.

On the due date in the afternoon Harold gave me the books and wished me luck. I didn't feel good at all. I went down the street to the library, stood in front of the closed door for a moment, took a deep breath and walked in. There she was, that awful, spectacled lady staring at me from the far end of the tunnel. I walked towards her, feeling a bit dizzy and faint, but managed to reach the desk without collapsing.

"I'm supposed to return these books." I was about to say 'for Harold Bruce' but decided in a flash to leave his name out of it. She opened the book covers, checked the due dates and said,

"Thank you."

That was it. Nice and simple. No problem. My halo was working. I turned around and quickly went towards the door not daring to look back. Lot's wife in the Bible looked back and turned into a pillar of salt. Once out on the street, I ran home.

Time moved on and I finally reached eighth grade. It had been a long haul. Old Lady Ballard was now our main teacher and I still sat behind Ruth Pryor with her flowing hair, but it didn't bother me much anymore. Old Lady Ballard had grey hair and took her job very seriously. Maybe that was what made her hair grey. Realizing that there wasn't much time left in Junction City Grade School, I did my best to concentrate on the subject matter being taught, and it was about time, because next year I would be going to Washburne High, the 'penitentiary' over on 6th Avenue. That was a whole different ball park, I was told. The top surface of my wooden school desk had lots of initials carved into it, so I added mine to the list, plus the crossbone symbol of the Hornibrook gang. Unfortunately, this act of classroom vandalism was noticed by Old Lady Ballard, and I was instructed to stand in the corner of the classroom and face the wall for the duration of the class hour.

There wasn't too much excitement that winter. A man came to the school grounds with a donkey and a camera. You could have your picture taken on the donkey for 25 cents and receive the photo a month later. There were no takers. Also an airplane passed over the school that January, and we all rushed to the windows to see it. But it was necessity of education that suddenly became paramount. We were all getting a little older - the teachers as well as the pupils. We had all moved up a notch, or as Harold said, one step closer to the brink. I didn't know what brink he was talking about, but it sounded serious.

Old Lady Ballard was an expert in geography and could rattle off the names of our forty-eight states with no problem. Her one requirement, apart from good education, was that kids come to school wearing acceptable footwear. She didn't like toes sticking out of shoes. This was a problem as some families were very poor. I remember the two Skovbo kids wore shoes that were in tatters. Then suddenly everyone had good shoes, thanks to a brand new innovative idea that just seemed to come out of nowhere.

It was a do-it-yourself idea made of materials that were readily available in large quantities. We took used, discarded rubber inner tubes from car tires and with scissors, cut them into 12-inch lengths. All car tires had inner tubes in those days. Using a large needle and stout string, we sewed the ends flat. Then we cut a round hole about the size of an ankle near the one end. You put your foot in the hole - and presto! The shoe was finished. Well, these new things caught on like wildfire. Girls wouldn't wear them, but the rest of us thought they were great. They were especially good for walking on gravel or on uneven pavement. I think inner tube shoes, as acceptable footwear, caught Old Lady Ballard off guard and also the school principal, Mr. Westinghouse, who wanted his pupils to be presentable at all times. Nobody really knew what to say about the black ugly things. The only problem we had was that roller skates couldn't be clamped to the shoes.

Apart from the strange appearance, there was something else. A new odor - that of sweaty feet, mostly noticeable in the eighth grade classroom where at least eight kids wore inner tube shoes. It was particularly bad on warm days - so bad, that Old Lady Ballard had to open all the windows. Tolerance prevailed for a while, but in the end - and we knew the end would come, a notice appeared on the bulletin board in the school corridor, stating that only acceptable footwear would be permitted on school premises. Innovation had been stifled. For us this was hard to understand, considering that education was supposed to broaden the mind, providing the groundwork for 'building better mousetraps' in the USA.

As the end of the school season approached, the glee club became active. We had to learn to sing an assortment of American songs for the final gala evening at the school where parents and students would gather in complete harmony for 'sign off' and possible award presentations. Definitely nothing fancy. How I ended up in the glee club I'll never know. There was very good attendance that final evening and one could feel a degree of excitement in the air. For months preparations had been underway.

Miss Taylor's class started the evening performance with an impressive display of kids dressed as flowers. A girl in a yellow paper tulip costume sang 'Springtime in the Rockies.' The fourth graders had a display of school artwork on a large easel, which happened to collapse just as they were setting it on the stage, resulting in the precious artwork flying all over the place. The fifth grade put on a play about the exploration of Oregon Trail. The two boys on stage, representing Lewis and Clark, were doing all right until Clark forgot his lines and had to be helped along by their teacher, before the exploration of Oregon could continue.

A piano was pushed onto the stage and a girl in a pink dress from sixth grade played 'Red River Valley.' Four girls from the seventh grade recited poetry. There was a speech by the school principal, Mr. Westinghouse, thanking everyone for everything and encouraging us all to have a bright, prosperous future, and the handing out of awards for achievement, good attendance, highest marks and other noteworthy happenings.

Finally we eighth graders gathered on stage with the American flag in the background to sing the songs we had practised - first 'Dixie,' then 'Yankee Doodle,' and then the one that was to bring tears to everyone's eyes, 'Hail ol' Grade School, we're leaving you now for High School.' This grand finale completed the evening entertainment, and was the cue for two kids to pull the stage curtains together while the audience clapped their hands enthusiastically.

Much as I disliked school, there was something about the last days in Junction City Grade School that made me want to stop the clock. Harold said I was nuts. In the end we all went home and they closed the school for the season.

Two weeks later, my father got the brainy idea that the American children of Danish heritage should attend summer school to learn the Danish language. He himself would be the teacher. The parents were enthusiastic about it all. The kids were devastated. The torture lasted two weeks and took place in the school assembly room where we pledged allegiance to the flag. But this was different. Our holiday was being ruined by this foreign stuff. The kids were restless. Finally my father had to give up and the school was closed for good.

It was also just in time. My middle name happened to be Cornaby - from my mother's side. But instead of being known as Visti Cornaby Favrholdt, someone in the Moore gang nicknamed me 'Whiskey Cornbeef & Cabbage Firehall.' This meant a declaration of war and the holiday was a perfect time for revenge.

Harold and I felt that something more than slingshots was necessary to scare the daylights out of the Moore gang. The idea of one shot at a time was simply not good enough if we were to have an edge on the enemy. I mentioned to the kids of our gang that what we really needed was a catapult which could hurl a volley of stones all at once. Harold agreed and felt a five-gallon can full of stones would be about right. For a period of two weeks we worked on detailed sketches in the clubhouse. It was Burton who brought to our attention that the whole idea was far too complicated, because no one in the club could even lift a five-gallon can of stones. It was just too much for a single volley. So we decided to settle for a one-gallon bucket. Other problems popped up. Since the catapult had to be operated from our territory, it would be necessary to hurl the stones over the houses on the east side of Highway 99 to the next street where the Moore gang's clubhouse was located - assuming, of course, that the battle took place there. Harold didn't think that we could built a catapult that could launch stones that high. However, if the catapult was on an elevated platform or something, we might be able to clear the roofs.

Our first solution was to build the catapult on our lookout tower, but we had no idea how to go about it. The tower was also too far back from enemy territory so that sort of solved that problem. It then became apparent to us that the stair landing of the Methodist church could be the perfect launch pad. It was just across the street from our clubhouse next to Miller's funeral parlor. It faced Highway 99 and the Moore gang's clubhouse beyond. The entrance door landing, which was twenty steps up from the sidewalk, seemed to be just the right height to strike at the enemy. We measured the landing and came to the conclusion that the catapult would have to be either mobile with wagon wheels so we could roll it up the church steps, or made in pieces that we could carry up and assemble.

Somehow I ended up with the problems of catapult design of which I knew absolutely nothing. Daddy and Mom also knew very little about catapults. However, the gang succeeded in finding a pair of old wooden wagon wheels on an axle, which was a start. With much effort, pushing and pulling, we got the wheels up the church steps to the top. We could hear the sound of the organ in the church - probably the organist practising for the next Sunday service. Some kids in the gang thought the whole idea was just too much hard work. If it took this much time and sweat just to get the wagon wheels up the steps, surely it would be next to impossible to get the whole finished contraption up to this height. We all stood on the landing thinking deeply. A man passed by on the sidewalk below. He looked at us and the wagon wheels and probably also was thinking deeply.

I don't know how it happened, but instead of trying to solve the problem, the kids suddenly got the idea that it might be fun to let the wagon wheels roll down the steps. Before I could get a handle on the situation, the heavy wheels bounced down the stairway, making a thunderous noise and rolled across the highway into a hedge on the far side. It was very exciting and dramatic. The organ music stopped abruptly and a moment later the church door behind us opened. I just caught a glimpse of a little old man peering out, before we ourselves tumbled down the stairs, scattering in all directions.

One Sunday morning during church service I noticed that Ben had opened his Sears, Roebuck catalog to a page about nuts, bolts and nails. A keg of nails cost four dollars - a lot of money, but also a lot of nails. It was one of our constant problems. We were always short of nails. There was enough lumber in town to build a hundred clubhouses, but no nails.

It was during the church prayer - the part where my father prayed for all the lost souls overseas, that I suddenly got the idea that I could pray for a keg of nails. After all, miracles did happen in the biblical days and perhaps they could happen again - right here in Junction City. With closed eyes, folded hands and very intense concentration I did my part during the church prayer to make things happen. It would have been better had the request for a keg of nails been an official part of the church prayer but then, the rest of the congregation didn't need nails.

Two days later, Harold's brother, Arden and Doctor Roger's kid cornered a skunk and, with the assistance of four barking dogs, managed to hold it at bay up a tree at Seventh and Washburne. The stink and commotion eventually came to the attention of Doctor Roger, who got a pistol out of his Ford Roadster and shot it. He kept the pistol in his car because he always carried so much money around. Doctors were considered wealthy. Harold and I heard the shot from the clubhouse and dashed down to Washburne to see what it was all about.

Immediately, Harold saw the dollar value in the skunk. He said if we skinned it and sold the fur to Mitchell's store we might rake in as much as four dollars. It was at that moment I realized that my prayer at church had been answered. I told Harold about the need for a keg of nails and he readily agreed that we use the four dollars for that purpose.

The next day we went to Washburne to retrieve the valuable beast. The stench was almost unbearable. You could smell it a block away. With difficulty we impaled the dead skunk on a long pole and carried it down to the clubhouse. Harold said that before we attempt to skin the skunk, it must be nailed to a wall, preferably in sunshine, so as to dry out and get rid of the smell. We nailed it to a barn door in the alley behind the Methodist church, adjacent to Miller's funeral parlor. Harold said that four days of hot sun should do the job. As the unbearable stench penetrated the neighborhood we knew there might be trouble. We decided therefore to keep an eye on the alley.

At two o'clock that afternoon we noticed, from our observation holes in the clubhouse, that Miller's parlor across the street was going to have another funeral. A couple of old Fords pulled up outside the parlor and dismal looking people dressed in black got out. They stood in a group on the sidewalk. Almost immediately, some of them took out their handkerchiefs and covered their noses. It was obvious that this was not due to emotion or sorrow. With such a stench around the funeral parlor one could only assume that the deceased, lying in an open coffin in the parlor surrounded by flowers, must be the cause. But why the deceased should smell like a skunk was anybody's guess.

The undertaker appeared at the top of the funeral parlor stairs all dressed in black, fanning his face with what looked like to be a copy of the Junction City Times. The odor was getting to him. He beckoned to the group of mourners on the sidewalk to come into the parlor, and they all went up the stairs and disappeared inside.

It was about then, as the sound of organ music filled the air, that we noticed a man appearing at the far end of the alley with a shotgun. He glanced to the left and right as though he was looking for trouble. He kicked over a couple of garbage cans, moseyed around a bit and then walked away. We wondered what he might be up to, and after pondering over this for about a half an hour, we decided to go down the alley to investigate. As we crossed the road we noticed that the sun no longer was shining on our spread-eagled skunk. Harold suggested we open the barn door on an angle so that it again would get sun. It was a good idea. The four-dollar beast now faced the sidewalk at the parlor, but that couldn't be helped.

We went the full length of the alley without seeing anyone or anything suspicious, but as we turned to go back there was trouble galore. The undertaker, who seemed to appear out of nowhere, slammed the barn door closed. Mourners, with handkerchiefs to their noses, peered around the corner to get a first hand look at the 'evil omen' nailed to the door. We dashed down the alley to lay claim to our property, when lo and behold, the man with the shotgun was on our heels hollering something about menacing rascals.

"Are you kids responsible for this?" the undertaker shouted angrily as we approached.

"It's our skunk. It belongs to us," I replied nervously.

"You're the preacher's son, arn't you?" The undertaker grabbed me by the collar. "Shame on you."

This was a messy state of affairs. Harold suddenly grabbed the skunk from the barn door with his bare hands and in a flash we ran down the street, leaving behind the undertaker with his mourners standing behind the man with the shotgun who was hollering his head off. We hid the skunk in the woods beyond Washburne. We had secret trails in the woods and no mourners or undertakers would ever find it there.

That night, Harold's mother, Mary Bruce made a bonfire in her backyard and burnt all Harold's clothes.

CHAPTER FOUR

It was during the early summer of 1933 that I sensed a slight disturbance to our lifestyle in Junction City. We were consistently poor but it now seemed to be even more so. I noticed members of the congregation frequently visiting my father and mother in the evenings. Behind closed doors there would be discussions in the front room. I didn't pay too much attention to what was going on. After all, that was the adult world. It didn't concern us, the children. Our world was different and much more fun. Personally, I had no intention of ever becoming an adult. However, at the age of twelve and with grade school now over, I had the funny feeling that things were not quite right. Opal Burgess was gone. Old Lady Ballard was gone. All the frustration, excitement, noise and activities of grade school were gone. A door had been closed. It was as though a faint breeze rustled through the leaves of the trees, breaking the stillness of the air. Maybe there was nothing to be alarmed about but somehow I felt uneasy.

Having to go to high school at the end of the holiday was in itself alarming. Washburne High was a dominating, wooden two-storey building that was bound to spell trouble. I did not look forward to it. In fact, I didn't really need it. Both Harold and I felt we knew enough to get by. After all, life in the Willamette valley wasn't that complicated and we had no intention of doing any work anyways, if we could help it. You could always get by, swiping fruit from trees for food, sleeping in a hayloft and going down to the river for refreshment and relaxation. The climate was always mild. There was never any snow to worry about. As long as we stayed in the valley and didn't go to the places that were in turmoil, like those my father mentioned in the church prayers, we would be all right.

So we started the summer holiday with the feeling of joy, confidence and abandonment, but also painfully aware of the looming presence of the high school - the place of confinement for the next four years. The only good thing I could see about that place, was that some of the kids who went there seemed to have 'tin lizzies,' which were old stripped-down Model T Fords painted in outrageous colors. A whole bunch of kids would pile into these tin lizzies and drive around town like yahoos.

Being the eldest in the family, I seemed to be assigned chores on an increasing scale. Once a week I had to walk to the creamery on Highway 99 just south of town and buy a pound of butter for fifteen cents. Another chore was the daily one mile walk out to a milk processing plant just north of town to fetch free milk. With Blackie and a tin pail, I was able to make the round trip in an hour. I found it absolutely uncanny how heavy a pail of milk became when moved from one place to another. Someday, I thought, I'll finish the bicycle I was making and then the round trip would be only twenty minutes. I had been working on the bike for two years, but all I had was an old rusty frame, handle bars and one wheel without a tire. Maybe part of this year's bean field money might be enough to buy the other parts at a bicycle shop in Eugene.

The daily one-mile walk for a pail of milk took me past the haunted house just off Highway 99 at the edge of town. It certainly was well known by all the kids as being a place where you could get into trouble. The reason was Guy King, an old grumpy man who lived in the place. The two-storey, tumbledown, dilapidated wooden structure was just about ready for the garbage heap. With sagging foundations, broken windows and a front garden full of weeds, it had all the indications of being the residence of ghosts, goblins and evil spirits. We had the impression that Guy King was in charge of these occupants and could unleash them at will, should we venture near the place. At the front of the house was a bay window turret with a commanding view up and down the street. It was here, peering out of the second floor windows, that grumpy Guy King kept a wicked, watchful eye on passersby, in particular kids like me. Yes, there was some justification for his concern, because as a dare, kids frequently took pot shots at the house with their slingshots. This really stirred him up. He would come dashing out of the front door, screaming and yelling with kids scattering all over the place like chickens. It was so exciting. But with my pail and Blackie, I kept my nose straight ahead every day as I passed the place and encountered no problems.

My daily chores and obligations seemed to somewhat deprive me of the reckless and carefree abandon of yesterday. I did, however, find some enjoyment watching the construction of the western branch of Highway 99 just north of the town when I went to get milk. It connected in the form of a Y to the existing highway to Harrisburg and was the only sign of any activity for miles around. After the concrete highway was completed it looked as dead as a tombstone, because very few cars appeared on the roadway.

Another project of major importance was Project Devastation. All Hornibrook gang members felt that the secret weapon was necessary in our on-going conflict with the Moore gang. This was about the same time that our president, Franklin D. Roosevelt got project New Deal underway to pull the United States out of the Depression. He was dealing with economic issues. We were dealing with defence issues. So lots of things were happening. In the woodshed behind the parsonage,

Harold and I started to construct a large wooden tank. Equipped with four wagon wheels, the big boxlike contraption, mounted on the axles, would enable us to advance on the enemy, and being inside the box, we could fire at them with our slingshots through small portholes. It would be propelled by pushing it from the inside. We hoped to have the mobile monster, called 'No Deal,' completed before the bean fields were ripe. After that there would be very little time.

Down by the river, past a place called Hentz's farm, was a grove of trees forming a little park. Frequently, the church had picnics there together with a gathering of Danes called the Danish Brotherhood. For children this was the place to be, for there were games to play, pop on ice, apple pies, Danish food and ice cream. The adults sat at picnic tables conversing while the young provided the energy and happiness all around.

It was here in the park, as we were having a picnic and eating apple pie, that the first inkling of a disturbance seemed to appear. At the picnic table we children were told by Mom, that Daddy was going to travel to Denmark to enquire about a job. Obviously, things were not going well here. It didn't look like there was anything to really worry about. He was just going to check on things. I figured the congregation must be in on this, because the money for such an expensive trip had to come from somewhere and heaven knows, we didn't have it. I wondered if this whole trip was accomplished by prayer alone.

A week later we all went down to the train station to see Daddy depart. With his hat and suitcase he looked like a successful salesman. As we stood there waiting for the train to come up from Eugene, I wondered how we were going to manage without him. It was a long way to Denmark - four days by train to New York and almost fourteen days by boat to that distant country, way up north on the other side of the ocean. I was told by Donald Dill it was as far away as Bethlehem, but much colder. If one looked at the sky on a clear night and located the last star of the Big Dipper - well, directly below that star here on earth was Denmark. It was at a place called the Far North.

It was very quiet after Daddy left. We didn't seem to make so much noise or quarrel as often as we used to, but Mom was cheerful as always and kept everything under control - just like her sister in England, who we called Auntie Annie. We had never seen Auntie Annie, only photos, but her frequent letters made us feel that she was part our family. She seemed to be positive and happy just like Mom. When we sent a letter to her, Mom always wrote on the envelope: *Postman, postman, don't be late. Auntie Annie cannot wait.* They both seemed to possess a flair for palm reading and similar unusual things as a harmless pastime - like the time I had a wart on my finger. Mom told me to get a needle, rub it back and forth on the wart, then bury the needle in the back yard and not tell anyone where it was buried. The wart should disappear within two weeks. I was very, very impressed when it did. I told all my friends about it and really spread the good news around. Now, had it been my father, he would have attempted to resolve the wart problem with prayer - but my mother was more practical.

Before we knew it, the bean fields were upon us. Whoever thought of putting bean fields in the Willamette valley sure caused a lot of trouble. Once again we had to go through the trauma of baking in the sun and suffering so much. I wonder who ate all those beans. We didn't. I couldn't even stand the smell of them. Harold and I debated whether we should play hookey like in school and skip the bean field season entirely, but then realised that such an action might label us as chicken. I thought Harold's reasoning made good sense. He said, whether we liked it or not, it looked like we eventually would grow up. When that happened, he would buy out all the bean fields in the valley and close them down. After that there would be peace for everyone.

During the summer a few things happened. A grain elevator on Front Street, just south of Main Street burnt down. It took three days to totally put out the fire due to the pile of smoldering grain. Also a tent show came to town setting up in a field behind Washburne High School. Harold and I helped the workers put up the tent and got two free tickets. At the evening performance we saw a couple of clowns, a man juggle balls, dogs jumping through hoops, a couple of horses and a tired looking elephant. Outside the tent there was a woman so fat that they had to bring her in by truck. She was on display as a freak.

There was also was a man on a platform, showing how you could stick pins through your cheek without pain, if you used a special secret remedy he was selling. You just rubbed on some stuff he had in a bottle and pushed the pins through your cheek. He had at least four pins going through his cheek without any indication of pain at all. As a bottle cost two bits it was quite expensive, but with that you got six free pins. The bottles were these flat curved bottles that fit in your back pocket, so it was very practical. I thought it would be a good idea for my father to show this in church when he got back. I was sure the congregation would be impressed and regard it as a miracle. There were so many miracles happening during the biblical days, but not any more. This would be a chance to restore the faith of the congregation. Unfortunately, I didn't do anything about it that day, and the next morning when I went over to the field where the tent show was, it was gone. All that was left was sawdust on the ground.

In August a man and his wife, who lived in a two-story house behind us across the alley, decided to burn the place down to collect fire insurance. It was a spectacular fire in the middle of the night. It took an hour to get the volunteer fire department together and by that time it was too late. All that was left the next morning were the foundations. Actually, it was good it burnt to the ground, because it broadened the view from the clubhouse lookout tower and they got their insurance money, so everyone was happy.

My birthday was also in August. Mom made a special cake for me with thirteen candles on it and she and the kids sang happy birthday. Suddenly I was thirteen years old which, as far as I was concerned, was an unlucky number. But the days passed by and I noticed I didn't really feel any different than when I was twelve, so I reckoned there was nothing to worry about. As a present I was given a yo-yo. This was very special. Yo-yos were the latest craze with yo-yo clubs being formed everywhere. So-called 'experts' from out of town would come to clubs and demonstrate advanced yo-yo techniques. Unfortunately,

Junction City was too far off the beaten track to be visited by an expert.

Unknown to me, Harold had embarked on a project of his own. It was the building of a rowboat. We certainly didn't need a rowboat in out endless battle with the Moore gang. But Harold said I had a one-track mind and this was for other purposes - like going up the river to Portland among other things. It suddenly made sense. We certainly had spent many hours on homemade rafts in the water filled garbage dump just north of town, so we both had navigational experience.

The six foot wooden boat had a flat bottom and Harold had given it a good coat of tar both inside and out. It was time to try it out. With a flip of a coin the privilege was mine. We selected a pond near the woods beyond Washburne Street for the moment of truth. Gingerly, I stepped into the boat, sat down and paddled away. A minute later the boat filled with water and sank to the bottom. Harold laughed his head off.

As we were drying my wet clothes over a wood stove we fired up in an abandoned house, I suggested we forget the boat, the river trip to Portland and instead concentrate on the Moore gang war.

CHAPTER FIVE

It was a warm summer evening and late in the month when Daddy returned from his long trip. I was standing on the front porch and suddenly saw him walking towards our house with his hat and suitcase. He had just arrived by train.

"Daddy's here, Daddy's here," I shouted, running through the house.

We all ran down the street to greet him. We were so happy to have him back, but it quickly became apparent that he did not find a job as a preacher in Denmark. Oh well, the main thing was that we were all together again. He prepared himself to resume his work as before, and for the rest of us, life went on as usual. The summer was just about over.

Three days later at the breakfast table, my mother said she didn't think there was anything to worry about, because last night she had a dream. She dreamt that a telegram arrived from Denmark with an offer of two positions in Denmark. She didn't know anymore, except that the one job location was where there was a tall, white tower. We all regarded her dream as merely an effort to comfort Daddy. He was quite tired after his trip and somewhat discouraged.

Harold and I resumed our work in the woodshed, building the tank. We were definitely behind schedule. High school was not far away. We found that the whole contraption was becoming much heavier than we had anticipated and consequently, more difficult to use as a mobile vehicle. We decided that a test run under the cover of darkness was necessary to verify our findings. With Hornibrook gang lookouts stationed on street corners, we wheeled our secret weapon out on to the street one evening. Four of us got inside through a trap door in the roof and we pushed it two blocks down to Doctor Roger's house and back. It was hard work. Changes would definitely have to be made.

We also had so much to do on the tower. It was now forty feet high, but

Harold said we should try to reach fifty feet before school started. He felt it was more important than the tank. There were still a number of buildings we couldn't see over from the lookout platform - including the church. He figured we would have to get it up to one hundred feet to be on the safe side. Hornibrook and Burton were of the same opinion, because the way it was now, the enemy could hide behind the church and we would never know it. We finally decided that both the tank and the hundred-foot tower must be completed by spring, 1934.

Next day at about two o'clock in the afternoon, as I was busy working on the tank, my mother came in and said that in four weeks time we were going to Denmark! I stood there, wondering if what I was hearing, was really what I was hearing. Suddenly the whole world stood still. The clock stopped. The universe was on hold.

"Are you sure?" I asked.

"Yes, we just got a telegram from Denmark and Daddy has been given a choice of two positions as church minister."

"I can't believe it. We can't jus' leave Junction City." I was stunned.

"Don't worry. Everything will be all right. It is best for us. We'll talk more about it at the supper table."

"But we belong here," I pleaded, as she left the woodshed.

Only four weeks! This couldn't be true. I stood there looking at my work, thinking feverishly. What should I do? We got this tank to finish. And what about the clubhouse and the tower? The tower was most important. We just had to get it up to one hundred feet. Who would run the Hornibrook gang? What about Blackie? Who would take care of him? Did this mean I would have to say goodbye to Harold and all my friends? What would I tell them all?

A whole nightmare of problems and questions seemed to overwhelm and confuse me. Harold was right. He warned me about the thirteenth year. He said I would continuously have to watch my step during that year, but darn it all, I didn't expect this. I went outside and sat on the woodpile to think some more. How about high school? It would start in a couple of weeks and that was where everyone would be - everyone I knew. This was awful. Blackie, forever faithful, came up to me, wagging his tail. I stroked his head. We just got to stick together, I thought. How could I get out of this?

At the supper table everyone was happy and excited except me. I could see Daddy was very relieved. All the worry and tension, that had been building up ever since he returned home, was gone. Mom was the same as usual. She was always happy. The kids were ecstatic - looking forward to a big train ride, seemingly indifferent to the consequences. Whichever way the wind blew was fine with them. After the table grace, Daddy added a prayer of thanks for our good fortune. I felt at that moment somewhat guilty about being so concerned with the unfinished tank and other things.

So Mom's dream came true. How did that happen? It had never happened before and frankly, she was not religious at all. She was like us children. None of us were religious. We, including my mother, just happened to be under the religious guidance and direction of my father and it was a very logical and natural environment for us. We talked about the strange dream. My father felt that it was spiritually inspired, but my mother didn't see it that way.

"It's just a coincidence," she said, "we all have dreams. But I must admit that I was surprised when the telegram came with the two positions."

"There's so much to do and so much to think about," Daddy remarked, taking the telegram out of his pocket to have another look at it.

"Now, let's see, the one location is at a place called *Sjaellands Odde* and the other is in a town called *Kolding*. Which shall we choose?"

Don't choose any, I thought. Those were awfully queer names and could only spell future trouble for us all. Why don't we just hang on and wait for Roosevelt to pull us out of our troubles with his New Deal program? We were Americans and Americans don't emigrate to other countries.

"I think it would be best for the children," Mom suggested, "if we choose the city rather than the country."

Darn it all, here was my future being decided right now at this very table.

"It would be better for their education."

"Yes, I can see that as being a very good point. What do you think, Visti?" Daddy asked, "Would you not rather live in a city than out in the country?"

"I guess so." What else could I say?

He ran his hand slowly over his hair, thinking deeply. He had very black hair, which was unusual for someone born in Scandinavia. Many years later I heard from Auntie Annie, that the reason his hair was black was because his grandmother, at the tender age of seventeen had an affair with an Italian sailor.

"Okay then, let's choose Kolding. It's a very nice place and I know we will all be happy there."

My fate was sealed.

"Oh, there's so much to do," Mom remarked, " and to think of all the canning I've just done. Well, we'll just have to give it away."

"With regards to school," Daddy pointed out, "I don't think the children need to go just for the sake of a few weeks."

"No, I think they should," Mom replied. "There's far too much to do with the children in the way, - but Visti can stay home and help."

There it was. No high school. Another nail in my coffin! The talking and excitement went on all evening, mostly as to what we should take with us to Denmark and what should be left behind. By bedtime, I had resigned myself to my fate and the departure from paradise.

The next morning Harold and I worked on the tank modifications for over an hour, before I mustered enough courage to spill the beans.

"Guess what."

"What?"

"We're goin' to Denmark."

"No kiddin'."

There were a few moments of silence after that. It took a little bit for the impact to settle in. Harold stopped what he was doing and looked at me.

"Yer not serious, are ya?"

"Yup, it's for sure an' there ain't nothin' I kin do about it, Harold. The fact is we're leaving pretty soon - in four weeks to be exact."

"Jiminy crickets, ya can't jus' leave everything. What about this here tank and the clubhouse? Does Hornibrook know?"

"Nope, I ain't tol' nobody yet."

"Well, let's keep this quiet, until we kin figure out what we're gonna do. No sense spreading the news around. Hey, I got it! Why don't ya go into hiding until it all blows over?"

"Ya mean they all go to Denmark and leave me behind here in Junction - 'cause they couldn't find me?"

"Well, sort of."

"Gee, I dunno. Someone else is gonna live in our house and where would I go? I can't live here."

"Maybe ya kin stay at our place. I'll ask my mom."

Suddenly the work on the tank became so unimportant. We went outside and stood around for awhile.

"D'ya know somethin'? I reckon we'd better move all this stuff to my place." Harold looked at the clubhouse with the impressive 27-foot lookout tower. "We can't leave the clubhouse here unprotected."

The clubhouse had a foundation of old railroad ties and built to last forever.

"I think we'll have to tell the gang 'bout me leaving, 'cause we can't move all this by ourselves. Wha'd'ya think, will ya tell 'em, Harold?"

He sighed. What a lot of problems for one day.

"Okay, okay, but think 'bout what I said. Hey, wait, I got it! Ya kin hide in Donald Dill's garage. We'll bring food in every day. Nobody will ever know."

"D'ya really think so?"

"Sure, what's wrong with that?"

We talked for another hour, but things got more complicated in my mind all the time. I did a lot of thinking. Eventually we parted and I went in the house. As soon as I felt the family around me, I knew I could not go into hiding in Donald Dill's garage. I decided the game was over. We would all be leaving Junction City together.

The news spread around fast. A day later the whole town knew we were pulling out. We were now in September and high school was just about to start. Everything became urgent. Moving the clubhouse to Harold's backyard would be an impossible task. To tear it down piece by piece would be most humiliating and would suggest that we had lost the battle with the Moore gang. It had to stay. We considered the tower to be just as important as the church tower across the street. They were both of equal height, but our tower served a better purpose, because it was a lookout. The church tower symbolized the serene life hereafter. Our clubhouse tower symbolized the concern for the present. The removal of the clubhouse and tower from the parsonage property would have been a great relief for the neighborhood as it was considered a community eyesore. However, there were many other junky-looking shacks and structures in town.

Friends of the family came to help with the packing and there was great activity day after day. I started to get caught up in the excitement of it all. A train trip and sailing on an ocean liner was certainly a lot more thrilling than anything going on in Junction City. Most kids had never seen an ocean liner. Our big heavy, upright piano from Boston was packed in a large wooden box. Underneath the keyboard where the pedals were was a lot of space, so that was filled with pots, pans, books and chinaware wrapped in blankets. We were sending all our belongings in boxes by boat via San Francisco through the Panama Canal to Denmark. The shipping company in San Francisco had advised my father that the shipment would go by volume, so the more we could cram into each box, the better. The huge box with the piano was packed on the front porch and must have weighed a ton, because overnight it sort of settled into the floorboards of the porch and was stuck there on a slant. The eight of us couldn't move it at all.

High school had started and it was a very strange feeling to be at home while everyone else was at school. I went over to Washburne High a few days before we were to leave and looked at the place, as the kids were coming out. I was on the far side of the street but some came over and remarked how lucky I was, not having to go to school. I didn't feel that way. I felt like an outsider - like having some sort of contagious disease or something.

A truck came to the house early one morning to pick up all the stuff for San Francisco. Almost at the same moment, a telegram came from the shipping company, saying that they made a mistake. The goods would be shipped and billed by weight and not by volume. This was a shocker for Daddy, because it meant that the box containing the piano, books, pots, pans and chinaware would cost a fortune. I really don't know how he managed things financially, but the two men who came in the truck couldn't manage things either. The piano box, stuck in the front porch, was like concrete. They tried and tried but nothing moved, so they told my father to get more help.

Daddy went down to the gas station at Main Street, bringing two men back with him. Together, the five of them managed to get the piano off the porch onto the sidewalk. Another man passing by also helped and together we all managed to roll it up on to the truck. The porch was damaged, but it couldn't be helped. All the other items went into the truck with ease and by noon, the house was empty. Daddy talked with the driver, signed some papers and shortly after that, the truck drove away down Highway 99 to San Francisco with almost all of our worldly belongings.

The kids now had a great time, running from one empty room to another, making all the noise they wanted. To me, it was as though we were eliminating ourselves from the face of this earth. We were burning all bridges and erasing all tracks. The atmosphere, sounds, activities and environment had just evaporated. Harold passed by to see how things were going and we both agreed it all looked pretty grim.

A farmer, at whose place we now were staying, passed by. He parked his old Model T Ford in front of the house. He and Daddy looked at the damaged porch and then went together over to the church to check on things. Mom told us to gather all the suitcases and our belongings and put them in the farmer's automobile. We checked the rooms for the last time and all went out on the front porch. Daddy and the farmer drove out to the farm with the suitcases. There was no room in the automobile for anything else, so the seven of us with Blackie sat on the porch step in the afternoon sun and waited for their return. It seemed so quiet. I think Blackie realized that something was happening that was not good, because he whined a bit and kept licking my face.

Half an hour later they came back and we all piled into the front and back seats of the Ford. It was a treat. Not very often did we get the opportunity to ride in an automobile. The farmer took the crank out of a toolbox on the running board and after a lot of vigorous cranking, got the engine running with explosions and smoke. He then jumped in behind the wheel to regulate the choke before it conked out. After a few jerks and explosions the vehicle started moving. We all took one last look at the parsonage and church, as we left for Dane Lane.

"I'll see ya at the station tomorrow," Harold said, waving his arm.

It was in the late afternoon of the next day. Our time had come. The leaves on the trees had turned golden brown and were falling to the ground, the loose hay was stacked high in wagons in the fields, the corn was ripe and so were the apples and pears. There was a lovely fragrance in the air as we headed for the station. It was harvest time in this beautiful valley - the time of hayrides to the barns, apple pie, corn on the cob, watermelons, Halloween pumpkins, Thanksgiving turkey and cranberry sauce - so much to experience and enjoy. The farmer's Model T chugged down Dane Lane to the train station, carrying the eight of us to our destiny. Another farmer in his vehicle, followed behind us with our suitcases.

There must have been at least fifty people on the platform at the station. I recognized most of them as being members of the church congregation. They flocked around as we climbed down from the vehicle. Harold was there. So was Donald Dill, Hornibrook and Burton. We had Blackie with us to give to Harold. He had said he would take care of him while I was gone. I had told Harold I would be back as soon as I could make it. Our suitcases were placed side by side in a neat row on the platform. My father and mother were very busy shaking hands with all our friends. My father thanked them all for the wonderful years we had with them and they did likewise, wishing us a wonderful trip. After that initial flurry of activity had died down, everyone stood along the platform facing the track, wondering what more there was to talk about. It was like waiting for a funeral to begin.

I looked at the rails - the rails that would remove me from Oregon. An idea came to my mind. I jumped down onto the tracks and placed six pennies on one of the rails, which was all I had in my pocket. Climbing up on the platform again, I told Harold to pick up the flattened pennies after the train had passed and give them to members of our gang 'in remembrance of me.' That was a phrase I had learned in church. I cuddled a bit with Blackie. So did the rest of the kids. He didn't know what it was all about. It was going to be hard not to have Blackie at my side, but it was all temporary. I would return and it would be very soon.

Right on time, the Southern Pacific appeared with the whistle blowing and surrounded by lots of steam and smoke. As it pulled to a stop at the train platform, all the excitement began. We all grabbed the suitcases, and there was lots of hugging and handshaking all around. One after another, we climbed aboard, running inside to find places at the windows, so we could wave to everybody. Faithful as ever, Blackie eagerly followed.

"Blackie's here, Blackie's here!" the kids shouted, excitedly with great concern, He was so happy to be on the train and jumped up on the wooden seat next to me. It was a most difficult moment. I had to lead him by the collar, back through the train to the steps, where Harold, realizing what was happening, took over. He grabbed Blackie's collar and held him back on the platform. My father came on board and made a quick count: one, two, three, four, five, six. Yes, we're all here. There was a brief pause of anticipation and then the train conductor shouted 'All aboard.' We looked at everybody on the platform through the open train windows and they all looked at us. So many friends. So many faces. In a minute or two it would all be only memories. It was a sad occasion indeed.

Nobody felt good. It was as though everyone had a stomach ache. And yet everything could be reversed. All we had to do was tell the conductor to hold everything, because we have changed our minds and want to get off. Everybody would light up and be happy. We could go back to the parsonage and have a big party.

The train whistle sounded. There was a lot of huffing and puffing from the big, black engine as it came alive with steam bursting out everywhere and then suddenly, we were moving. Everyone started waving frantically with their hands, arms, handkerchiefs and hats. We stretched our arms out of the windows, touching hands for the last time. This was it. History in the making. The final chapter. Paradise over. It was November 4, 1933.

The train gathered momentum. Before we knew it, the station was behind us. We started to pick up speed. Leaning out of the window, waving my arm, I shouted to Harold,

"Take care of Blackie. I'll see ya soon."

Harold shouted back, but I didn't hear what he said. As I looked back at the station, with all the people standing there, the whole picture grew smaller and smaller until it eventually became just a speck at the end of the rails. It was all over. Goodbye, Junction City.

We sat back in our seats, slightly bewildered. I had my suitcase next to me on the seat. It was a very important suitcase, as it contained my slingshot plus a special slingshot Harold gave me, four bottles of rootbeer extract from Pete's grocery, two jigsaw puzzles, my yo-yo, a bag of glass marbles, my geography book from school, my toothbrush, the American flag with a flag pole, three photos of the clubhouse, some clothes and my beanie cap - which by the way, had nothing to do with bean fields.

We were somewhat silent now, just for the moment, sitting in our new environment. The huffing and puffing up front and the clicking of the wheels on the rails were the only sounds, providing a steady rhythm that would be with us for the next four days. There was also a visual rhythm - that of telephone poles flying past like a picket fence. There was no doubt, things were happening.

In Portland that evening, we changed trains - from Southern Pacific to the 'Portland Rose,' the train that would take us all the way to Chicago. In the dark we left Oregon, the most important state in the Union. From now on we were on our own.

CHAPTER SIX

At bed time there was a bit of disturbance in our Pullman sleeping car, as to who should sleep in an upper berth and who should sleep in a lower berth, but my mother solved the problem by saying, that we would all take turns sleeping upper and lower and also take turns as to who might sit next to a window in the daytime. The first night it took a long time to fall asleep.

Next day I decided to find out where we were heading. I took the geography book out of my suitcase and opened it to the last two pages, that gave all the information one needed to know about the rest of the world. There were a couple of world maps in the front of the book that showed country borders and the annual rainfall, but it was in the back of the book that the nitty gritty facts were given about foreign countries. Going through the book, it was easy to see that the United States of America was more important than all these foreign countries, since there was so little about them and so much about us. And that was why everyone wanted to come here. Really, with this trip we were bucking the tide. We were going the wrong way.

On the second last page under index D, it said: *'Denmark is a little country in Scandinavia. The land which is at sea level, is flat and it is surrounded mostly by water. Fishing and agriculture provide the livelihood for the small population.'* It wasn't too much to go on. Fishing would be okay, but this word 'agriculture' sounded like there might be bean fields there. I looked back at the world map. Yes, it was awfully far away from Oregon. It might be harder to get back than I thought. And another thing, being way up north, who knows, there might even be snow. We might even have to wear winter clothes. Well, we didn't have any, so that solved that problem.

We crossed the Rockies, amazed at all the spectacular scenery and color, and descended into a landscape of sand and sagebrush that seemed to go on forever and ever without change. Passing through towns in Idaho, Wyoming, Nebraska and Iowa, poverty was evident, but it wasn't until we arrived on the outskirts of Chicago that the real severity of the Depression appeared.

As if in a different world of our own, we looked through the train windows at a passing panorama of abandoned stockyards, dirty streets and brick buildings, dilapidated, unpainted, wooden shacks with garbage everywhere, telephone poles, wires, clotheslines with laundry between buildings, hobos standing around, breadlines, empty back streets, empty stores, For Sale signs on walls, litter on sidewalks, in doorways and in alleys - a panorama of destitution amid squalor and pollution. Hundreds of men were standing at the side of the tracks, waiting for passing freights, but we had only quick glimpses of their faces as our train passed them by. It took us an hour to thread our way through the maze of railroad tracks in Chicago's backyard, before we finally reached the Dearborn Station.

We emerged from the door of the train, down the steps on to the crowded platform in the cavernous building, and Daddy made a quick count to see if all of us and our suitcases were off the train. It was here in Chicago we were to change trains for the last leg to New York. I noticed, standing on the platform that the name on the side of our Pullman car was Hiawatha. After verifying that all twelve items were in one spot - six children, five pieces of luggage and Mom, he left us to find out what train we now were to take.

We all stood close together with our suitcases around us and waited. It was sort of like a circle of covered wagons on the prairies, providing protection from the Indians. This was a very crowded place - something like when you remove a rock and see millions of disturbed ants scurrying around. And really, all this activity was unnecessary if everybody had stayed at home - like we should have done.

Daddy came back with information and instructions and we all followed him like quail with our suitcases to another train platform. He found a bench where we could sit and wait for our train, which he said, should be here in about one hour. Time seemed to go rather quickly as we sat there, because there was so much to look at.

Suddenly Vita said she had to go to the bathroom! Panic erupted! In twenty minutes the train would be here. Where was the bathroom? We all got up and looked around desperately.

"Can't you wait?" pleaded Mom.

"No, no, I got to go now." Vita wailed, jumping up and down. This was an awfully big station and from where we were standing, there was no sign of a bathroom, washroom, restroom or whatever they might have called it in Chicago. Daddy reacted immediately. Time was of the essence. He grabbed Vita by the hand and together they rushed down the platform, disappearing in the crowd. Three minutes later he was back with Vita still jumping up and down.

"I found it," he shouted, "but I can't go in with Vita, because it says 'Ladies' on the door."

Without hesitation Mom grabbed Vita and once again there was a rush down the platform into the crowd.

No sooner had they left, than our train came in easing to a stop at the platform. We looked at the clock overhead. There was still a full ten minutes before departure time. Daddy put the five of us and the suitcases on board the train and stood on the platform waiting, looking very concerned. We all leaned out of the open train windows, looking down the platform for a sign of Mom and Vita. The overhead clock changed almost unnoticed to five minutes. With his hat in his hand, Daddy ran down to the conductor at the other end of our rail car. I could see he had a lot to say, the way he was using his arms and now and then pointing in the direction of the public restrooms down the platform. The scheduled time for departure suddenly arrived. We kids expected the very worst to happen. The big engine way down at the far end, was sort of simmering, with steam oozing out all around, impatient and ready for action. We were extremely upset, especially Xenia, who I thought was on the verge of an asthma attack, but Daddy came back to us, calming us down somewhat by saying the conductor told him they would hold the train and wait a bit. Other people were also hanging out of windows, saying goodbye to their friends in anticipation of prompt departure. Five minutes past the scheduled departure time, Mom and Vita reappeared, running towards us with great haste. Daddy, standing at the steps, helped Mom and Vita aboard and followed closely behind them. The conductor was next to follow, blowing his whistle as he waved toward the engine. Almost instantly the train moved. What a relief! We were all together again.

Mom explained that the reason for the delay was that there were coin operated locks on the toilet doors. She couldn't open them and she had no money. Eventually she found an attendant who opened one of the doors after noticing how much Vita jumped up and down. This whole episode was almost enough to generate a heart attack. As we pulled out of Chicago we became more relaxed. It was getting dark now. We closed the windows, sat back and waited for meal time in the dining car. Dearborn station was a place we would not soon forget.

At the end of the fourth day we arrived in New York. But although we could see the famous skyscrapers as a skyline, we ended up on the other side of the river in Hoboken. I have no idea how my father found such a cheap run-down place for our last night in North America. It was a three-storey, brick rooming house, squeezed in between a number of other questionable brick buildings, all of them on a dark street that looked like a breeding ground for gangsterism. I figured we were in this sleazy place because it was dirt cheap. After all, we were pretty poor. Daddy must have been given the address from someone in Junction City. For much of the night, the flashing neon lights of a diner directly across the street kept me awake.

The luxurious ocean liner was called *Frederik the Eighth*. It was big. It had two masts, one with a crows nest, and two large funnels. The ship must have been about 600 feet long. We arrived at the docks on the New York side of the Hudson River about noon, after having gone under the river by subway and after a quick visit to the Chrysler building. There were a few formalities with papers that my father took care of at the dock and we went up the gangplank, but for my part, not before I prepared myself for this historical moment of departure from American soil. I wished newspaper photographers were there to take pictures or maybe even a reporter from Junction City Times, to record the very moment I lifted my foot from American soil. But, of course, there was no one around.

I would have liked to have seen a write-up in the Junction City Times under the photo, which would say: *Young American leaves the United States temporarily. Visti Favrholdt, who has been such an asset to our community over the years, is currently on an overseas trip. We have been informed that he will return to*

Junction City shortly. I knew, of course, that this was wishful thinking. It was more likely that a write-up would consist simply of two words: *Good riddance.*

I stood at the bottom of the gangplank on the ground as long as I was permitted to do so. Everyone else seemed happier on the ship. But the time for farewell had come. I was compelled to get on board. The gangplank was taken away, the ropes pulled in and an earth shattering blast from one of the funnels, signaled our departure from the land where we belonged. We eased down the Hudson River, assisted by tugboats, and then were let loose to find our way to Denmark.

For the next hour I stood by a railing at the stern, keeping my eyes fixed on the Statue of Liberty. My mother came and asked if I didn't want to join the rest of the kids who were having so much fun elsewhere on the ship, but I said,

"No, I'll stay here a little and see the last of America."

"Well, take care you don't catch a chill and don't be too long."

"Okay, I'll be up in a little while."

She left and I looked at the trail of white foam from the ship all the way out to the horizon. The Statue of Liberty was definitely getting smaller. The configuration was clearly defined, but it was very far away. It almost looked like it was waving goodbye. The lower part of the statue disappeared first, sinking into the ocean. And then the top part, the head and arm holding the torch, just faded away ever so gently. I stood there for a little while longer. I felt that an important part of my life was now a memory.

Frederik the Eighth, named after a Danish king, was a floating palace. By the standards of the day, it probably didn't rate very high, but for the poor passengers from Oregon, it was luxury unlimited. To be served lavish, three course meals with real tablecloths and silver cutlery by waiters all dressed in white, to have your bed prepared with fresh linen every day, to be treated like royalty with nothing at all to do - these were blessings my mother had never experienced before. I, for my part, looked forward each day to the scrumptious desserts consisting of Napoleon tarts, Othela cake, fruit and ice cream. There was a small library on board and even a grand piano. We were living in fantasy land.

We passed Cape Race of Newfoundland and I was told that we would be heading over the top of Scotland and then sail down to Denmark. Why the captain decided on this route, when my geography book clearly showed that a straight line from New York to Denmark was much shorter than a curve, I could not figure out. I was sure Old Lady Ballard would have agreed with me.

I spent many hours up on deck, standing at the railing watching the waves, the seagulls and in particular, the seaman standing alert in the crows nest, a basket attached to the forward mast, about fifty feet above the deck. His job was to watch out for anything ahead that might present a danger, such as a whale, iceberg or another ship. Every quarter of an hour he had to ring a bell above the crows nest, to indicate that he was still awake. The constant vibration of the ship's propellers, the bellowing black smoke from the red painted funnels, trailing along in the wake for miles behind us, the gentle roll of the deck, the sound of the waves and the sea breeze in my face - all this gave me a feeling of being on a very special voyage at a very special time, but still in a state of limbo, suspended between two worlds.

It wasn't long before the many passengers on board started to mingle. I met a boy my age from New Jersey. He said his Dad was fed up with New Jersey and all the hassle there, so he and his family were now on their way to Russia, where there was no depression. I didn't know where Russia was, except that it was in the same direction as we were going. He had a sister, a bit younger, who was very beautiful with brown hair. My heart fluttered every time I saw her. But then she got seasick and I never saw her again.

Time passed by rather quickly. The day of reckoning was not far away. I did not have the slightest inkling as to what lay ahead, but one thing I knew for sure, it would not be another Junction City. Certainly the climate would be different. Already, on board this ship, I noticed that the weather was getting colder and we no longer spent much time outside. Also, we were losing time going east. The hour hand of the clock in the ship's dining room was moved one hour forward every day. Oh well, I would get the lost time back, when I returned to Oregon.

To keep the passengers entertained, the ship's address system broadcast music. Since they apparently only had a couple of gramophone records, the repetitious monotony of the music was almost too much to bear. 'The Blue Danube' and a melody called 'The Whistler and his Dog' were heard every day all across the Atlantic. I wondered what the seagulls thought of it all, flying with our ship all the way to Europe.

After being on the ocean for eleven days, extra cheer came our way in the form of the Captain's Dinner, a grand finale to our life in fantasy land. Here we saw the captain in person, smartly dressed in his white uniform with gold buttons and trimmings - the person responsible for getting us across the vast expanse of ocean - and finding Denmark, probably the next day. We were not privileged to sit at his table as we were not important enough, but we were in the same room and it was considered an honor to be in his presence.

Little did the captain know, that in five years time, this mighty ship, with all its power, glamor and luxury would be sold as scrap metal to England for the making of cannons for World War II, and he probably would be joining the list of unemployed. But right now he looked very important, and the ship was in one piece with a purpose and a destination.

That night our ship entered a fjord in Norway.

CHAPTER SEVEN

Standing on the deck in the cold of the night, I could distinguish lights some distance away on both sides of the ship. It was clear we were in a kind of channel. Another passenger said it was a Norwegian fjord. How he could tell, I didn't know, because it was pretty dark out there. But one thing was very clear. The captain of our ship, for all his golden buttons and stripes, must have got lost because he was supposed to find Denmark. Columbus could have done better.

I stood there in the dark and thought about the matter for awhile. Maybe someone should speak to the captain. Maybe we could give up searching and head back to New York.

About midnight we arrived at the harbor in Oslo. I had gone to bed, but woke up suddenly, because for the first time in eleven days, the ship was not moving. Also we heard the strange voices of dockworkers - strange, because they spoke words I did not understand. It was icy cold and there was snow below us on the illuminated dock and on the roofs of nearby buildings. We were only there an hour, but looking over the railing, it was long enough to give me a taste of what was to come. I decided to be on the defensive in this hostile, foreign environment. I then returned to my bunk, feeling that as long as I could keep my wits together, I would survive.

Unfortunately, the next day the captain found Denmark. It was just as cold as Norway. Copenhagen suddenly appeared - a city with red tile roofs, fancy church and castle towers and all sprinkled with snow. It all looked very strange. There was no resemblance at all to anything American. This was scary. Very slowly we approached a large harbor area, where other large ships were at rest. A space for our ship appeared, we nudged into the dock, the rope lines were cast and after a review of the whole situation, a gangplank was brought into position. We looked at the proceedings through portholes. It was too cold to be on deck.

We left the ship a short time later, walking down the gangplank with our suitcases, and staying together as much as we could. It was very windy and we could feel the chill. There were buses at the dockside to take passengers to the railway station. Daddy helped us into one of them, and we children quickly realized that the trip was not yet over. The bus ride through Copenhagen was a cultural shock - strange looking buildings, narrow crooked streets, thousands of people on bicycles, signs on stores that I could not read, funny looking yellow streetcars, cobblestone squares, frozen fountains and snow everywhere. Through the window I looked at it all apprehensively. I thought to myself, 'Boy, wait till I tell Harold about this.' Daddy, Mom and the kids, on the other hand, had no problem adjusting to these new images.

At the large train station in the center of the city we went down some stairs to our platform and the waiting train. It wasn't exactly your Pullman Sleeper, but at looked like a train and was warm inside. Unlike American trains, there was a corridor running down one side, with sliding doors into compartments with two opposite seats. We filled one compartment completely. Each rail car had only four wheels. The little black engine was the type you see in crayon books for children. It also had only four wheels, but to make up for all its shortcomings, it featured a slim, black smoke stack at least three feet high. The train whistle had the sound of a flute. Just a little shrill pip. There was no feeling to it at all. It sounded like it needed to be oiled or overhauled. Our American train whistle on the other hand, had depth and meaning. The mournful, lingering sound with changing pitch seemed to communicate with the surrounding landscape. It conveyed a message and was very American. Oh well, I thought, the inventor of this funny Danish whistle will probably some day realize that it takes more than a shrill pipsqueak to communicate with feeling.

I was gradually accepting one revelation after another without too much hostility, partly because there was so much happening around us and partly because everything was so different. The train chugged along 'like the little engine that could' and the winter landscape moved past our window without much sign of life. We were out in the country. All was white. The farmhouses, deep in snow, were very isolated. Most likely, everyone was inside waiting for spring. The sky was grey. This was indeed the Far North that Donald Dill had talked about.

A conductor, wearing a strange looking, black uniform and a funny cap with a red stripe opened the door to our compartment. Nothing like our conductors, I thought. He checked our tickets and spoke a little to my father in that funny language, which I knew to be Danish. After he left, Daddy told us that we were informed that this train went on two ferries and would take us directly to Fredericia, our destination. We were actually on an island and had to take the ferry to a second island and then another to the peninsula, called Jutland, where the town, Fredericia was located. They weren't kidding when they said this place was surrounded by water.

After many hours of ever-changing scenery and impressions, we arrived somewhat tired, in Fredericia in the late afternoon. My uncle Anders, who we children had never seen before, was at the train station to greet us and to take us to his farm. He had his arms full of coats, mittens and scarves. There was a happy exchange of greetings and then, bundled up in all the additional clothing, we followed him out of the station. I don't know what made me think there would be a car waiting outside the station, but here was an open sleigh with two big horses! One would think we were going to be on our way to the North Pole.

We all climbed up into the open sleigh where numerous blankets were wrapped around us to keep warm. My uncle took the reins, cracked the whip and the horses headed down the street, making new tracks in the falling snow. We passed through the town, just as foreign looking as Copenhagen, and found ourselves on a country road, leading out into the middle of nowhere. The snow was quite deep, but compact on the road surface. Daddy told us that this was the worst snowfall they had experienced in years. It was also unusual to have snow so early in the winter. It didn't matter to me, because everything was unusual and one thing more or less didn't change the picture much. It was all gloomy and dismal, anyways.

It was getting dark and windy when we finally arrived at the farm - at the end of our long journey, sixteen days in all. Another historical moment and cultural shock. Another impression to absorb and digest - and who knows, maybe another nail in my coffin. The farm consisted of four one-storey, brick buildings with whitewashed walls and thatched straw roofs, positioned around an interior cobblestone courtyard. Three were farm buildings and the fourth was the living quarters. Light through the windows reflected on the snow. It all looked as being from the middle ages.

The sleigh came to a stop at the weather-beaten kitchen door of the farmhouse. Sonya, Ben and David were all fast asleep at this time. For them, it had been too much for one day. On the other hand, I was very alert. I had to be. This was all such a drastic change for me. The kitchen door opened, the sleigh was bathed in light and my uncle's wife came out, excited and with outstretched arms, welcoming us all. Her two children were right behind her. It was a great moment for them and a great moment for Daddy and Mom. For me it was just another moment. The commotion woke up Sonya, Ben and David who didn't have the slightest idea where they were.

We were all ushered into the farm house, with a lot of talk in Danish, the funny language. I could instantly see that this place was behind the times. The kitchen had a stone floor and there were oil lamps, the kind with wicks you adjust, so they don't smoke. There was no electricity. There was no plumbing. The iron kitchen sink had a pump, with a large curved iron handle for pumping water from a ground well far below. Hot running water was nonexistent. To me the whole place was like entering a strange museum. I estimated they were one hundred years behind times. If this was the situation elsewhere in this strange country, then either we were going to be in for a rough time ahead, or maybe we should bring in American know-how from Junction City and make a fortune.

We took off the overcoats, scarves and mittens. A lot of big iron pots were steaming away on a large wood-burning stove and there was the smell of a meal being prepared. Mom combed our hair and made sure we all looked presentable, as we entered the dining room from the kitchen.

The table was set for dinner. It looked like it was going to be a banquet. It was our welcome party. We were many at the table, in all eight of us and four of them plus two farmhands who were employed there. The glasses were filled with red wine for the adults and apple juice for the children. This was the second time in my life that I had seen wine served at a table - the first time being on board the ship. I always thought red wine was made only for religious purposes - like communion. However, you had to be an adult to drink red wine. There was a lot of talking going on during the meal, but I understood nothing.

Eventually, it was decided by Mom that it was time for us children to prepare for bed. In good old USA it was a simple matter. Mom would simply say 'It's time for bed. Go to the bathroom and remember to brush your teeth at least two minutes. I'll come and tuck you in later.' But here it was different. There was no bathroom. We had to put on heavy overclothes and go outside.

It was decided that Vita should go first, since she was the one who, at the mere mention of the word 'bathroom,' found herself jumping up and down. Mom dressed her up in an overcoat, scarf and a pair of wooden clogs that were in the kitchen, and she herself did likewise. Together, holding a lantern, they opened the kitchen door and went outside into the dark of the night and a raging snowstorm. Daddy quickly explained to the rest of us that it was an outhouse they were heading for, but that it was located in the farm building next to the pig pens, so it wasn't too cold in there.

While they were out, the rest of us prepared ourselves for our turn to brave the elements. The overclothes and wraps given to us, didn't fit very well. The clogs I had on belonged to one of the farmhands and were much too large. But all this didn't matter much. It was merely a matter of getting from point A to point B without freezing.

The farm building had an aisle going all the way down the middle with pig pens both sides. There were posts here and there holding up the straw roof and a partition, separating part of the building from the pen area. The toilet seat arrangement, located at the partition, was simply a wooden board with a hole in it flanked by a wall each side for privacy but with an open view of the pens. The pigs made a lot of noise when I entered. The lantern, which I hung on a post, formed eerie shadows on the whitewashed ceiling and walls. I noticed that the toilet paper was old Danish newspapers. As I sat there in this cold place, looking at my oversized wooden clogs, listening to the oink, oink of pigs and the howling wind outside, I really felt the cultural shock of my first day in Denmark. What would Harold or the rest of the gang say, if they saw me here. They probably would laugh their heads off.

I woke up the next morning, feeling like a pancake. The eight of us were in two bedrooms in the upper storey of the farmhouse, an area that had been closed off for the last twenty years and was as cold as an ice box. Since all the windows were frozen solid, the stale air inside was probably also twenty years old. We breathed that stuff all night, as we lay crushed under the weight of the feather beds, which were huge cotton bags filled with chicken feathers and heaven knows what, weighing at least a hundred and fifty pounds each. You crawled into bed with this mountain on top of you and felt like you were under a rock. However, next morning we did feel better than the night before and were happy to see the sun was shining. Also, it looked like the snow was melting. At the breakfast table we were asked if we all slept well. Mom translated and we replied, 'Very well, thank you.' We each got a bowl of hot oatmeal with a cube of butter in the middle and milk all around. This was not in my opinion, as nutritious as white bread and jam for breakfast, the way it was in Junction City, but my uncle and his family looked healthy enough.

We spent the first day on the farm looking at the horses, cows, pigs, ducks, roosters and chickens and playing in the snow. There was nothing to resent or be startled about, so I had no complaints. Daddy left us, spending a few days at the town called Kolding to get things ready. He had to find us a place to live and start his new position as minister of the Lutheran church there. In this country there was no such thing as a preacher. 'Minister' was the correct title and the state financed the church and paid the minister's salary. This was a great relief for my father, who no longer had to rely on charity and a few coins in a collection plate. I am sure they paid for our trip from Oregon, because I couldn't imagine any other source to cover that expense. Even at my young age, I realized that the move from America probably was best for the family, but personally, I was a displaced person and was only here temporarily. It was all a matter of time before I would leave the nest and return to Junction City.

Our cousins did their best to entertain us and make us feel happy but the

THE GATHERING STORM

language was a problem. They could say very little in English and we knew no Danish at all. The boy was three years older than I and had many farm chores to do every day, so I didn't see too much of him. In a little back room off the kitchen was a table with a radio on it, complete with earphones. It was a wooden box with some wires inside and a crystal on top, that looked like a small piece of coal. With a wire, you touched the crystal, and if you were lucky you might hear a voice or maybe even music. I noticed I was able to get different stations depending on where the wire touched the crystal, but it was all far away. This was about all there was for me to do on the farm, so I spent hours tinkering with the little box. I had noticed a number of soup dishes side by side on top of a cupboard in the room. They had been there quite a few days. I stood up on a chair and took a look. There seemed to be something like white paint in the bowls. Lots of strange things in this place, I thought. One afternoon when I entered the room they were gone. I just about fell off my chair at the dinner table that evening when I discovered that each one of us had one of those bowls placed before us with a spoon. It was a shock. I whispered to Xenia,

"Don't eat it. As far as I can figure out, it's paint."

"Really? I wonder." She sniffed the bowl. "It doesn't smell like paint."

"Don't take chances. Let the others start first," I said, looking around in a sneaky manner.

Everyone was taking their places and Daddy was waiting to say grace. I managed to whisper another warning to Xenia,

"This stuff has ben sittin' on top of the cupboard in the other room fer a whole week."

"Really? I didn't know that."

With folded hands, we all bowed our heads as Daddy thanked the Lord for the food we were about to receive, asking Him in His name to accept our most humble gratitude. All the adults said 'Amen,' picked up their spoons and started eating. So did Vita, Ben, Sonya and David and my cousins. Xenia and I decided to wait a little bit. It was better to be on the safe side and see what might happen.

"Visti, what's the matter with you?" Mom said suddenly, "Aren't you going to eat?"

"We don't know what it is," Xenia replied, coming to my defence.

"Don't be silly. It's curds and whey. You will like it. It's good for you."

Curds and whey! What in the world was that? Xenia, hesitantly took a small mouthful, swallowed it, sat there as if in a trance for about five seconds and then, turning to me, said that it was okay. Knowing that all eyes would be upon me, if I didn't take the plunge, I closed my eyes and swallowed a small spoonful. I didn't like it. Not at all. Strange stuff. So I decided to be difficult. I simply refused to eat it. It was only the first course, so I did get my fill, eating other things that were more normal. And I think they learned a lesson - not to serve strange food to an American kid, who is old enough to decide for himself, what tastes okay and what does not.

Every meal was a discovery. Some things I found acceptable. Some things were not. I liked the apple sauce cake with whipping cream, but I hated the pudding, made of malt beer and pumpernickel bread. I liked potatoes and gravy, but didn't like eating raw fish. Also having to eat a chicken that, only a few hours before, was alive and well, took some adjustment. It was one morning, that my uncle grabbed a chicken in the farmyard, and with a hatchet, chopped off its head. The headless chicken dashed out of the farmyard and ran down the road for about a half a block, before it keeled over and ended up in a ditch.

After spending about a week on the farm, everything seemed to be ready for our move to Kolding, which was only about thirty kilometers away. That was another funny thing - kilometers instead of miles! Wonders never ceased. Kolding was a town of about twenty-two thousand, situated at the end of a fjord. Most of the snow on roadways was gone by now, but it was still cold and windy. There was never a day without wind from somewhere.

We said 'thank you,' and 'see you soon' to my uncle and his family at the farm. We were supposed to go by horse wagon to the train station, but there seemed to be a problem with the aging horse, so a taxi was called at great expense. As there were eight of us, plus suitcases and driver, the taxi barely made it to the station.

In United States during the thirties, it was very popular to try to break records, like sitting on top of a telephone pole for 60 days, flying an airplane upside down from Chicago to New York or eating 20 watermelons, one after the other. There was also Charles Lindberg, who flew across the Atlantic. In the case of this taxi trip, we broke another record. We were packed in like sardines.

The train trip to Kolding only took half an hour. We passed through hilly country and saw a couple of windmills along the way. Coming around a curve near the fjord, we caught our first glimpse of Kolding through some fir trees. It was at the end of a fjord surrounded by hills. An old castle and two church towers, one in the center of town and the other on the far side of town, projected above the red roof tops. One church tower was dark red in color. The other was white. Daddy said the white one was our church.

Immediately, Mom lightened up and said that was the tower she had seen in her dream. Uncanny! I didn't know what to think and neither did Xenia. The rest  of the kids didn't worry about it. Mom didn't speculate about the dream either. It was just one of those things. But as far as Daddy was concerned, he reminded us again that the dream was religiously inspired. On our arrival at the station we were met by a member of the church congregation, who arranged for a taxi to take us to our place of residence.

We drove along quaint, winding streets and arrived twenty minutes later at an apartment on the second floor of a old building in the middle of town. This was our new home. It was on a street called Haderslevgade. Haderslev was also the name of a town thirty-two kilometers farther south. Little did I know at the time, but that place called Haderslev would later shock the daylights out of me. The front windows of the apartment faced a noisy street and the back windows in the kitchen faced an enclosed yard surrounded by other buildings. In the middle of the yard were garbage cans and a row of outhouses. Number twelve was ours and it even had a padlock on the wooden door. There was no toilet in the house. It was the same thing all over again. Not like our house in Oregon. Our boxes and crates from San Francisco had not yet arrived, but the apartment was furnished, albeit sparsely, and we had a few belongings.

Every time I opened my suitcase and looked at my few possessions, I was reminded of Junction City, but here outside it was a different world - a world I caught a glimpse of as we drove through town and now must face. Today it was comforting to be inside with the family. Tomorrow I might venture outside.

The very first thing that had to be done, was to prepare myself to face the strange environment out there on the street. I thought a lot about this and realized what I needed was something with which to protect myself. So at my request, Daddy wrote on a piece of paper *Jeg kan ikke tale Dansk,* which, translated said 'I cannot speak Danish.' I put this in my shirt pocket and intended to have that with me at all times. If someone stopped me on the street and started to ask questions in the funny language, I would simply show them the piece of paper and they wouldn't bother me anymore.

That evening, looking out of the window at the street below, I saw a man on a bicycle carrying a ten foot long pole with a hook on the end. He cycled up to a street lamp, inserted the hook into a wire loop under the lamp and pulled. Presto! The gas lamp was lit. What would they think of next? In Junction City we had electricity to light up the main street, although I would have to admit that most of Junction City was in darkness at night. I watched this man with his pole, ride his bike down the street to the next lamp and turn that one on. I wondered how long it took him to cover the whole city. And then another thing - he had to come back in the early morning and turn them all off again. There must have been thousands of these lamps in Kolding, because just from the apartment window, I could see at least six of them. Here was a man who could truthfully say 'Let there be Light.' He was called a Lamplighter and without him the town would be in darkness.

CHAPTER EIGHT

Next morning was the day of discovery. Instead of looking at cows, pigs and chickens, I could now see what my new world around me was like. I left the apartment and walked down the busy street, carefully looking at all the strange sights and people. I was very much on the defensive.

The first thing I noticed was that everyone was riding bicycles. There were very few cars, but lots of horse drawn wagons. Most of the winding streets were cobblestone. Many of the stores had curly wrought iron hooks projecting out above the store entrances, holding up artificial samples of the merchandise they sold. A bookstore would have a book hanging from a chain. A baker would have a Danish cake called a *Kringle.* A watchmaker would have a clock which didn't actually work, being just a piece of wood. A shoemaker would hang up a boot and a hatmaker would display a hat. A butcher would display a wooden head of a cow and a tobacco store would have a cigar. All roofs were red tile and some of the houses had the eaves so low, you could almost touch them. I noticed policemen wore black uniforms with silver buttons. They wore white gloves and had helmets, similar in appearance to the soldiers of the Roman empire period. They carried black sticks in their belts.

I stopped at a toy shop and looked in the window. Never in my whole life had I seen such a display of exciting toys. Everything was decorated for Christmas. It was a beautiful sight. This looked promising. Someday perhaps, I would be able to buy some of these things and take them back with me to Junction City.

Just then, someone tapped me on the shoulder. I turned quickly around and found myself facing a policeman! There seemed to be an emergency. He said something to me in the funny language. I grabbed the piece of paper in my pocket and held it up for him to see. He looked at it and then looked at me and then looked up and down the street, wondering what to do next. I certainly didn't know and felt very nervous, not knowing what I had done wrong. Maybe I was trespassing or something. Just then, the owner of the toy shop came out, glanced at me and said something to the policeman. They talked a bit and the store owner turned to me and said in my language,

"Do you speak English?"

"Yes, I do," I replied.

"Well, this policeman wants to know why you are not in school."

"Gee, I dunno. We jus' came here yesterday. I'm from America."

The two of them talked some more. Then they both laughed, the policeman patted me on the back and walked away. Yes, school was something I hadn't even thought about yet. I could see now, there were no kids on the streets. Here we were in December. Maybe Daddy would let me skip this school year. I continued down the street with a little more confidence. That piece of paper I had in my shirt pocket really worked. I decided I would use it continuously, until I returned to Junction City.

A couple of hours later I was back at the apartment. Daddy was at the church, Xenia was helping Mom in the kitchen and Vita, Ben and Sonya were down in the enclosed yard, playing with some Danish kids. They were all bundled up, as it was cold and windy. I decided that I had better look for the letter I had written to Harold. Somehow it was lost. I eventually figured it was left at the farm. In the letter I told Harold about the long trip, the awful, terrible shock of arriving at this strange, cold country and about our stay at my uncle's farm. I called the letter *An American's tragedy,* but never found it.

During the next few days I did some more exploring and found out that the castle that we saw from the train, was right in the center of town. Built in the year of 1268 by a king named Erik Glipping, it looked like it had been through a lot of battles. Most of it was in ruins.

I also saw some kids come out of a school one afternoon. I stood inconspicuously in a doorway as they passed by and was able to get a real close look at them. They were about my age and were carrying their schoolbooks. There was no doubt that they looked foreign. First of all, they all had blond, golden hair and all the girls had long braids down their back with white ribbons. The boys all wore funny looking pants which I later found out were called knickerbockers. They were baggy and made them look like sissies. All the kids wore wooden clogs and were talking in the funny language. They went to a school bicycle shed and each picked out a black bike from the hundreds of black bikes in the shed and pedaled away.

I wondered if I ever could mingle with them. Well, one thing was sure. I would fight it all the way. I looked different, my thinking was different, my clothes were different and I had absolutely nothing at all in common with them. I almost felt a shudder, thinking that I might be forced into a school with them. On the other hand, Daddy and Mom surely would not do a thing like that. They were always on my side. I decided I had better write a second letter to Harold immediately while there was still time, because the future looked like it was going to be a disaster for me.

Dear Harold,   *December 9, 1933*

I reckon ya will never git a letter from me where I say I ain't got nothing to write about. I got so much junk to tell about that my brain is nearly busting to flinders. How's Blackie? Does he miss me? Have ya had any scraps or fights with Kelso yet? Ya don't know how tough it is to be here. I ain't got no friends and I can't understand what people are saying. I feel terribly, ripping, blasted, awful, hopelessly lonesome and homesick fer Junction City and I don't mean maybe. Do ya miss me much or am I jus a faint diminishing shadow in yer memory? I feel like I'm trapped, but don't ya worry, I'll find a way to git back real soon. In the Hornibrook gang we learnt how to git out of fixes and I'll use that experience here.

There's lots of things that are really dizzy here. Danish money has holes in it and theres no ring to a coin when ya drop it on the sidewalk so, fer all I know all the Danish coins could be conterfeit. Doors have door handles instead of door knobs, but I must say that these handles are very praktikal, cause ya can open a door with yer hand, yer elbow, yer little finger, yer head and even with yer foot if ya have to. Windows open outward instead of up and down. I don't think the people here have ever heard of the American kind. Horses are used everywhere to pull wagons cause there's hardly any cars around. Clocks have 24 hours on them instead of 12 which makes it impossible to tell the time. Suppose, Harold, somebody said to ya it was 23 minutes past 19 o'clock. Holy smoke! would ya ever be confused. Well, that's the way it is here and my mother says it's very praktikal. As far as I can figure out it jus means more rithmatik fer everyone. Now I gotta carry a piece of paper and pencil in my pocket all the time jus to figure out the time and I can't stand rithmatik. I think the inventer of the silly clocks made em jus to hurt peoples feelings making them do more rithmatik.

They got chimney-sweepers here in Denmark. Ya always gotta have yer chimney done by a chimney-sweeper. There are only bout 5 in each town so it's pretty good bizness. They have the blackest clothes on and wear a hat like a preacher has got. They are mighty black with soot and carry alot of brooms and different things and also some rope. They ride around on bikes like everybody else. When ya are a chimney-sweeper ya never have to bother washing yerself  *cause ya get dirty all the time so thats kinda conveniant.*

A real crazy thing here is the writing. I hain't seen much of it, but what I've seen is pretty awful. The people don't write with their arm like we do in America. No, they write with jus their fingers. In America we believe in having nice round curves in our handwriting like we did at grade school, but here they believe in a stiff, pointed handwriting that looks like a bunch of crawly dead spiders on the paper. It almost makes ya want to vomit. And then they have three extra letters in their alphabet which makes it impossible to learn their darn language. Another dizzy thing, they don't slant their paper when they write. If that ain't what I call silly and dizzy, I don't know what is. Jus try to write without slanting yer paper and see what a heck of a job it is. I think if Opal Burgess was here she could help straighten things out. They really need help.

The policemen here wear white gloves and black suits with silver buttons on them and they wear black roman empire helmets. They stand on the corners of the main streets stopping the traffic and telling em where to go. They don't do any hollering but only make moshuns with their hands. The policemen are also a real noosence. In Junction City when ya licked Raymond Mosegaard they warn't any cops to boss ya around - was there?

No, of course not. Thats cause the cops don't want to interfere with free enterprise. But here it's diferent. Boys can't fight without the policemen interfering. I can't shoot kids with my slingshot either. A kid can't do a blooming thing without these windbags bossing em around.

Here in this dizzy place the houses are built of brick. Another dizzy thing is that the roofs of houses got tiles on them and they are always red. It's a shame that the houses h'ain't got shingles cause I can't make arrows or airplanes and the other things we used to make out of shingles in Junction. 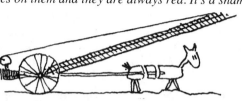 *It is also a shame cause it makes it so that there ain't no houses on fire. It was much more fun in Junction where houses burnt down at least once a month. And what a fire department they got here! It's crazy!*

The ladder wagon is pulled by horses and they got an old ford which carries the fire hose, which ain't no thicker than an American garden hose. There's never any fires but they got fire practise all the time. The firemen are the silliest lookin men in all of Denmark. They are short and powerfully fat. They wear black uniforms and red belts and roman empire helmets like the policemen here but with a wider rim. Everytime they finish fire practise, they go parading around town. Some of them got horns and drums to march along with and then they sit together on the ladder wagon in the middle of the street and drink beer. It's good in a way there's no fires cause nobody would know were to find the firemen when they are out parading all the time all over the place.

Drug stores don't have soda fountains, they only sell medicine. There are speshal stores that sell only cigars and cigarettes and speshal stores that sell only magazines and noospapers. The candy stores and bakeries are perfect. The only good reason to stay in Denmark is on account of the cakes at the bakery. They are loaded with whipping cream and jam.

The wind here is a real noosence. It never, never stops. If it don't blow from the east then it blows from the west and if it don't blow from the east or west, then it blows from the south and if it don't blow from the east or west or south, then it blows from the north. It's hard fer the thousands of people riding bikes here cause no matter where they go, the wind is always against them. Kettles here have whistles on them so that when the water starts boiling, the whistle blows.

My father has been powerfully busy at the new church. He's only been there a couple of days and he's already had 3 funerals, baptised 8 babies and 2 marriages. When somebody gets married in the church, the janitor (who is dressed as slick as a whistle and very partikuler) puts speshal carpets on top of the every-day carpets and he puts a genuine turkish carpet by the altar. The are only fer the bride and bridegroom to walk on, cause the first day of their marriage is a happy day and thats when they are speshal. There are two churches here in Kolding and they got two bells apiece in the church towers. Every morning the bells ring at six o'clock to wake everyone up fer a new day and at six in the evening ya hear them again and it's to tell everyone it's supper time. It's always nice to know. Tomorrow we're gonna go to the church fer the first time.

Bicycles are very, very, very, very, very common here in Denmark. Every single person rides a bike which is the policemen, the workers, the school teachers, the doctors, the postmen and everyone else. Even the poorest people got bikes. There are speshal paths fer jus bicycles to go on. The bikes got funny lights fixed to a contrapshun called a dynamo that touches the front wheel. When the wheel goes round it makes elektricity. A pretty good idea. This reminds me, Harold, the bike ya got stolen - I'm sure it was Kelso or someone else in the Moore gang. Maybe ya should spy around a bit and shadow Kelso. I bet a dollar he stole it and sold it to one of the bicycle shops in Eugene.

The streets in Danish towns wind in and out all over the place like a jigsaw puzzle and that is fer a good reason, cause in the olden days when the enemy attacked a town they would git lost in the streets and couldn't find their way out and then people in the town could capture them all.

There's just oceans of German poodle dogs here in Denmark. They look like long sausages with very short legs - like they grew up under a bed or a cupboard or something. I guess they had a hard time keeping them down in Germany.

Xenia, Vita and Ben are gonna start school pretty soon but maybe not me, cause my dad and mom hain't made up their minds what school I gotta go to. Maybe they will decide I don't have to go to school at all, considering that I don't intend to stay here very long. And I have decided that I'm not going to learn the silly language they got over here. It would be a waste of my valuable time, cause I'm coming back to Junction very soon. I don't like this place at all. It stinks - except fer the cakes in the bakery and some toys I saw in as store window.

By the way, Harold, how high have ya got the tower now? Is it gitting close to a hundred feet? I jus happened to think theres some lumber in the alley behind Morgans house. If ya run short of lumber fer the tower ya might borrow a little of that. I don't think they will ever know the diffrence. I don't reckon its stealing cause we'll give em the stuff back when the Moore gang war is over and when we don't need the tower no more.

Fer yer information every word in this letter is the honest-to-goodness plain truth but I guess I'll quit now cause I'm so tired and this place makes me as depressed as the bottom brick of a skyscraper.

Yours till I rot - Visti

CHAPTER NINE

It was Sunday. It seemed as though the church bells had been ringing all morning but that was normal here. We were dressed in our Sunday best - which were the same clothes we had been wearing all the time ever since we left Junction City. Until those darn boxes and crates arrived from San Francisco we were stuck with what we had. Daddy left for the church about a half hour before us because he had to get everything ready for the ten o'clock service. As we walked up the street, the church came into full view. It was huge. The square, white tower with the church building behind, was at least seven stories high. It was set back from the street about a hundred feet. Twenty-five steps, also a hundred feet wide, led up to an impressive entrance under an archway that spread across the front to two residences, one each side. The church's caretaker lived in the left one and the church's first minister lived in the other.

Yes, the church had two ministers, the first one being the Dean, very privileged, honoured and respected, who conducted the Sunday afternoon service, which in itself was a privilege because it meant that he didn't have to get up early in the morning on Sundays. Also his place of residence, being part of the church property, was rent free. His name was Rosen. My father was the second minister, received no special privileges and his residence was wherever he could find one and he had to pay for it. Daddy conducted the morning services. The only way he could ever become first minister was if Dean Rosen kicked the bucket. However, but I should point out that this was not Daddy's observation, but mine.

As we entered we were completely overwhelmed by the majestic beauty and the size of the interior of the church. There must have been thirty rows of pews each side. The center aisle alone, with the plush red carpet, was as wide as the whole church in Junction City. Talking about Junction, it made that place look like a chicken coop. This one had marble floors. That one had a squeaky wooden floor with bugs underneath. This one had a statue of Jesus twenty feet high. Back in Oregon it was only five feet. This one had twelve beautiful stained glass windows in lavish marble window alcoves. That one had plain cheap window glass in wooden frames that needed painting. This one had a beautifully decorated arched ceiling that was about seventy feet above the floor. In Junction City you could never get a belly stove pipe to go that far up without collapsing. There was no stove pipe here and no stove. They had central heating. The length of this church, when you stood at the entrance and looked down towards the altar at the far end, was about the same distance as from first base to third, maybe a little more. In Junction City the length was less than the distance from home base to first.

And the pulpit! This was really something. No old wooden staircase behind this important spot. Nope, here the minister emerged from a special secret room behind the pulpit, parting the black curtains like in a Turkish harem, as he entered. The pulpit was almost the size of one of the rowboats on the our ship, *Frederick the Eighth.* There was certainly enough to look at. Montgomery Ward and Sears & Roebuck catalogs were not needed here. It seemed to me that if the lavish extravaganza of a church was a measurement of the congregation's devotion to God, then these people here in all this splendor, stood a much better chance of getting to heaven than those in Junction City where the church was not much more than a wooden shack. Well, time would tell. In a hundred years from now we would all know for sure.

We sat in the middle of the church which was almost full. I guess everyone wanted to see what the preacher from America looked like. The service was just like in Junction City, except that the hymns were different and sounded more like a funeral. Also, it was all in the funny language and lasted a full two hours. I yawned all the time and was completely exhausted when it was over.

The next day, big decisions were made. Daddy and Mom had talked it over and decided that Xenia, Vita and Ben would go to public school straight away and I would not go to public school due to my age. That suited me just fine. It couldn't be better. But then my mother went on,

"We think it would be best for you to have private school lessons to start off with and then school later. What do you think?"

"Sounds okay to me. Where's this gonna be?"

"Well, we had long talk with your Uncle Magnus in Haderslev, which isn't too far from here. He's a school teacher, you know."

"Never heard of him."

"Oh, that's right. I guess we haven't talked about that. But anyway, we feel that it would be a good arrangement if you stayed at his home in Haderslev and he will teach you Danish and other school subjects."

"You mean at school down there?"

"No, this would be at his home, after his work at the school."

I thought about this for a minute or two. It didn't exactly sound like paradise, but at least I would be on my own and not have to be with all those foreign kids with their funny language. I looked at Daddy and Mom and said, "Sounds okay to me."

"Good. I think you will be happy there. It will only be for a few months and you will be able to come home on weekends."

"When am I s'posed to start?"

"Oh, not until after Christmas - so you still have time to look around town and see things."

Daddy was glad I accepted. Everything was going to be fine.

Dear Harold   *December 14, 1933*

I guess yer wondering how come I'm writing another letter to ya when ya jus got the last one. Well, that's cause I jus made an important discovry. It's a spy mirror they got over here that we could use on the clubhouse. Almost every house has one. It's a small mirror mounted in a frame at 45 degree angle outside yer window and then ya kin sit in a chair and see whats going on down the street without being noticed. A lot of little old ladies sit by their windows and spy on what their naybers are doing and then they kin tell their friends whats going on. My Mom says it's called gossip. Never heard that word before. But it sure works cause Missus Brunn who my Mom knows said that she saw the milkman go in a ladys house and didn't come out fer a whole hour. Now if she didn't have the mirror she would have to lean out of her window and then she would be noticed.

Well I was kinda thinking if we had a mirror like that on the clubhouse we could spy on the Moore gang and they wouldn't know we were there. I reckon we need a drawing of this so I'll git something going. Here's something else. I don't have to go to school over here right now. I'm gonna stay at my uncle's place in another town fer awhile so we kin breathe a sigh of relief.

Yours till I rot. Visti

It was now very close to Christmas. The winding streets were decorated with fir branches and store windows became framed pictures of luxurious delights, radiating light on the wet pavement. There was very little daylight at this time of the year. It wasn't light until about ten o'clock in the morning and then about two-thirty in the afternoon it would be dark again. Cold, wet, dark and windy - that was little Denmark in December and even in this hostile environment, bicycles were everywhere with dark silhouettes of bundled-up images struggling against the wind and darkness. Why they wanted to keep this up was more than I could figure out. The Statue of Liberty not only welcomed suffering humanity to freedom, but also to a better life in places like sunny California and Oregon.

Before we knew it, Christmas was on the doorstep as they say in Denmark but we were prepared. Each one of us children would get one present and that was fine with us. The big day in Scandinavia is the 24th of December. That's when everything happens. The traditional sequence of events starts with church service at four o'clock in the afternoon for those so inclined, while mother slaves away at home getting the turkey ready. The Christmas dinner takes place that evening and following that, there is dancing around the tree, the singing of Christmas songs and then the opening of the presents. The 25th is hangover day for some, sleep-in for others, and continued church services for the rest. And Santa Claus is replaced by little elves, who somehow hide up in the attic at Christmas time.

Being a preacher's son, it was expected that I volunteered for basic church duties on special occasions such as at Christmas time and Easter. I did this without question. It had always been this way. As early as two o'clock in the afternoon of Christmas eve, together with the caretaker, I went up in the church tower to ring the bells. During the Christmas season the bells in the tower were set up to make a continuous chime sound rather than the normal bell clang. This was achieved by turning a crank, one for each bell. With church service starting at four o'clock, we started the bells at two o'clock, cranking nonstop for the full two hours. The sound could be heard all over the city. As I turned the crank, looking at all the lights around us below, it was easy to get into the spirit of Christmas. It was also easy to get a headache and become deaf, being so close to the two big bronze bells. All I knew was, when we walked down the one hundred and fifty-three tower steps, I couldn't hear a thing.

Following this, my next duty was to help light the candles on the two very large Christmas trees at each side of the altar. They were so tall that long step ladders were used. The afternoon Christmas church service was short - just a little over an hour. The reason for this was, that everyone wanted to get home for the Christmas dinner and also because the candles on the two trees at the altar didn't last for more than an hour. Until somebody invented electric Christmas lights, that was the way it would have to be. This church service was of special interest to me, because when the candles burnt down, the flames seemed to flutter and then fall to lower branches before the flame went out. As I sat there in our pew, I wondered if anyone else noticed how close we were to a possible fire. I was hoping something would happen and also hoping that nothing would happen. There was the potential for a disaster.

The Christmas dinner was at six-thirty with the turkey, all the trimmings, candlelight and passages read from the Bible by Daddy. Clearing the table and washing the dishes took place between eight and nine, during which time Daddy was in the living room. Unnoticed, the Christmas tree had been brought into the living room and for the last two days this part of the house had been locked and off bounds. The decoration of the tree, the arrangement of the presents under the tree and the lighting of the candles were done only by Daddy, who was the master of the house. We had made many of the tree decorations but they were given to Daddy to put on the tree. While we all helped Mom wash the dishes in the kitchen, there would be one ring of a bell from the living room. This was the signal that we should get ready, but there was still time. A little later there were two rings of the bell. We all became more excited and finally, having just finished all work in the kitchen, three rings of the bell signaled permission to open the doors to the living room.

With great anticipation and excitement, we children were greeted for the first time to the splendor of the beautifully decorated Christmas tree in the middle of the room, complete white candles and gift wrapped presents around the base. The live candles, being the only light in the living room, created a very intimate, festive atmosphere. We circled the tree holding hands and, following the Danish tradition, danced around the tree singing Christmas songs. After a lot of hoping and pleading to finishing the singing and dancing, we children finally were permitted to dive under the tree and get our presents. Christmas was a very delightful and happy time for all of us.

No sooner did the Christmas tree come down, than we moved to a second floor apartment on another street called Valbygade. This place had a real bathroom with hot and cold water and I also had my own room. I guess Daddy figured I was soon to be an adult, which entitled me to more privileges. Actually I was growing up, because I had to borrow his shaving set every two weeks. I was still only thirteen, but felt the same as grown-ups.

Our boxes and crates finally arrived. For the next week we had so much fun unpacking. Every little item reminded us of Junction City, but to me, no matter how we arranged things in this new place, it did not look like it was the natural setting. We could remove ourselves from Junction City, but all the images were still with us. Looking at all the things in the boxes and crates made me feel lonesome. For Daddy and Mom, this was a new chapter in their struggling, but happy life. For Xenia, it was a change, but being close to Mom, she had no problem adjusting to her new life. For the rest of the kids, anywhere was okay.

One problem I had was that I was unable to share any thoughts or activities with Daddy, because he was busy at the church all the time, practically seven days a week. We were all together at mealtimes, but it could hardly be called a father-son relationship when, sitting at the head of the table, his presence demanded respect from us all. It also seemed that there was a lot more to do in this big church than in Junction City. He was under a lot of pressure.

Every evening, just before bedtime when we were in our pyjamas, we respectfully had to enter the study, one by one and be blessed by Daddy. It went according to age, with me being first. He would be seated at his desk as I entered. Standing before him he would lay his hand on my head, saying,

"May the Lord bless and keep you; May the Lord make his face to shine upon you and be gracious unto you; May the Lord lift his countenance upon you and give you peace; in the name of the Father, Son and Holy Ghost."

Then I would leave, telling Xenia as I came out of the door that it was her turn. And she, in turn would tell Vita and so on. All of us, since the day we were born, had received this daily blessing. It was as natural as brushing our teeth before bedtime. But it did not make for a close relationship with my father. It created an atmosphere in which he was the minister, his children were the congregation and Mom was the caretaker. In our eyes he was not just an ordinary, ordained minister. He was chosen. Even his first name, being Elias Marius, sounded religious. My mother's first name, Bertha, sounded more suitable for her position as caretaker.

I found myself becoming very isolated. It was comforting that I could talk to Mom, even although our conversations were mainly about daily obligations and happenings. She never mentioned anything about religion when we talked together, other than to show respect. But there were many thoughts and feelings that I kept to myself and they certainly had nothing to do with religion. The problem was really that I knew no one apart from the family. I also noticed my voice was changing, becoming deeper, as if I had a cold or something and at times I felt kind of funny. Maybe a visit to a doctor might help, but for the time being I decided to refrain from telling Mom about it. I certainly wouldn't want to go to hospital.

And so it was, as we approached the new year, 1934. Outside it was dark, cold and windy. With only four and a half hours of daylight each day, it was hard to feel lighthearted or enthusiastic about anything. The future looked dismal. In the distance was the place called Haderslev. That was another change coming up, which gave me more to think about.

CHAPTER TEN

It was a Sunday afternoon and the second week in January when Daddy took me to the bus station for the uncharted trek to Haderslev. The bus driver knew the way, but for me it was the big unknown. Mom had said goodbye at the apartment. She couldn't very well leave the children. Daddy assured me everything would be all right, and that my uncle would be meeting me at the bus station in Haderslev.

"He knows what you look like, so just wait at the entrance door to the waiting room at the station. He will find you."

"Okay."

"Oh, one more thing. Remember to bow when you shake hands with him. You must remember to be polite."

"Okay, I will."

"Well then, we will see you again next weekend."

He gave me a fatherly hug. I got on the waiting bus. As the bus pulled away, I waved to him through the window. I had two suitcases with me - one with my clothes and shoes, the other with all my treasured items from Junction City. Even although it was only thirty-two kilometers, this was the first time in my life that I was traveling alone. I sat in the front of the bus so I could look out of the window ahead. We passed a windmill and a number of farms. The countryside was still under the grip of winter with snow everywhere, but the highway was clear. We made a stop at a small town called Christiansfeld, where some passengers got off and others got on. As we continued, I noticed that the architecture of some of the roadside houses looked different than in Kolding. I found out later it was, because at one time, this part of Denmark belonged to Germany. This whole area was called Southern Jutland.

Haderslev was situated at the end of a fjord in a valley between rolling hills. It had a harbor and a military garrison. We approached the town from the north, coming down a long hill. Passing the garrison, we went down a couple of narrow streets around a corner, arriving at the bus station. The driver eased to a stop, pulled on the handbrake and turned off the motor. I got off the bus with all the others and stood at the entrance to the waiting room. There was a lot of activity as passengers were being greeted by friends, and others were running around, gathering their belongings to get on the bus. I was quite used to this atmosphere, having experienced it at all the train stops across United States. People seem to react the same everywhere, regardless of nationality, culture, language or appearance. We all have a number of basic things in common - like going to the bathroom, combing our hair, tying our shoelaces and scurrying around at bus and train stations.

Eventually, everyone found out where they wanted to go. Those from the bus walked away with their suitcases and friends, and those who wanted to get on the bus were now sitting in their seats with their noses pointing forward, waiting for departure. Everything was in its proper place. The bus left the station, scattering a flock of seagulls. It was now very quiet. I sat on one of my suitcases and waited. My uncle was obviously delayed.

A mailman came around the corner of the station on his bicycle. Mailmen distinguished themselves from the masses by wearing red uniforms and black caps. They carried the mail in a black bag and always rode a black bicycle. To complete the picture, mailboxes were red. I thought about it for a while. The uniforms of policemen, firemen and chimney sweepers were all black and they also rode black bicycles. Only the postman was different. I was later told it was a very respected position and once you became a postman, it was for life. You wished nothing else.

Mind you, it would be life on a bicycle, but that was the way it was for almost everybody in this cold, windy country - and when you died your title and your name would appear together on your gravestone. It might say: *Postman Hansen. Rest in Peace.* Actually, you just might need a rest after thirty years in the King's Postal Service. I figured out, that riding a bicycle eight hours a day, six days a week would amount to 75,000 hours of pedaling and most of this would be with a head wind, but still, it was a prestigious profession.

A little, middle aged man in a dark overcoat, scarf, hat and ear muffs came around the corner pushing a bicycle. He wore spectacles that looked all steamed up and he was huffing and puffing. The bicycle had a flat tire. Upon seeing me his face lightened up and with outstretched hand, he said,

"Velkommen, velkommen til Haderslev!"

It was Uncle Magnus. Although I knew no Danish, I was able to understand him. I stood up, shook his hand and bowed as I was supposed to do. Then, helping me with the suitcases, he said in English,

"I am so sorry I am late, but as you can see, my bicycle has a flat tire." We both glanced at the tire. "Did you have a good trip?"

"Yes, very good, thank you." Daddy said I should say 'thank you' whenever it was appropriate to do so.

"Well, we will arrange your suitcases on the bicycle and be on our way."
We put one on the back carrier and the other between the handle bars. He
took some string out of his coat pocket and tied the back one down.

Together, we pushed the bike through some snow at the station around the
corner to the roadway which was clear.

"Our villa is not far from here. We should be there in about half an hour.
Well, what do you think of Denmark, may I ask?"

"It's different."

"Oh, yes. I can believe that. We have it good here in little Denmark but we
also work hard to make it so. Have you noticed how hard people work here?"

"Not really," I replied, thinking of the firemen I saw drinking beer on the
ladder wagon.

"Well, I am sure as you grow older, you will be able to observe many good
things about little Denmark. A good education makes all the difference. In a few
months time we will have you speaking Danish like a native."

I was about to say 'over my dead body,' but in a flash changed my mind and
said,

"That will be nice."

"Not only nice, but necessary. You cannot survive without devoting a good
part of your life to educating yourself."

We passed a red brick cathedral right in the middle of town that must
have been eight hundred years old. I found it very intriguing, with its spooky
walkways and arches. I would have liked to have taken a closer look, but my
uncle kept forging ahead with the loaded bicycle.

"You must keep in mind, Visti, that boys your age in Denmark know that
they must study hard. In school they learn three languages besides Danish,
and at your age they are well advanced, having had language studies for years.
What languages did they teach in Junction City?"

"American."

"No, what I mean is, other than English, or American as you call it?"

"That was it. We don't need no other language to live in the USA."

This conversation was getting a bit too much to handle. I found myself on the
defensive and I hadn't even had my first school lesson yet. Maybe this was the
first lesson. We walked in silence for a minute or so and then he patted me on the
back, saying,

"Well, don't you worry. We will just take one step at a time and I am sure
you will be able to catch up to the others."

I helped him push the bicycle, one step at a time, most of the way, to help
cut down on all his huffing and puffing.

"We might have to include an English lesson or two. Yes, I think that would
be worth considering. It would be of help to you, you know."

I couldn't figure him out. Americans don't need English lessons. Mom and
I spoke the same language. Mom had a slight accent, being from England, but it
wasn't her fault. She just happened to grow up there.

We arrived at the villa. I was wondering what a villa looked like, but it was just a fancy name for an ordinary brick house with a red tile roof on a residential street. His wife greeted me at the door with a hug, which just about knocked me out, considering I had never seen her before.

"Velkommen, Visti. Kom inden for."

I figured out what she said, bowed and walked in, followed by Uncle Magnus and the suitcases. Huffing and puffing, he said to her in English,

"Yes, we are a bit late, because I got a flat tire."

I got the immediate impression that she didn't know what he was saying in English. We entered the hallway and she helped me take off my coat and scarf while saying a few things in Danish that was all Greek to me. They seemed very happy I was in their home, having never had children of their own.

They were both about a half century old. I noticed now that Uncle Magnus was bald. He seemed to be the master of the house in charge of everything. His wife's name was Agnes. She had grey hair and looked like she at one time might have been in charge of everything - probably when she was young and beautiful - but that was hard to imagine.

"Let me show you your room," Uncle Magnus said, carrying the suitcases. We entered a small room, with a window facing the street. The room had a single bed, a small desk and a chair. There was a lamp on the table and a picture on the wall.

"You will like it here. It is nice and quiet," he said, going to the window, "and the window opens easily as you can see."

He opened and closed the window so that I could see how it was done.

"Always sleep at night with your window open. Fresh air clears your brain and makes you feel morning fresh when you wake up."

Agnes had set the table for dinner and I could see she had tried to make everything very presentable. She could speak English, but not very well as I later found out. She didn't say too much. It was Uncle Magnus who decided everything, or at least acted like he did. She looked a bit worn out like an old car, but it was probably due to her age. As we were taking our places at the table, I noticed a picture of her on the mantel piece of the fireplace. There she looked more like a spring chicken, but time takes its toll.

"Vaer saa god, tag plads," my uncle said, pulling out my chair. It was all just a lot of garble, but I figured this was an invitation to sit down. They sat at opposite ends of the rectangular table and I was placed at the side. Agnes passed the dishes around. We started with soup.

"Visti says he had a good trip," Uncle Magnus said in English, looking at Agnes.

She smiling politely.

I couldn't figure out why a thirty-two kilometer trip was so significant, but maybe they never traveled anywhere.

"How is family?" she ventured in English.

"Fine. They're doing fine."

"Visti says he finds things different here in Denmark."

"Oh," she said, cutting the meat.

"Yes, and I would think so," he continued, "there are not many places like Denmark. Not many places where you have it so good."

Agnes said something to him in Danish. He replied in Danish. Then she said something again and I felt that we might be having an emergency situation at hand, judging from the tone of voice. Turning to me, he explained,

"Agnes was just asking when was I going to fix my bicycle tire. I need the bicycle to go to the school tomorrow. I told her it will be done. No need for concern. Not to worry. It will be done in time. How is the food?"

"Very good."

I could feel, from the way they looked at me during the meal, that they were not impressed with my American table manners.

"Perhaps this is a good time to discuss your schedule." Uncle Magnus took a sip from a glass of water, and continued,

"Today, being Sunday, we won't start lessons, so this evening will be a time of rest - also tomorrow morning when I will be at the school, but in the afternoon we can start. Now, I had a talk with your father and we both agreed that a few household chores would be in order, to help you earn your board and keep. You understand that, do you not?"

"Yes."

"Tomorrow morning you can help Agnes around the house. She always has so much to do on Mondays."

"Every day much to do," she remarked.

"Of course, of course, ahem - er, well, we will see how we can balance things out. Maybe a little housework everyday, and then your homework until I come home and then lessons till suppertime. How does that sound to you?"

"Okay, I guess."

"We will be able to do this five days a week. On Saturdays you go to Kolding, but that can be Saturday afternoon, which will give us the morning for homework. Then you don't have to do the homework when you come back on the following day. Don't you think that is a good arrangement?"

"I guess so."

After the meal it was suggested, that maybe I might want to unpack and get settled in my room. Also, if I wanted to go for a short walk, I was welcome to do so, as long as I did not stray away too far from the house. It was now dark outside and they wouldn't want me to get lost. I retired to my room and lay on the bed - thinking. What a day. It look like I was trapped. I would just have to bite the bullet.

I gazed at the framed photograph on the wall at the foot of the bed. It was the portrait of an elderly lady, somewhat like Queen Victoria. Most likely it was Agnes's mother or grandmother. The more I looked at it, the more the eyes seemed to stare at me. I got out of bed, went over towards the window. This was uncanny. The eyes followed me. I tried the other corner by the door. Same thing. This was too much. I decided to go for a walk. Later in the evening, having brushed my teeth, said goodnight and opened the window as I was told to do, I took the picture off the wall before going to sleep.

A week passed. It was Saturday, thank goodness! I thought it would never come. Agnes said I could borrow her bicycle to go to Kolding, so as to save the bus fare. In my pocket I had an important letter to Harold, telling him about my latest troubles. He would be thirteen very shortly and I felt I should warn him about all the things that could happen to him - just like me. I left the villa at about one o'clock.

Dear Harold   January 12, 1934
    Harold, ya don't know the trouble I'm in. It's jus awful. I'm warning ya. The 13th year is scary. I'm stuck here in a dinky ol place called Haderslev and gotta stay at my uncle's house fer about 3 months, maybe longer. It's a torture. It's all gotta do with that they don't think I know nothing. This is a rotten time and a terrible hardship. 'Course it ain't half as bad as in the pioneer days, but the pioneers had exciting hardships and mine are so grim and dismal. Anyways it's better than going to public school.

    My uncle is what ya might call a gentleman. We didn't have any of them in Junction and who needed them anyways? He thinks a powerful lot bout manners, politeness and neatness and all that junk. My manners are nothing compared to his. He says I don't do a blasted thing right. 'Course he didn't say it jus like that, but I certainly ain't gonna write like a gentleman jus to suit him. Things are jus awful. Every morning I'm called up out of bed at 7:30 and gotta take the top covers off my bed so that everything can git air and then I gotta comb and brush my hair. If I don't brush or comb it good enough, I gotta do it over again and then if it ain't good enough, Agnes does it. She's my uncles wife and is real corny looking. She never gits mad at me if I don't do it right. Then I gotta brush my clothes and then I gotta go into the kitchen and dip my whole face in a bowl of icy cold water to git the sleepyness out of my eyes. I even have to do it even if there's no sleepyness in my eyes. After that I knock on the door to the dining room and walk in. They are already seated at the breakfast table which has been set neatly and perfectly when I come in. The first thing I have to do is say 'good morning' in Danish and then I can sit down and unfold my serviet and begin to eat my porrige with a silver spoon. We've had hot porrige fer breakfast fer five days now. The first thing I am asked is - have I ducked my head in icy cold water and if I have, everything is okay. If I havn't, then I gotta go and do it cause I can't tell a lie and say that I did do it when I didn't cause I'm a preacher's kid and they ain't allowed to tell lies.

    My uncle says that I don't do nothing right. He says I don't hold my fork right, I don't hold my knife or spoon right and I don't hold my cup right. I am not allowed to hold the cup in my left hand. He says in Denmark all people hold their cups in the right hand and when I eat bread I should only eat a little piece at a time and I must never have my elbows on the table and never talk if my mouth is full and if I talk its gotta be in Danish. So I seldom open my mouth except to eat and drink. And he says I gotta sit up straight and when I chew food I gotta keep my mouth closed. I can tell ya, Harold, this place stinks. Whenever I pass food to anyone of them at the table I gotta say 'Vaer saa god' which means 'please.' Jus imagine, three corny words jus to make one American word! And then after we finish eating and get up from the table I gotta say 'Tak for mad' which means 'thanks for food' which is kinda silly to say when nothing else is on the table except food, so jus 'thanks' would be enough.

Then my uncle gets on his bicycle and goes to work. He's a school teacher and comes home at 2 o'clock in the afternoon. And after breakfast I gotta clear the table, wash dishes, make my bed, sweep all the floors and do lots of other

UNCLE MAGNUS

work fer Agnes until 10 o'clock and then I gotta sit in my dinky room and study until 1 o'clock. I can tell ya, after three solid hours of pants-pressing work - cause thats what my pants look like when I finally get out of the chair - just like when ya look at peoples pants when they walk out of church after two solid hours of sermons - full of creases, well then I gotta go into the kitchen and peel spuds fer dinner. When my uncle comes home he gives me lessons until 6 o'clock. Then we eat dinner. My uncle eats so mannerly. After that I gotta do all the dishes and clean up and then I'm allowed to go for a walk fer one hour to git exersize and then I gotta come back and sit in my room until bedtime which is 9 o'clock. Then I say my evening prayer which I do alone cause it ain't none of their bizness and then the very last thing I do is take a picture off the wall in my room cause it's of an ol' woman and it looks like she's staring at me and I can't have someone staring at me all night when I wanna git a decent nights sleep.

I ain't told ya half the stuff that goes on here cause it makes me too darn depressed to talk bout it. But I know ya wanna know so I guess I'll write some more tomorrow or when I feel better, which might be a long long time. Maybe I better sign off now cause I might die in my sleep from depreshun. Who knows what can happen in this dump. How's Blackie? And how bout the tower? How high is it now?

Yours till I rot. Visti

It took a full two hours to get to Kolding on the squeaky old bicycle. I was so glad to see the family and they likewise. It seemed that the kids were doing well in school, which was more than I could say. It was such a relief to be here. It was though I had been in prison all week. Here I could do what I pleased with complete freedom for twenty-four hours. At the supper table we all had so much to talk about and it made no difference whether we had food in our mouths or not. I told them about Haderslev.

"We know it's hard on you," Daddy said, "but it is only for about three months. It is to help you adjust to the Danish ways and get you started."

"When do I have to go to school?"

"Well, Mom and I thought in the beginning of April."

"What's our uncle like?" Xenia asked.

"Kinda funny looking. He calls himself a gentlemen."

"Hey, Mom, what's a gentleman?" Vita intervened.

"It is a man who is polite and has good manners."

"Is he bald?" Xenia asked.

"Yeah, kinda bald. Mostly on top."

"I hate bald men."

"Xenia, that is not a nice thing to say," Mom said, "he is your uncle and is helping us in many ways. He is a very kind person."

"I still hate bald men."

"Shame on you," Daddy said sternly, "we can't have you saying things like that. Now eat your food, and be quiet if you do not have better things to say." Xenia started to get sulky and decided in defiance to refuse to eat. Mom, fearing that one of her traumatic asthma attacks might be coming along, tried to comfort her, coaxing her back into a state of tranquility.

"Is there anything you need in Haderslev?" Daddy asked.

"Gee, I dunno. Maybe a couple of my books to read in the evenings."

"I can feel, Visti, that this is a little hard for you, but every day you will find that things become easier. The three months will go very fast. Did Mom tell you we got a letter from Mrs. Bruce?"

"No. What did she say?"

"Well," Mom answered, "everything is much the same in Junction City and Harold will be writing to you, but unfortunately they had to put Blackie to sleep."

"What! How come?" I felt very upset. They must be joking.

"Well, you can read the letter. It seems that Blackie ran to the train station every time he heard a train coming, and then on Sundays, when he heard the church bell, he would wait outside the church door and look at everyone going in and coming out - so he was a very unhappy dog."

"Gee wizz. This ain't fair. They could have at least asked me for permission, and d'know what? I would've said no."

"I guess we will never really know the details, but he must have suffered after we left." Mom was trying to ease the pain.

"We should have taken him with us, like I said."

I didn't feel good at all. It was as though another link with Junction City had been broken. The rest of the afternoon was a quiet one. It took me a while to get over it. I wondered what Harold would have to say about it all. I was sure he did what he could. Who decided this anyways? He was my dog.

That evening we worked on a new jigsaw puzzle that Daddy had bought for us. It was of a Danish castle and took all evening to assemble. The next day, being Sunday, was taken up with the morning church service and I noticed the smaller kids were getting fidgety and restless during the service. They needed some new catalogs or something to keep them busy, and so did the rest of us, because there was absolutely nothing that we could understand. It would probably take years before we could understand Danish, and I certainly had all intention of being back in Junction City long before then. The two hour church service was two hours too long. I felt very tired.

After lunch and about two o'clock in the afternoon, I had to leave for Haderslev to be there before dark. I gave Mom my letter to Harold which she promised to mail for me.

The second week in Haderslev was harder than the first week. I was given more to study and lots of homework. I think my uncle regarded me as having the potential to become clever, but since I lagged so far behind the rest of the world, a crash program was necessary. I didn't know what confidential arrangements Daddy might have had made with Uncle Magnus, but judging from the intensity of what I had to do, I figured he was told to make me into a Dane in three months. It wasn't just the studies. I also had to learn how to behave in public, when to bow, when to say thank you, when to speak, when not to speak, how to speak and so on. Chances of appearing in public and applying any of this stuff was very remote, because I was stuck in this house all the time. When I went out for the evening walk it was dark and nobody was out there. I just walked a mile down the road, came back again, and that was the end of public association for that day.

In some ways, Uncle Magnus was like my father. Dedication was a common trait. For my father, religion was just as intensive at home as in church. For Uncle Magnus, education was now, thanks to my presence, just as intense at home as in his school. I could feel he was very interested in his new pupil. It was, of course, a pity that his pupil was only interested in returning to Junction City.

I had the evenings to myself. Apart from the one hour daily walk there was not much to do so I would sit in my little room alone, read my books from Kolding or draw pictures. I felt I was getting better at drawing. It was real fun to create something out of nothing, especially pictures of clubhouses and of the Hornibrook and Moore gangs, fighting each other. I still had things to tell Harold, but did my writing in secret. Uncle Magnus and Agnes always sat in the living room in the evening. Frequently, I would hear them argue over something but, being all in Danish, I didn't know what it was about.

Dear Harold   *January 17, 1934*

I jus heard that someone killed Blackie. That's terrible cause he was my dog. I know ya didn't have nothing to do with it and I guess it happened when ya wern't around. Do ya think it was the Moore gang? Maybe this is the time for revenge. When I git back we'll look into it together. It sure makes me mad. This 13th year is getting worser and worser.

Unfortunately I have to tell ya more gloomy things cause thats all there is to write about. Every morning I got all the silly housework to do. Agnes does some work too. She shows me how to do things. She always looks tired and worn out like an ol' car but thats mainly from the endless work thats gotta be done in this goofy place. We don't talk much together because we're so busy cleaning house and she doesn't know too much American and I only know 10 Danish words by heart. Sometimes she has to go in and lie down in the middle of the day cause she's so tired, but she is always up when Uncle Magnus comes home cause that's when things happen. This week he's taught me all about manners which it seems they need here in Denmark. First of all he doesn't like the American clothes I wear. He says they gotta go and I say no. So

we have a problem, but fortunately I got my Dad on my side. All Danish boys dress up neatly when they play, go to school or do anything but they wear knickerbockers and wooden shoes and there ain't no way I'm gonna wear such junk. I don't wanna look like a sissy. Could you imagine the Hornibrook gang running around in knickerbockers and wooden shoes! Holy cow! The Moore gang would laugh their heads off fer sure.

Both my uncle and his wife keep telling me all the time that I gotta keep very clean. Every night I have to wash my hands and face so clean in soapy water that my towel will never ever git dirty. My uncle says I wash in a girlish way, which is a lot of bunk cause a Hornibrook gang member would never do a sissy thing like that. He said I gotta use a lot more soap and hot water cause thats how a gentleman washes. Every morning I gotta polish my shoes. I'm not allowed to wear shoes in the house so I have to wear slippers. Ain't that silly. I always have to have my fingernails cut real short and make sure they are powerfully clean. They are so short that it makes my fingers bleed when I peel an orange.

One time Agnes noticed the dirt in my ears. So she got a match and a washcloth which she put over the match and then she poked around and got dirt out by the buckets full. She also hauled out a lot of wax. I thought the wax was in our ears so we could hear better. And I thought we had fingernails so that we could pick stuff out of our nose and pick up needles and bugs and things. Agnes and my uncle don't know nothing how to use nature. Yesterday Agnes washed my hair. Ya should have seen how she scrubbed and rinsed it time after time until it was as clean as the Willamette river. It really shook me up, but this was nothing compared to when she started wiping my hair. She kept on wiping until it was as dry as a book full of rithmatik. When she was finished it felt like straw and really hurt. I'm mighty powerful glad it's over.

My uncle says if I pass somebody on the street that maybe I might know, I am supposed to take off my lid and bow. Gals don't have to take off their hats, but they gotta curtsy. Well, the truth of the matter is, I ain't got no hat. I got my beanie cap, but I ain't allowed to wear it here in Haderslev.

Another thing, if a guest comes into the room I gotta stand up and bow and shake hands with them. Can you imagine if somebody came into our clubhouse and we would have to stand up and bow. The guys would laugh their heads off. I tell ya, this place is a goner!

This is a brick house and is powerfully clean inside. I hain't seen a single speck of dust nowhere, But Anges sure does. She can spot a single speck of dust a block away. She's got me dusting like mad all over the place with a rag every day and thats besides all the other stuff I gotta do. Magnus says that dust fogs up the brain so ya can't think straight. Course ya and me know this is a lot of hooey cause when we played ball and went skidding into second or third base all that dust we kicked up didn't damage our brains.

Even although I gotta wear slippers in the house, Agnes don't want me walking on the rugs more than absolutely necessary cause it might make marks. Agne is cleaning the house all the time when she's not resting and is always afraid I might bring in a pinhead of dirt from somewhere by mistake. She's always got a dust rag stuffed in her apron pocket jus incase she sees a speck of dust floating around. She also gave me a dust rag to carry around jus incase I might see something somewhere. We are both on the lookout. You never know. There jus might be a single speck floating around somewhere but I hain't seen none. I only do what is strickly necessary around here so that I don't cause trouble - cause I can sorta feel that Agnes is about to become a nervous wreck. There's so much to do in this villa that it makes her as tired as a dish rag every day. Even when I sit alone in my room with the door closed I can hear her chasing around in the other rooms looking fer specks of dust. And when she's not chasing around she's lying exhausted on the sofa. Harold, this dump is enough to make a guy croak!

Well, as far as my educashun goes in this crummy place, I might learn a few more Danish words, but 20 is gonna be the limit. After that it's curtains. I hain't told uncle Magnus bout that cause he would probly blow a fuse. It looks like he's heading fer a nervous breakdown jus like Agnes cause he's overloaded with work and me. Anyways I'm coming back soon. I git one krone a month from my dad as pocket money and so far I've saved up 11 kroner fer the return voyage. I can hardly wait to git outta here.

Yours till I rot - Visti

Another week had passed and I was back in Kolding. The trip was terrible with cold wind and icy rain. The wind never blew from the back. It was always against anybody who rode a bicycle. I was soaked. Daddy and Mom, of course, wanted to know how I was making out.

"So and so," I replied.

"Do you get enough to eat?" Mom asked.

"Yup, but I don't like the food much. It's strange stuff."

"I'm sure it's all good food. Make sure you eat well."

"Yeah, but one day we got beer soup. Looks like mud and tasted jus' awful."

"Visti, that has nothing to do with mud. Beer soup is made out of malt beer and pumpernickel bread."

"Well, it still tastes awful."

"What's Agnes like?" Xenia decided to join in.

"Okay, I guess."

"Does she boss you around?"

"A little bit, but it's okay."

"Is she ugly?"

"Gee, I dunno. Maybe a little. Mostly corny looking."

"I bet she's real ugly."

Mom could hear which way this conversation was going, so she decided to break it up.

"Why don't you all go out and play now and then later you can all come in for a nice cup of tea."

Next morning I used Daddy's shaving set. It was fourteen days since I shaved last. Daddy had left for the church. The kids were in the other room.

Mom came to the bathroom door and said that Daddy had a bit of pain during the night below the stomach, but this morning it went away. She seemed somewhat concerned. I said it was probably something he had eaten. She told me not to mention it to the other kids, but if it came back he would go and see a doctor. At lunch time and later in the day when I had to leave, I did not get the impression that there was any problem with Daddy. I think Mom also felt everything was now okay. So everything was back to normal - or as normal as it could be in Denmark.

Back in Haderslev the daily grind continued. I had begun to read books in the evening, because there was very little to do in my room. One evening Uncle Magnus noticed a few things that seemed to disturb him. I had my American flag on the window sill. It had been there from day one. I guess he never noticed it before, but you could see it from the street. Anyways, he came into my room and politely asked,

"I see you have your flag at half mast. Is the string too short?"

"No, that's the way it's supposed to be."

"Well, here in Denmark we always have the Danish flag at full mast. Only in the event of a tragedy would we have a flag at half mast."

"That's why I got it at half mast. When I get enough money in my cookie jar fer the return trip to Junction City, that's when I'll raise the flag."

He looked at the jar on the desk, which now had twelve krone in it. I could see he was disturbed. He then noticed a book on the bed that I had been reading. It was Huckleberry Finn and I was reading it for the fifth time.

"I really think you are too old to read that book. It is not proper English. I suggest you put it in the garbage can and instead read some good Danish books. We have many right here in the house."

"This is my book and I like it."

"Visti, you are never going to learn to read Danish unless you try. What you have there is trash. You have a long way to go before you catch up with Danish children your age, so it is best you listen to good advice."

"This book is from Junction City and it is very valuable."

"Yes, Visti, I understand how you feel, but reading American books is certainly not going to help us master the Danish language."

It was obvious that my uncle wasn't too happy with my progress, but I resented the environment I found myself in. Each day was much the same as the previous day. I had no real contact with the outside world, except for the one hour daily walk in the dark by myself. Agnes was gradually changing, looking upon me as a burden - more to cook, more linen to wash and more house cleaning. I did as much as I could, but found if I spent too much time helping her, my studies for the daily afternoon lesson suffered, with Uncle Magnus asking why I couldn't manage the assignments. It was absolutely amazing how much work had to be done in that villa. Every morning there were dishes to be washed, potatoes to peel, silverware to be polished, rugs to be cleaned - and the endless dusting. If I suggested that it was time I started on my homework, she would frequently get emotional, saying that there was so much work to be done and so little time to do it. It would make me feel guilty as if I was letting her down.

In my room I could be by myself, but I experienced a terrible feeling of loneliness, sitting there hour after hour trying to make sense of Danish words and grammar. My mind kept wandering all the time and I would gaze out through the window, listening to the wind blowing through the trees and feeling very unhappy.

I think Uncle Magnus also had his problems. His life was not a bowl of cherries or a rose garden. Every morning after breakfast he would put on his overcoat, hat, scarf, mittens and boots, put his prepared lunch in his old leather briefcase and get his bicycle out of the basement. He was always late. Agnes would receive a henpeck kiss on the cheek, and he would be off on his bicycle with his briefcase clamped in the carrier, steering with one hand and holding an umbrella with the other. Through my window, I would watch him pedal away into the darkness, fighting the rain, sleet, snow, hail and wind, or whatever nature could provide to make his life uncomfortable. He taught school six days a week, and with the additional work of teaching a difficult pupil in his spare time plus coping with his emotional wife, the pressure was on.

Agnes was her husband's servant. Meals had to be on time. His clothes had to be cleaned and pressed. All housework had to be completed by the time he came home in the afternoon. Twice a week she would ride her bicycle to town and do the shopping. Seldom did they have guests, because he was always so busy and when he was not busy, he was so exhausted and so was she. In the evening he would sit in his chair and doze off after having read the newspaper, while she sat in her chair, knitting in silence.

The lady next door spoke to Agnes once in awhile, but this was not enough to put any excitement into her life. In the beginning, I think my appearance created a feeling that something unusual was happening in the house - like a breath of fresh air, but now I was an obstacle, like an extra piece of furniture that didn't fit in anywhere. I also noticed, that the two of them seemed to argue often about small things - more than before. I didn't understand what they were saying but the tone of their voices told everything. I felt sure that my presence in this awful villa was part of the problem.

On one occasion, Uncle Magnus came into my room and apologized for the disturbance that took place in the kitchen. He said it was a rather difficult time for Agnes at the moment, because she was going through her 'memopause.' I found that strange, because I hadn't seen her pause to write any memos. In fact, what would she be writing memos for in the first place? And even if she had to write memos, why get so uptight about it? This was becoming a peculiar place.

That weekend, as I cycled home towards Kolding, the warm sun came out just as I approached the small town of Christiansfeld, the halfway mark. The days seem to be getting longer, but it was still a long way until spring. I was told it didn't come before May.

It was a refreshing feeling to get out of that house in Haderslev. No matter how many hours I spent there I still felt like an unwanted guest. It was not my natural territory. Well, in two months time it would be over and I would be back in Kolding. Then the big worry would be public school. The terrible thirteenth year would be over in August. I was sure by that time I would somehow be able to return to Junction City and hopefully with the family.

I was just cycling through the narrow main street in Christianfeld, when suddenly a window opened up on the second floor of a house across the street - and a beautiful girl with a well endowed bosom, leaned out, shaking a white pillow case. I just about fell off my bike! I had never seen such loveliness. She was even bathed in sunshine. It was over in an instant and the window closed with a bang.

A few feathers drifted gently to earth like snowflakes in the afternoon sun. I got off my bicycle, ran out in the middle of the street and managed to pick up six of the fluffy feathers before the traffic cut me off. I felt a bit dizzy and in a dreamy state as I continued along the street pushing the bicycle. This was unbelievable. I just happened to be at the right place at the right time. Maybe she had another pillow case to shake.

I decided to turn around and sort of check up on things. I parked the bicycle against a wall nearby and stood casually and inconspicuously, leaning against a tree with full view of the window across the street. There was no way she could shake another pillow case without me taking it all in. I waited for over thirty minutes. Nothing happened. Either she didn't have any more pillow cases to shake, or she had spotted me and refused to shake pillow cases while I was hanging around - so, I continued my long, lonely trip to Kolding somewhat frustrated, but also enlightened. Agnes's squeaky ol' wreck of a bike almost seemed to have wings. It was something to remember.

Xenia was resting when I arrived at our apartment in Kolding. Mom said that she had just had an asthma attack, so we all had to be quiet for an hour or so. I asked how Daddy was. Mom said he was okay, but I could feel that she was still concerned. He had a work schedule that was becoming more demanding all the time. The kids were all doing well at school and picking up Danish words at an amazing speed. They knew a lot more than I did. They even had Danish playmates. I had no one. I was beginning to question the reason for my isolation, but decided that I would keep it to myself and weather out the storm without complaining. I was now one third of the way through the process of being transformed from an American into a Dane. I might play the game, but it wouldn't be for real. My thoughts and feelings would always be my own.

Daddy told me, that when I finished in Haderslev at the end of March, I would be going to public school straight away. It was no surprise. I did not look forward to it, but what else was there? I had no control at all over my own destiny. I was a misplaced person.

Arithmetic was added to my studies in Haderslev. As much as I disliked that subject, it was more acceptable than Danish. How the Danes themselves ever managed to learn their complicated language was beyond me. I really wondered if I ever would be able to say complete sentences and converse with another person in Danish. It was so hard to concentrate. Uncle Magnus continued to encourage me to work harder and refrain from engaging in frivolous activities. The only frivolous activity he had so far discovered was Huckleberry Finn. The other books I brought with me from Kolding were acceptable, but reading Danish books would have been better.

He wasn't too happy with the subject matter of my drawings which I did as recreation. It was acceptable for me to draw pictures of nature and beautiful things, but the drawing of cartoon figures like Popeye and Mickey Mouse didn't go over well. Secretly, I had started to make drawings of a new clubhouse design for the gang and also some new ideas for the wooden tank, but I kept these confidential documents in my suitcase under my bed.

Dear Harold   *February 10, 1934*

I ain't dead yet but its gitting close. This place is murder. I reckon yer scratching yer noodle wondering why I am sending this letter when ya jus got one. Well thats cause this ones speshal. As ya will notice theres a secret ducumant in the envelope and I want ya to keep mum about it till we iron out all the rinkels. Its how we can make the tank lighter so it ain't so doggone hard to move around and how we can improve the firing posishuns. What we gotta do is rip out all 2x4's that ain't serving no perpose and then use thinner boards.

If ya sneak over to Guy Kings place ya'll see that the boards in his fence are real thin and I think we will be doing him a favor by borrowing some of those boards cause his fence ain't much to look at anyways. His whole place looks like a dump.

Then the next thing we gotta do is to fix up the firing slots. As ya know we were figuring on using our slingshots to fire through the slots. If six guys inside the tank used slingshots all at once like we were figuring, we would be stuck fer space and ammunishun would be flying all over the place inside the tank cause we would be handicaped. Well, I done alot of thinking and it ain't gonna work cause we don't want to hit the inside of the tank somewhere instead of through the slots so what we gotta do is have the tracks I've drawn up. These tracks are nailed in each slot and ya can turn them and aim in any direcshun. Then ya put the stone in the end of the track inside and pull back the rubber band thats fixed to each of the firing slots and lo and behold, ya fire! If that ain't gonna scare the living daylights out of the Moore gang, I'll be a squashed hamburger.

So hang on to these secret drawings and cross yer heart and hope to die if anything leaks out. If ya want ya can wait with the tracks until I come and meanwhile work on the rest of the tank when ya ain't working on the tower.

The best way to git the fence boards from Guy Kings place is to git some of the other gang members to start a lot of racket in the alley behind his place so that Guy King will go out to see whats cooking while ya take some boards out of his fence in front. This is called a distracshun. I read it in a book once.

Yup, I'm still here at my uncles place and its awful. Now his wife Agnes has got me hauling the carpets outside and trying to bang dust out of them on the clothesline. I can't understand why she wants to go to all the fuss and bother when the only dust around anywhere is in her head. I had to move all the furniture out of the way to git the carpets up and Agnes got so tired and worn out half way through the job just giving orders and direcshuns that she had to go and lie down. When I was banging the carpets outside the nayber came out and yelled at me over the fence. Since I'm American I don't aim to figure out what these foreigners are squawking bout, but I reckon it had something to do with disturbing the peace. Well, after all that ballyhoo I had to haul the carpets back in the house and spend a powerful lot of time gitting all the furniture back in place which was a major hardship cause I warn't allowed to walk on the carpet - not even in those silly slippers. I could only work from the edges. It was a hard nut to crack.

Agnes is gitting to be a real slave driver and if she doesn't cool off she might end up in a cookoo house. Well, we jus managed to git all the stuff back in place when in walks Uncle Magnus. He greeted Agnes with his usual henpeck kiss and then walked right in on the carpet! I jus couldn't believe what I was seeing after all that work I done and when I warn't allowed to put my foot on it. But I know the reason. Its cause women ain't allowed to boss their husbands around. Its the law cause husbands are masters of the house and can do anything they want and don't have to ask for permishun.

Well, all this unessesary work didn't do me no good cause I didn't have time to do my homework and even though I tried to cover up, Uncle Magnus found out that I warn't ready. I told him that was cause there was all this housework and there warn't time, but he said I gotta make time. Well how in the tar nashun kin ya make time when it ain't there. And why do I have to learn this depressing foreign stuff anyways. I'm not gonna use any of it when I git back to Junction.

When Uncle Magnus discovered that I didn't do my homework on account of the housework and all, he said a whole pile of danish stuff to Agnes and she did the same to him and it sure sounded like they was quarreling to beat the band. I could feel that Agnes warn't gonna take this lying down, but then she got emoshunal and upset and had to go into the bedroom and lie down anyways. Uncle Magnus warn't feeling too good either and tried to go in and comfert her but she warn't intrested. Somehow I seemed to be the cause of all the trouble. When ya really ponder over things, Harold, who would ever think that a Hornibrook gang member would end up in a horrible villa in a foreign country!

Well, its only temperary, thats fer sure. Let me know what ya think bout the secret drawings and don't let the other guys in on it yet. Ya never know they jus might blabber bout the secret by mistake and the word will git around what the Hornibrook gang is up to and we might git in powerful trouble. I'll see ya soon.

Yours till I rot, Visti

CHAPTER ELEVEN

One day at the table Uncle Magnus said that they would be having guests for dinner the following evening, at which occasion I would have the opportunity to meet a Danish boy my age. Somehow I smelled a rat. This was probably rigged. Anyway, I was told to help Agnes as much as possible in the kitchen and when the guests arrived to make sure I looked tidy and clean, with my hair

DOOM AND GLOOM

combed and also to display proper manners in their presence.

Daddy and my uncle had probably discussed my situation and came to the conclusion that I should be given the opportunity to meet someone my age. I was sure it was planned. They obviously realized that I was somewhat isolated. I could have told them that long ago. The awaited guests arrived right on time at seven o'clock the following evening. I could hear them in the front hall with Uncle Magnus and Agnes exchanging greetings and niceties, as they were taking off their overcoats. It reminded me of gobbling turkeys. I stood at attention in the far corner of the living room, tidy and clean with my hair combed, ready to display proper manners.

Uncle Magnus invited them into the living room and, saying something in Danish, gestured with his arm towards me. I heard the name Mr. and Mrs. Jensen. I bowed. They bowed and we shook hands, bowing again. Mr. Jensen then turned around and brought forth his son, who had been hiding in the background. He was a kid my age. From the exuberant introduction in Danish, I managed to salvage the name Carl Henry. I bowed, he bowed and we shook hands. His handshake was as limp as a dead fish.

I looked at this kid, sized him up and came to the immediate conclusion that I did not like him. He was dressed in a dark suit that he had completely outgrown. He wore shiny black shoes, a white shirt, blue bow tie and had curly red hair and horrible looking glasses. He was the true picture of a sissy according to Junction City standards. Feeling uncomfortable and very much ill at ease, we stood side by side in dead silence while the adults engaged in conversation.

Agnes seemed happy and relaxed. At the moment she had no problems regarding the memos. Uncle Magnus also seemed to be at ease, enjoying the entertainment of guests in his home - and Mr. and Mrs. Jensen were happy to be invited out with nothing to think about. Everything was mellow and in harmony, except for the new kid and myself. We had one thing in common. We both wished we were somewhere else.

Agnes and I had spent over an hour preparing food and setting the table just right, so when guests entered the dining room, all was ready. Uncle Magnus directed us all to our assigned seats with the flair and decisiveness of placing chess pieces on a board. Carl Henry and I were placed directly across from each other, so as to entice us to become acquainted. Uncle Magnus, as usual was at the head of the table. He rattled off the grace as if it interfered with the business of eating and then said *Vaer saa god* which was the official permission to open up the serviettes, place them on our laps and start passing plates of food around. Conversation was brisk during the meal. Only Carl Henry and I sat in silence, staring into our plates as we ate - and with good reason. I simply didn't know enough Danish to form a single sentence and also, even if I did, what would we talk about?

Uncle Magnus suddenly asked Carl Henry something in Danish. He replied and then Mrs. Jensen said something. Then Carl Henry said something again. Then Mr. Jensen said a couple of words, followed by Uncle Magnus who said several words. A single word was then said by Mr. Jensen, and Carl Henry,

81

looking up from his plate, asked me in English,

"You live next door to Charles Lindberg in America?"

I could feel it was an effort on his part to say all that in English. I would also say it took courage to ask such a stupid question. On the other hand, it was possible. I guess Lindberg could have lived in the vacant house across the alley behind the woodpile. I replied,

"No, we lived in Junction City and he lives somewhere else."

Uncle Magnus explained the conversation to Mr. and Mrs. Jensen. They both must have thought it was funny because they laughed, but then Mr. Jensen became serious and said something to his son that sounded like a scolding. Carl Henry looked down into his plate, obviously defeated.

We didn't talk any more during the meal, but the adults sure did. After a couple of glasses of table wine they whipped up quite a party and seemed to forget the reason why they got together in the first place. Carl Henry and I became part of the decor in the dining room, as they carried on, toasting glasses, talking and laughing as if there was no tomorrow.

Eventually dessert was served which kept us all quiet for about ten minutes. Scraping his plate clean, Uncle Magnus then came up with a brainy idea. In English, he said,

"Visti, you and Carl Henry may be excused if you wish. I suggest you show him your room."

Everyone was relieved as Carl Henry and I pushed our chairs back, stood up and said 'Tak for mad' which was the custom to do. I led the way out of the dining room. Opening the door to what I called my jail cell, I showed him what was there. He saw the American flag, the money jar, the desk, the chair, the bed and the picture of Agnes's grandmother and then I invited him to sit down, wondering what to do next.

"Do you live far from here?" I asked.

"Thirty minute."

We sat in silence for a few seconds - both of us somewhat uncomfortable.

"Hey, I know what we can do. I got a jigsaw puzzle." I reached under the bed and pulled out my old suitcase. I opened it on the bed and took out a few things.

"Is it hot in America?" he suddenly asked.

"Are ya kiddin'? There's this guy in Nevada who was going to the barn with his horsewagon full of corn an' it was so hot that the corn started popping all over the place an' the horse thought it was snow an' froze to death."

There was no reaction on his part. I don't think he understood a single word. On the other hand maybe he did, but didn't want to let on that it sounded stupid. And then again it just might be true, because anything is possible in good old USA. It certainly was food for thought. Anyway, there wasn't much more to say about the matter, so out came the jigsaw puzzle. I dumped it all on the desk in a big pile and said,

"This is a jigsaw puzzle of the famous Boston Tea Party."

Again no sign of intelligence, but he seemed interested, because he said,

"Tea party in Boston?"

I figured we might as well give up trying to hold a meaningful conversation, so we started putting the puzzle together. About an hour later, Uncle Magnus stuck his head in at the door to see how we were making out, and he was happy with what he saw; two contented boys having a good time together in harmony. Except for the puzzle, I had nothing in common with this kid, Carl Henry. When we eventually finished the puzzle, he asked in broken English,

"No tea party. No people tea drink?"

"Yer right. This is a different kind of party."

It would have been impossible to explain why the tea was thrown overboard in Boston harbor in 1773. We both had a language problem. Carl Henry did not seem to be one of those bright Danish students Uncle Magnus was always talking about. The kid didn't know anything about America.

The evening then passed without further excitement and I was greatly relieved when they left. Uncle Magnus said he was glad things worked out so well between us, which was something I did not know. He said that the Jensens would like us to visit them in the near future, which would give me another opportunity to be with Carl Henry. Just the thought of another meeting was appalling and almost made me shudder.

Back in Kolding, the two hours I had to spend in church every Sunday were becoming increasingly boring. Not understanding anything that was said in church, I could only sit there in my own thoughts. It was the same for the rest of the kids. Ben took the telephone book with him to church every week. He was becoming fascinated with numbers and with pencil and paper did a lot of calculations during service. He loved arithmetic. Vita was developing an interest in interior house design, and in church, worked on plans of furniture arrangements for her future home. Xenia did not take anything to church. She just sat there, probably thinking of her music.

To pass the time I started counting things in the church. I figured out there were 425 ceiling tiles, 572 small window panes, 1586 small rosettes around the perimeter at the ceiling, 82 vertical pieces in the railing at the altar, 64 marble slabs in the window sills, 120 light bulbs in the three large chandeliers, 27 of these were not working, 1200 marble floor tiles, 29 rows of pews accommodating 580 people, 16 different shades of color in the interior design of the walls and ceiling, 890 linear feet of gold trim around the windows with 36 rosettes, 720 small glass droplets in the chandeliers, which worked out to 6 per light bulb, 48 window panes that could be opened, with 96 brass hinges and 39 leaves on the wreath that adorned the pulpit. Unfortunately, I could not turn around to count how many pipes there were in the big organ up in the balcony, but I decided that in the near future I would bring a small mirror with me to church and in that way see what was behind me. I kept all this data on a pencil pad in my pocket. It was the kind of occupation that made no disturbance.

As I sat there checking up on chandelier details, ceiling tiles and the like, those in the congregation who forever were adoring the minister's children and looking at us, could only assume that I was gazing towards heaven, deep in religious bliss. Everybody had to look somewhere while the sermon was going on and if you didn't look at the pulpit, then looking up towards heaven was a natural choice. But I noticed some with their heads down - probably asleep. Ben made an amazing discovery in church about the number 9. The psalm numbers of the church service were posted on a board on the wall next to the pulpit. He noticed that the posted numbers were 3, 9 and 27. So he quickly figured out that $3 \times 9 = 27$ and that $2 + 7 = 9$. So he tried with $4 \times 9 = 36$ and found that $3 + 6 = 9$. I agreed with Ben that it was uncanny. I was sure even Daddy would have found that this was a revelation - especially since it was discovered in a church.

I was aware that there were many at the service who, had they known what we were doing, would have said 'How shameful - carrying on like this with their father in the pulpit!' But it was the language problem that isolated us and I did not feel it would deprive us the chance to walk through the Pearly Gates when the time came. We would all make it. The positive side of our activities during church service, was that it provided us with a foundation for our future professions.

Life in Haderslev dragged on. It became apparent to Uncle Magnus at the end of the second month that I had made very little progress. I knew about 30 Danish words, but was unable to form sentences. The only Danish I heard around me, was the exchange of words between Uncle Magnus and Agnes and most of that sounded like it would be inadvisable to translate. Often he came home from the school very tired and I could feel he had no desire to put in another three hours of teaching. Nevertheless, we plodded along with very little enthusiasm. It was simply the call of duty for both of us. I felt sorry for him and he felt sorry for me. I was also becoming increasingly aware of the consequence of learning so little. Already I was far behind other kids my age, having not attended school since we left Junction City. That was a half a year ago. I didn't have the slightest idea how I was going to make out when faced with public school and all those strange kids.

I felt comfort opening my suitcase in the privacy of my room and looking at things that linked me with my past. I would spread all the things out on my bed and play with the glass marbles , try out the yo-yo, test the slingshot and look at the photos. I really didn't have much, but it was American. I now had thirteen kroner in the cookie jar.

Suddenly a ray of sunshine!

Dear Visti   *February 28, 1934*
I aint no good at writing cause by the time I look round for paper and pencil I can't remember what I was gonna write about. Yep, it looks like theres trouble over there . If I were you I wouldnt waste no more time at yer unkels place. In fact I wouldnt waste no more time in that country. I guess you heard that Blackies gone. Its too bad cause he was a good dog. I didnt know nothing about what happened until it was all over. It was somebody out on Dane Lane that did it.

I dont know but things aint the same no more after you left. The clubhouse is ok but I cant get the other guys to work on the tower cause they aint got time on account of high school and things. Hornibrook got a gal friend and so has Burton so I told em to get lost. Well I guess thats all thats happened round here. If you are coming back maybe you kin tell me the date so I kin be at the station. My mom dont think you will be back but then she dont know the inside story.

Yours truely - Harold

I decided that upon my return, we would reorganize everything from scratch, throw out ol' Hornibrook and all the sissies, and call our gang 'The Black Band.' The sooner I could get a letter to Harold about this, the better. We couldn't have girls undermining the very foundation of what took so many years to build. It was good the clubhouse was still in one piece.

Sunday came again. Another two hours at the church. More ceiling tiles counted. More and then we all went home for lunch. Following that, we kids played dominos until it was time for me to go. On the way back to Haderslev, it was tough going with a cold wind blowing the wrong way. When I came to Christiansfeld, I stopped at the pillow case window and waited for about fifteen minutes, but nothing happened.

I did a lot of thinking on those weekly bicycle trips. Fortunately, I did not feel sorry for myself, but I was unhappy. Uncle Magnus's remarks about how clever Danish kids were and how far behind I was, did not entice me to roll up my sleeves and get cracking. It almost had the opposite effect. I resigned myself to the fact that Danish kids were in a different ballpark and I just happened to be out of my ballpark temporarily.

It was Uncle Magnus's idea that I should drop in and see Carl Henry on the way back from Kolding that Sunday afternoon. Once again, everything was arranged. I had no say in the matter. I was given the address of the Jensen family and it turned out to be an apartment in the center of town. This was not anything to look forward to. I had nothing at all in common with this kid, Carl Henry, and actually thought that the first meeting we had was going to be the last, but Uncle Magnus wanted the 'friendship' to blossom. To keep the peace, I decided not to fight it. I did not want negative reports about my conduct to leak through to Daddy. He had enough to think about, just running that big church.

On the third floor of the apartment building, I found the door with the name Jensen on a brass plate. I rang the bell and after a short wait, Mrs. Jensen opened the door, greeted me cordially but seemed a bit upset. I was ushered into the parlor and she invited me to sit down on the sofa. She could not speak English but surprisingly I could understand, from what she was saying, that Carl Henry was not around. I got up, suggesting that I should go but she said a whole lot of stuff in Danish that led me to believe it was best to sit down again. She then left the room and I sat and waited.

The parlor was overflowing with antique furniture and large potted ferns. The sofa faced a window which was almost covered by heavy looking, dark brown drapes with tassels. Oval framed photographs of the previous generation were everywhere on the walls staring down at the present generation, and numerous items such as ashtrays, miniature bronze figurines, vases and ceramic knick-knacks occupied every horizontal surface. The low table in front of the sofa was partly covered with a white lace table cloth upon which was a large, crystal glass bowl of imitation fruit. There were grapes, two bananas, three apples and a pear. The apples looked almost real. Two large, upholstered chairs faced the sofa. All three were the of the same design, which looked like some sort of faded rose petal pattern from the fourteenth century, and they were loaded down with hand-embroidered cushions. A Persian carpet completed the decor, but was hardly visible with so much placed upon it. Although everything was tastefully arranged, I felt like I was in a storeroom from the seventeenth century.

Mrs. Jensen appeared between the ferns, carrying a tray with chinaware, coffee and cookies. She poured two cups, placed herself among the cushions in a chair opposite me and made a sincere attempt to explain why Carl Henry was not around. I looked at her intensely, doing my best to figure out what she was saying. At moments like this, it was apparent that two and a half months of tutorship had not helped me much. If only she could speak English, it would be so much easier. She picked up her cup and sipped some coffee. I could see she was trying to figure out a way to get through to me. Suddenly she put her cup down, said something, opened her mouth and pointed to her teeth. Eureka! That was it. Carl Henry was at the dentist! With this major breakthrough in communication, we were both relieved. I then thought to myself, this must be an emergency since he was at a dentist on a Sunday.

After we finished the coffee and cookies, I thought it was time to go, but again with gestures, she suggested I stay and wait for Carl Henry. To keep me entertained, she now brought forth a large photo album and sat down beside me on the sofa surrounded by all the cushions.

Opening the album, we started on page one. There was a photograph of Carl Henry, one month old in the nude. Mrs. Jensen explained to me all the wonderful things about this precious baby, but I didn't understand a word. Then she slowly turned the page, taking one last look at her angel, and now we had a double spread of photos, all of Carl Henry. He was now about five months old and could sit up by himself. There was one of him in his crib where he was hanging on to the railing, another where he was in a bathtub and a few photos, taken at various angles, showing him peeking out of a buggy. Very cute.

Mrs. Jensen jabbered away in Danish and I pretended to be greatly impressed with this wonder child. After five minutes of this, she slowly turned to the next page, making sure I got one last opportunity to take a lingering look at this beautiful creature - and then, lo and behold, another double spread of Carl Henry! This was almost too much. He was now about two years old and could walk. Amazing! Mrs. Jensen pointed to individual photos, explaining in great detail all the exceptional things about this child. I don't think she realized I hadn't the slightest idea of what she was talking about - except, of course, that it must be about Carl Henry. Again, a page was turned and he was now about four years old, having entered the age of great discovery - not so much of Carl Henry discovering the world, but rather of the parents discovering Carl Henry. Judging from these photos, he seemed to possess great intelligence and talent. There was a photo of him where he was seated at a piano with his fingers on the keys - probably in the middle of a concerto, and another photo showing him reading a newspaper. The newspaper was upside down, but that revealed even greater ability and intelligence. Very few people can read a paper upside down. There were a couple of photos of him on a bicycle. His feet didn't reach the pedals and the hand holding the bicycle at the back fender hadn't been completely removed from the print, but it sure looked like he was on his own. And there was a photo of him in an oval frame - just the head and shoulders, with some sort of a fake background, as though it was taken in a studio. He looked very stern and undoubtedly this photo would, in a hundred years or less, end up on the wall with all the other ancestors.

The last picture of Carl Henry on this double spread, showed him sitting at a desk with pen and paper - perhaps writing his memoirs. Mrs. Jensen's continuous jabbering created a dramatic background to this impressive record of her son's life. And there was more to come!

I had an awful time refraining from yawning from total boredom, but managed to keep my mouth closed through a yawn, resulting in tears in my eyes. I took out my handkerchief to wipe them away. Mrs. Jensen, noticing this, thought I was being overcome with emotion. She herself felt the emotion of yesterday's memories, and so we stopped for a moment while she poured another cup of coffee for both of us.

The next double spread showed him as a successful boy scout with many badges. He looked to be about nine. Three other photos revealed that he excelled in sport. He was sitting in the front row of a soccer team, holding a trophy in one of the photos, obviously the leader of the pack, and the other two photos showed the team in action. The last picture on the page was a misplaced baby photo, where Carl Henry at the age of two, revealed the early ability to hold a conversation on the telephone. Time, place and age was written under each and every photo, thus providing a well documented record for future generations.

I could hardly stand any more. Also, this place was stuffy and Mrs. Jensen never stopped talking. I made a move, suggesting I would like to go now, but again she gestured me to remain seated, because there was much, much more to look at. I wondered if the real kid was ever going to turn up. Time dragged on. I was beginning to feel very tired and had to do my utmost to avoid yawning continuously. This was a torture.

Half an hour later, as we were looking at a photo, where Carl Henry, at the age of just one year, was able to push his own buggy, there was a noise in the hallway and in came Carl Henry in person with a swollen face, supported by his father. He looked quite sick. Upon seeing her poor son, Mrs. Jensen jumped to her feet and rushed over to comfort him. A flurry of panicky words were exchanged between Mr. and Mrs. Jensen, and together they hustled the ailing Carl Henry out of the room to bed. It all happened so fast. I was witnessing an emergency. There must have been complications in the dentist's chair. I picked up the photo album, which in that brief moment of panic had fallen to the floor. Placing it on the lace covered table next to the bowl of imitation fruit, I sat among the cushions and waited.

Mrs. Jensen eventually came back into the parlor looking like an emergency case herself and said something to me in Danish. I nodded, got up and went towards the entrance door in the hallway. We both bowed to each other, shook hands and I left, greatly relieved. This was the last opportunity I had to be in the presence of the child prodigy, but that's the way the cookie crumbles.

Dear Harold   *March 12, 1934*

I got yer letter last weekend when I was at home. Fer a while I thought ya were dead. Jiminy crickets, Harold, what ya said bout Hornibrook and Burton makes me wanna vomit. We aint supposed to intrested in gals cause we dont wanna be sissies. Maybe ya kin talk Burton out of it. I dont trust Hornibrook anyways so lets start a new band. We kin call it the Black Band and its main purpose is devastashun and to build the tower higher. I'm gonna come back as soon as I got enough dough, but I've ben thinking I might need some help. Maybe ya guys kin start a collecshun.

Yesterday at supper my uncle Magnus gave me a terrible long lekture about health. He told me I gotta eat about 10 pieces of ryebread and 2 cups of milk at supper time. In the same lekture he told me that I should do an hours exercise each morning in the yard such as jumping, running round in circles streching and the like. It was hard for me to digest all that at the supper table. When he was finished I told him and Agnes bout all the rats we had in Junction City and how we killed em with our slingshots. Agnes didnt like that so Magnus said we gotta only talk about nice things at the supper table and if I talk its gotta be in danish which I dont aim to do. They sure eat dizzy things here. They let milk go perfektly sour until its lumpy and then they sprinkle little pieces of black bread on it and some sugar and then they eat the whole blasted contrapshun and think it tastes awfully good. They call it "Tyk Maelk" which means "thick milk." I hate the stuff. I only like white bread and jam like we had in Junction.

Uncle Magnus made me meet a danish kid whos gotta be the awfullest sissy I have met in my whole darn life. He didnt know nothing bout nothing and he was a pain in the neck. I dont need to know anybody here cause its all temperary. I reckon in a half a year I'll be on my way back. I'll live in the club house. This letter is kinda short cause Magnus is putting the pressure on and says I'm wasting too much time. Well, I never waste a minute. Women waste time but men dont.

Yours till I rot - Visti

Liberation day finally arrived. It was a happy day for me and also for Agnes and Uncle Magnus. With the room cleared out, my suitcases packed and wearing coat and scarf, I said goodbye to Agnes in the doorway. It was no tear-jerking farewell. After all, Kolding was only an hour away by bus, but neither she or I felt any desire to share kitchen duties anymore. Uncle Magnus helped me put the suitcases on his bicycle and we headed for the station. The snow was gone. Spring, he told me, was only one month away.

As we waited for the bus at the station, we both had time to reflect on the achievement of the last three months. I don't think Uncle Magnus was too happy with the results of his work. It could have been better. I did learn good manners and some arithmetic, but the most important subject of all was still on the ground floor. I knew about thirty words in Danish, which was not enough to form sentences or hold a conversation. However, I was no longer afraid to walk on the street alone and I did have some confidence in myself, even though I was lacking in intelligence - according to others.

The bus came to the station. All the passengers got out. Uncle Magnus took the suitcases from his bike and gave them to the bus driver. We shook hands and I thanked him for 'the good time' together and he did likewise, although neither he nor I thought it was very good. It was just a formality so we could depart in peace. Through the bus window I waved goodbye. I thought he looked somewhat pathetic, standing there with his bicycle. Now he could go home to his Agnes. For me it was freedom.

Dear Harold   *March 30, 1934*

Well, ja won't know what happened, but I'm out of jail. That place called Haderslev and my uncle's house is now a faint memery. He gave up on me when he discovered ya can't change an American. The trees are begining to get green and springs a-coming here pretty soon. I feel awfully home-sick fer Junction. There haint ben a day here in Denmark which I haint thought bout ya and thinking of things like the time we that b-b gun war with Reymond Mosegaard and Dick and all those noodleless brats.

I jus found out that a foreigner ain't allowed to stay in another country fer more than a certain mount of months, but they won't be beable to kick me out again, cause I'm not a foreigner and if they say I am cause I've ben in Denmark then I'll go into hiding. As soon as my time is up and when they git tired a-hunting fer me I will appear again under a different name. I'm sending you a photograph of me which Xenia took. I'm blasted sorry fer not looking happier in the picture but theres reasons fer it that any guy would know if he had ever ben in this blamed, rotten land of trouble.

Every sunday here round Easter I helped the janitor of our church chime the bells which is harder than plain ringing. It's fun to go up in the church tower and be allowed to make so much racket. There are two bells and they both have verses on them and are supported by huge ties, iron an bolts. We fix a rope onto the iron knobs of the bells when we chime. The chimings done quick so that it sounds like one long note. The whole contraption fer chiming is a speshal invenshun invented by the janitor. Jus think, Harold, I'm the only boy in town who is allowed to go up in the church tower to ring the bell. My, ya should see my muscle from all that chiming. It aint one of them sissy soft muscles, no-sir-ee. It's a real regular hard muscle, the kind a person kin be proud of. I'm also pretty strong now. I'm gonna let my hair grow long and see if it makes me strong like it did fer Samson. If it don't work then I will know they made it up. I've done a lot of thinking and that's not the only thing they made up. I know ya would rather read Zane Grey cowboy books, but it says in the bible that Cain built a city. Well, who needs a city when theres only four people in the world? Anyways I got all my strength from jus ringing church bells. I'm 5 feet and 6-3/4 inches tall now and I'm growing awful fast. I'm gonna be a six footer or bust. I sure am aching fer a scrap and am gonna start one 'for long. Some day if I ever git time I'm a-gonna show some of these sissy boys I've seen round here a few things.

Theres something I fergot to menshun in my last letter. Its bout gasoline wagons and matches. They don't have gasoline trucks over here. They have gasoline wagons pulled by horses instead. I think that's to save on gasoline so its not all used up when they git to the gasoline stashun. The matches here are jus perfektly awful. There is only one kind of matches in all of Denmark. The matches kin only strike on a danish matchbox and nothing else in the whole world. I'm sending ya a match. Ya kin try to strike it on anything ya please and I bet it won't work. A guy could be in real trouble if he was out in the cold wilderness and had his bonfire ready and his match, but then fergot the match box at home.

Well I got a rip-roaring headache and my arm is dog-tired on account of thinking of the dismal future thats jus round the corner so pardon me fer ending this here letter.

Yours till I rot. Visti

CHAPTER TWELVE

It looked like a big prison, four stories high. The dismal, grey brick buildings seemed to cover a whole city block. The only entrance was through a portal, which led into a very large courtyard, surrounded on all sides by the grey facade. A great number of windows faced the yard and also concrete steps with iron railings, leading up to four or five different doors, which were about three feet above ground at first floor level. It all looked very old. The day of reckoning had come. This grim place was to be my school. Daddy was with me to arrange for my registration and together we found the door to the school office in the portal area. I was very much on the defensive.

There were no kids around, but I knew they were there - hundreds of them, somewhere in these grey buildings. Daddy talked to an elderly lady at the counter in the school office. Then we sat down on a bench at the wall and waited. Daddy said we would be seeing the principal shortly. For me, it was worse than a dental appointment. It was now nine in the morning according to the clock on the school office wall. The school day had started at eight, so somehow I was late, but for what I did not know.

The principal came into the office and we stood up. He shook hands with Daddy and then with me. I bowed as I was supposed to do. We were ushered into his office and sat facing him at his cluttered desk. Behind him on the wall was a large photograph of the *King Christian the Tenth*. Daddy and the principal talked at length. Now and then the principal would look at me in a way that made me feel like an additional problem to the school system. Finally he stood up and we did likewise. Daddy shook his hand and, turning to me, said the principal would take me to the class. However, Daddy added, the principal suggested I should start in a lower class to begin with, so as to catch up on a number of subjects that I must learn to be at the educational level of others my age. It was no surprise.

For quite a while now, I had realized that my Junction City grade school education was okay for Oregon but not worth very much in this foreign country. If the three month period I endured in Haderslev accomplished anything at all, it was to make me aware of my shortcomings and the dilemma I now found myself in. Daddy gave me a fatherly pat on the back and left. I was now officially enlisted and at the mercy of the system. This place was called *The Latin School.*

I followed the principal like a dog across the school courtyard. I could hear the voices of kids somewhere, reciting or saying something in unison. We entered one of the doors facing the courtyard, walked up an old, antique looking staircase to the third floor and then down a dismal school corridor. There was no doubt this was an institution. The wooden stairs and floors were worn down from the trampling of generations of reluctant school children. The wooden knobs on the stair railings revealed management's disciplinary attitude. Frivolous activities, such as sliding down stair railings served no purpose in this place of learning. Along the corridor walls were framed photographs of past teachers and principals, but not of pupils. It seemed obvious that the status of management was more important than that of those to be educated. After all, school children passed through like manufactured products on a factory assembly line, but management stayed on forever. Halfway down the gloomy corridor we stopped at a classroom door. Everything looked so foreboding. If there ever was a time to be on guard, this was it. The principal knocked on the door and we entered.

A shock wave hit the classroom. The sudden, unexpected presence of the school's principal standing in the doorway brought the class and teacher to immediate attention with everyone standing up, facing the principal like tin soldiers. This was the moment of ultimate respect and fear. The principal said something to the school teacher and I was pushed into the foreground. After some more words where I heard my name mentioned, the principal left, with me standing alone facing the class and teacher.

I felt absolutely awful. I quickly noticed that all the kids in the room were only about nine or ten years old! The teacher, a thin man with spectacles, a long pointed nose and a stick in his hand, told the class to sit down. Addressing the class, he said something about my presence and almost immediately the kids started snickering. The teacher slammed his stick on a desk and the snickering stopped. He then turned to me and said in English,

"Please, name on board."

I took a piece of chalk from a tray and printed my name on the blackboard. The awful, dead silence, the squeaky chalk, and knowing that all eyes were following every movement of my hand, for a fleeting moment gave me the satisfaction of feeling very important. But this all faded immediately as I was escorted by the teacher to the back row in the classroom and placed on a school bench next to a little kid, who immediately moved away from me. There was some more snickering, but a whack with the stick on the desk in front of me put a stop to that. I considered myself fortunate to be placed in the back row. Thus, I was able to size up the situation of everything in the classroom without being stared at.

There were twenty-six kids in the room, half of them girls. Almost all of the kids had golden hair. The school desks were made to accommodate two pupils each. I don't think anyone knew why it was so. The desk and bench were too small for me. Discipline and obedience was the foundation for all learning here and the teacher, armed with his stick, kept everyone on the edge of their seats and wide awake.

This first hour in this Danish school was a disturbing experience. I sat there feeling grim, angry and very much alone. There was absolutely no way I would ever resign myself to anything going on here. It was a nightmare in progress. I would have to let Harold know about all the trouble. Maybe he could think of something to get me out of this jam. Not only was there something rotten in the state of Denmark, it was hairy scary.

Dear Harold,   *April 8, 1934*
Well, like I said in my last letter the gloomy months at my uncles place is now jus a faint memery. My uncle and his wife were always tired and worn out. I didn't

learn nothing there. I was stuck in that blooming place all day long with all the house cleaning and homework. And then they tried to git a boy friend fer me but all they could find was a sissy who almost made me shiver. The way these guys dress over here is enough to make ya wanna throw up. His name was Carl Henry and I know ya won't believe it but I had to sit in a sofa with his mom and look at baby pictures of him. Wotta nightmare. Well anyways, my uncle and his wife were glad to git rid of me and I was glad to go, so we were all happy.

CARL HENRY

But I was only happy for five days cause then on April 2nd I had to begin school here in Kolding. That was the most dreaded day in my life. I reckon ya know it's bad enough to have to change from one American school to another, but to have to change from an American school to a danish school is awful. It's enough to scare the living daylights out of ya.

The school I go to is terribly old. It has stone floors. The floors in the halls are like shallow troughs from continual walking on them. The staircases are wood and the steps are completely worn out jus like the floors. The railings got knobs on them to prevent kids from having fun sliding down a railing. They don't want any fun here cause it interferes with learning. Ya can feel there is fear everywhere in the building. It's jus like a jail.

The desk and benches are black and much wider than American desks so that two kids can sit at the same desk. They usually have a boy and a gal both on one bench so that there won't be wispering, cause it ain't no fun to wisper to a gal. Lots of gals have long braids with big ribbons on the ends of em. The boys tease the gals by pullin their braids and tying them in knots. Well, as I was saying, the first day at school was the awfullest day of my life. The principal put me in a class with little kids. Its like going from the 8th grade down to the 5th grade in Junction City, but I figured out they got alot more subjects here even in this 5th grade. They have rithmatik (pardon me while I choke a little), German, English, religion, geography, natural sience, history, chemistry, mathamatics, geomatry, drawing and French and alot of other rot. The only ones I know are drawing and English and stinky old rithmatik. My dad says that they are gonna try me out in this grade, but if it don't work then I gotta go down to 4th or 3rd grade where the kids are 8 and 9 years old. Its not jus that I gotta learn all this junk, but I first gotta learn Danish so I can understand how to learn all this dismal junk. I almost feel like commiting suicide, but I can't do that cause I'm a preacher's son. Instead I gotta bite the bullet.

Well, anyways the principal put me in this class and when I entered the room all the kids stood up cause they gotta do that when anyone comes in. I sit next to a boy in the back row who only comes up to my shoulder and we both hate each other. Well I jus happened to enter the classroom during a rithmatik period. As soon as I knowed that, my heart fell ker-plunk into my stomak. Jus think, Harold, rithmatik is my worsest subject and school is my worsest place, so everything was perfektly awful at that dreadful moment. The teacher was a nightmare. He's got the worsest lookin face ya can possibly amagine. All the teachers in Junction City were women which is the way it should be, cause ya don't wanna be fighting a battle while yer studying, but here they got men teachers who are real tough and only want to give ya a hard time. They jus want to scare the kids all the time so that they will have nightmares every night.

Well, this rithmatik teacher looks like he was born by mistake. He's as skinny as a rake. He wears specticals and has black greasy curly hair which he keeps well oiled and perfumed so he stinks like a bottle of stale vinegar. He also smells of cigarettes and his fingers are yellow from all the smoking he does after school. He has a long pointed nose that kinda seems to jab into you. It might be okay for ringing door bells, but looks awful on his face. And he's got a couple of extra large teeth sticking out over his lower lip which reminds me of a donkey. He wears those silly lookin pants they wear over here like a guy playing golf and he has a vomit colored jacket on top of a sickly brown sweater. He's got a big frown on his face all the time and carries a stick to fracture kids bones with. He's got a temper a million times worse than Opal Burgess. He's hollerin all the time. He thinks everyone is deaf. I bet he hates rithmatik as much as we do. He hollers as loud as he can, even when the pupil is right under his long pointed nose. When he screams and hollers its so loud that us kids have to hang onto our seats fer fear the noise and racket will blow us away. He uses the stick to slam on kids desks when he talks about rithmatik. He's powerful fond of pulling kids out of their seats by their hair and also by their ears. He takes hold of their shoulders and shakes them until they are jus about seasick.

When he stands in front of the class and asks a kid a rithmatik questchun, the kid is in big trouble if he gives the wrong answer cause the awful teacher then gits into a terrible rage, digging his fingernails into his hair and grinding his teeth and gitting powerful red in his face fer a minute or more. Then he goes tearing

down the aisle to the kids desk and yells at him in rage and if the kid says anything in protest then the crazy teacher slams his stick on the kids desk making everything shake, and then he hollers and screams and yanks the kid out of his seat by his hair or ear whichever is the handiest, and shoves him into a corner of a the room where he has to stand fer at least an hour facing the wall like a statue. I can tell ya, Harold, this guy is a real headache maker. If this nut was in America we would call the cops. I don't know how much more I can stand of this crazy place. I jus gotta git back to Junction City. I simply don't belong here.

One of these days I'm gonna play hookey. I know it's against the law over here to play hookey, but I can't stand anymore. It was much better in Junction where it was okay to play hookey. Even the teachers did. I remember Miss Taylor in the first grade played hookey once a month.

I was gonna ask ya, Harold if ya have any ideas how I can git out of the fix I'm in. There ain't no clubhouses here so I can't go into hiding. Do ya think if all the gang over there started a collecshun that maybe ya could git enough dough scraped together fer my trip back to Junction? I would pay everybody back real quick cause I would work real hard in the beanfields and earn piles of money.

Ya can send the money in an envelope but make sure its a thick envelope cause I don't want anyone to hold it up to the light and see whats inside. Remember this is an internashunal emergency!

I feel like squashed hamburger in a garbage can so I better quit, - but the nightmare continues and continues.......!

Yours till I rot -Visti.

The sound of a bell in the school corridor brought the 'rithmatik' hour to a close. All the kids got up and dashed out of the room. The horrible teacher gathered up a couple of books on the front desk, and with his stick clutched in his hand, walked out. I just sat there wondering where they all went, but then realized it was a recess period. Sure enough, going to the window, I saw all the kids down there, pouring out into the school yard and running around, making a lot of noise. There must have been a thousand of them. I had no desire whatsoever to go down and be in that yard. It was safer here.

I returned to my bench near the back wall of the classroom and waited. The bell rang again. I went to the window to see what was going to happen now. The kids started lining up in different rows according to their classes. I noticed at

94

least three lineups, where the kids seemed to be my age and even some that looked older. And then there were the lineups for the eight, nine and ten year olds. There was absolutely no way I would appear in public with those little kids. I could see 'my' class all standing at attention in the school yard ready to march in for another hour of slavery. At the head of each line-up was a teacher. The arithmetic teacher was not there. It was a different teacher. I wondered what subject they were going to have now. It was good I didn't have to be part of anything. That was one good thing about being dumb.

There was a lot of racket in the corridors as all the kids returned to their classroom. Suddenly kids poured into the room and I didn't recognize a single one. This was a whole new bunch of ten year olds! A kid came to the back row where I was seated and looked at me as an intruder. It was his seat. I got up, extremely bewildered. Other kids noticed me and probably thought I was a thief, having entered the classroom during the recess period. The teacher, an older man, entered the room, saw me and asked me something in Danish. Not knowing what he was saying, but realizing it was a question as to what I was doing in the room, I replied in English,

"I'm American and I just started school here."

To my surprise he responded in English,

"What class were you assigned to?"

"I dunno."

"Well, I am sure there is a mistake. How old are you?"

"Thirteen and a half."

"I see." He thought about things for a moment. "Come, I will take you to your proper class. Can you remember if it was A, B or C?"

"I think it was B."

"Good, that is right here on this floor."

We walked down the gloomy corridor, leaving behind a giggling, noisy class. We stopped at a door near the stairwell. He knocked and we walked in. About two dozen boys and girls my age stared me right in the face! The teacher spoke to the other teacher. They seemed perplexed. They looked at me as though I was a new piece of furniture. I knew I was in the wrong place and so did they. The first teacher returned to his classroom where things sounded like they were out of control, and left me standing here with this new class which just stared in silence, but probably were doing a lot of thinking, wondering where I came from. The teacher then asked me in English,

"Do you know the way to the school office?"

"Yes."

"Well, I suggest you go down there and register. They will then assign you to a class."

"Okay."

I turned around and left the room. This first day was turning out to be a real mess. It was good the teachers could speak English. I went down the stairs and walked across the school yard to the school office in the portal area. I was just walking up the stairs to the door when the principal came out.

"What are you doing here? Why are you not in class?"

"I can't find where my class is," I replied, feeling very nervous.

He turned around, and went into the office with me at his heels. Checking a school schedule at the counter, he turned to me and said, "You are in class 5 B. Please remember that. At the moment they are in the gymnasium. Do you have running shoes and gym clothes?"

"No."

"That you must have. The gym teacher will instruct you what to do. Now, I am going to take you there. From now on stay with your class."

Again I crossed the courtyard - this time to a different building. On the second floor was the boys' gym. The principal spoke to the gym teacher and left me in his care. He couldn't speak English, but it didn't matter. He let me sit on a bench in the gym and watch. It was just as well, because I would have looked out of place running around with those little kids.

The bell finally rang and all the kids went out into the school yard. This time I followed along, but tried not to be with them. During the recess I stood alone in a corner near a basement staircase. With hundreds of kids milling around no one noticed me, so I felt very fortunate. This was indeed a peculiar situation. I was probably in the same grade as Xenia and Vita. They went to a different school. I wondered why it was so hard for me to get a grasp on things, as compared to them. They were doing fine in school, spoke a little Danish, understood a lot of Danish and had playmates.

I must admit I knew quite a few Danish words by now, but I was unable to form sentences. It was very difficult to grasp what others were saying. The language sounded garbled as though something was stuck in their throats. I knew no one and always had to be on the defensive, guarding myself against trouble which seemed to be everywhere. I figured the solution to it all was to take one day at a time, weather the storm, stay out of trouble, keep calm, watch my step, be on guard, tread softly, don't rock the boat, play it by ear and eventually - with a little luck I would find my way back to Junction City.

What a moment that would be! I would write and tell Harold the exact train I would be on. It would probably be the Portland Rose. All the kids would be at the station to greet me - Harold, Burton, Donald Dill, the two Skovbo kids, Jimmy Hansen, Freddie with his dog Jiggs, Pete and even Hornibrook, although we would deal with him later. From the train station we would all go straight to the clubhouse. There would be so much to do. The first thing would be to change the name of the gang, since we were kicking out Hornibrook. The name 'The Black Band' sounded good. That would certainly shake up the Moore gang, scare the living daylights out of them and keep them on their side of the tracks.

The sound of the bell brought me back to reality. All the running around in the school yard subsided as the kids started forming queues according to grades and classes. Confusion gave way to order. I recognized some of the small children of my class and reluctantly took a place in line with them. With all the queues eventually formed, faced by a teacher at the head of each, a certain calm prevailed over the vast school yard. I stood out like a telephone pole among the small kids in 'my' queue, and immediately this unusual sight was noticed by hundreds of kids throughout the school yard! Suddenly I was the center of all attention and there was lots of laughing and jeering that seemed to echo between the surrounding walls. I was actually on display. It was the most humiliating moment of my life. Boys in other queues pointed their fingers in my direction and thumbed noses at me. Girls held their hands up to their faces and giggled. There was nowhere to hide. I felt embarrassed. I tried to act natural, but looking down on the head of the little kid in front of me as our queue moved forward, I knew that I was misplaced, displaced and had absolutely nothing in common with anything or anybody. This was all enemy territory. It was a great relief when we reached the outside steps and passed in through the doorway of the building, leaving the mockery behind me. The inside of the school was almost a haven.

Back in the classroom I felt really shaken. I never suspected this kind of hostility. It was like a bad dream. What I really needed was a gang of kids to back me up, all armed with slingshots. The Black Band could do the job. We would show them a thing or two the American way. Nobody pushes an American around.

As I sat there in the back row in my own thoughts, I suddenly became aware that the class was reciting in a strange language and that the new teacher had written mysterious stuff on the blackboard that definitely was not Danish. Maybe it was German or French or Greek. Oh well, whatever it was, it had nothing to do with me. I was just a spectator, watching a show. And there were better shows. The guy in Junction with his secret lotion and pins through his cheek - that was a better show, and the exciting films in Junction City show house - those were the best of all. For the rest of the hour I just sat there next to the little kid I didn't like, and feeling pretty grim. I decided that I was not going out in the school yard anymore. If I couldn't stay in the classroom during recess, then I would look for some place to hide. I just had to keep track of where the little kids would be going after this foreign language hour. It couldn't be another gym class.

The bell rang and all the kids scrambled for the door. I followed, but half way down the corridor I slipped into the boys' washroom, entered a toilet cubicle, locked the door and waited. It worked. All the kids emptied out into the school yard and here I was, safe and sound. Apart from a dripping tap, it was nice and quiet. Ten minutes later there was the bell again and shortly after the corridors were again full of kids. Some came into the washroom, but in all the commotion I slipped out unnoticed, saw some of my classmates and returned with them to the classroom. This was a good idea and worked well. I would do it every recess from now on. I already felt better.

After school was over in the afternoon, I managed to slip out of the class-room door ahead of everyone else, and I ran like lightning down the stairs, out of the door, across the school yard, through the portal and out on the street before any of the kids could corner me. Obviously, my training in running away from overturned outhouses on Halloween nights in Junction paid off. They would have a hard time catching me.

Fifteen minutes later at our apartment, I felt protected and safe. Mom greeted me in her comforting way,

"Well, how did school go today, dear Visti?"

"Not very well. I got a headache. I don't feel good."

"Really? How did that happen?" She put her hand on my brow to see if I had a temperature.

"You certainly don't have a fever. Looks like you'll live. I suggest you go to your room and rest on the bed and we'll hear more about your day later. It's nice and quiet at the moment."

I went to my room, lay on my bed and pulled a blanket over my head to shield myself from the outside world.

At the supper table, when the eight of us were together, there were many questions as to how my day went - mostly from Xenia, who always liked suspense and drama. After my account of the 'nightmare' at the school, I almost expected Daddy and Mom to recommend that I quit that school and together we would try something else. Instead, Daddy said,

"I realize it has been a hard day for you, Visti, but for each passing day, the easier and more acceptable everything will become. The Lord will always protect you. I want you to know that."

Mom was more practical. She could have soothed me with her usual pearl of wisdom -'Don't worry, you'll soon be dead,' but she never said that when Daddy was present. So instead she said,

"Cheer up, Visti. You are quite normal and five years from now, all these unpleasant incidents will seem so far away."

While my father always referred to the Lord for comfort, my mother relied on the time factor to take care of things. However, one way or the other, the present arrangement was here to stay. With the Lord's help everything should be okay five years from now.

Xenia also gave good advice regarding all the heckling in the school yard.

"I think what they did to you was awful. If I were you I would report them all to the principal."

"Gee, that would be hard 'cause it was almost the whole school," I replied.

"Imagine having to hide in a washroom. I think that's disgraceful. We don't have any problems at our school."

Xenia could hardly contain her indignation.

"Hey Mom," Vita pitched in, "how come Visti can't go to our school? We don't have any big kids making trouble."

"Yeah, that's a good idea," Xenia added, "he could go in our class and then we would all be together."

"Yes, I know, girls, but you see, Visti is older and the school he now goes to is also a high school. It is best that he can meet boys his own age."

"But it's not working out that way," Xenia remarked.

"Yes, but in time it will. We must try to be patient," Mom concluded.

Well, whether or not I had patience was really irrelevant, I thought. The best thing was to be on guard at all times and not let anyone push me around.

I certainly would not want to be in a school that only had small kids. Although I hated the kids in my school, those who were of my age at least provided me with a feeling of identity - something I could relate to. I would probably have to take them on one by one somewhere after school and teach them a thing or two. They were not going to get the best of me. It was just a matter of time.

The next morning I was in school yard at a quarter to eight. I had forgotten to reckon with the situation concerning the arrival at school. I couldn't get into a washroom to hide before the school opened and yet, I had to be at the school for the beginning of the school day. So here I was in the yard with all these kids running around. I sat down in a corner of the school yard next to the basement stairwell that could provide me with means of escape if things got rough, but most of the kids arrived about five minutes before eight, so only when the bell rang, did I become the object of ridicule. Whether it was because the kids were still half asleep or had passed the stage of the initial shock, the intensity of ridicule was considerably milder than the day before. I just looked straight ahead as our queue marched forward into the building, but I definitely felt all eyes upon me and there were some teasing remarks from boys in the line next to ours.

The first hour of the day was all Greek to me. I didn't even know what the subject was. It could have been history or perhaps religion. But I passed the time in the back row drawing pictures of a new tower for the 'Black Band' club house. It would be three feet taller than the old one we had, and have a top platform large enough to hold both Harold and me. We would probably need extra bracing, but that was no problem. I also figured it would be a good idea to have some method of communication from the tower to the gang members in the club house. Maybe a rope could do the job. If there was danger, the lookout guy on the tower platform would pull the rope and those inside the clubhouse would know that something was up.

Before I knew it, it was recess and obediently, I filed out of the classroom with the rest of the kids. Heading for my hiding place in the washroom, I discovered, much to my dismay, a broom and a pail blocking the entrance. A couple of workmen were doing some repair work in there. I wouldn't say panic set in, but I frantically thought of alternatives. Finding none, I ended up in the school yard where I kept myself close to a wall. For the first few minutes all was calm. Then two boys about my age appeared and tauntingly made faces at me. One of them became more aggressive and gave me a shove. The other one held his finger to his head and shouted in English,

"Dumb American!"

That immediately brought other curious kids around, who now got a closer look at this strange creature in their midst. I had black hair and brown eyes. Most of them had golden hair and blue eyes. Furthermore I wore long legged pants of the same material as American overalls. They wore baggy pants called plus fours or knickerbockers and they wore wooden shoes. I wouldn't be found dead in that attire. And then, of course, I didn't speak their language, which in their opinion, probably made me a real freak. With my back against the wall, I felt cornered. The kid, who gave me a shove, seeing he now had an audience, did it again, almost knocking me over.

As a Hornibrook gang member, I was not going to submit to the role of being a sissy or chicken, so I lashed out at him and a moment later we were both on the ground engaged in 'mortal combat.' The kids cheered him on and the whole scene became the main attraction in the school yard. He really gave me a rough time, but for a long time afterwards, I liked to think he was saved by the bell - and by the awful arithmetic teacher, who came running up at that moment to break up the fight. A moment later we were all in the queues. I had a torn shirt sleeve, scratches on my arms and dishevelled hair, but otherwise felt okay. As before, there was a lot of jeering and laughter directed my way, but at least I clearly demonstrated that I was no sissy.

Back in the classroom, I felt restless and frustrated. It didn't help that the awful arithmetic teacher was there. We all had to stand at attention at our desks until told to sit down. As soon as the teacher saw me, he came to the back, grabbed me by the collar and brought me to the front. As I stood there, facing the class, he slammed his stick on his desk to create the proper atmosphere for a lecture on discipline. At least, that's what I think it was. He addressed the class, shouting most of the time and emphasizing certain words with his stick slamming the desk. Then he wrote something on a piece of paper, folded it, sealed it in an envelope, gave it to me and told me to go and see the principal. Going down the stairs and out into the school yard, I thought - this whole place is awful. If I had my slingshot now, I would plaster every window in this darn school. Everybody was trying to make problems and trouble. There was no happiness anywhere.

The principal read the message, as I stood before him in the school office. I suddenly got the feeling that it could be about me. Sure enough, it turned out to be just that, because he then said in English,

"Please keep in mind that we expect good behavior at all times here at our school. We cannot have fights in the school yard. I'll let it go this time, but if it happens again, you will have to be disciplined and your parents notified. I am sure you understand that."

"Yes Sir, but I didn't start it all."

"That's beside the point. From what your teacher says, you were involved. That will be all. Return to your classroom."

What a crazy world! They couldn't even see straight. Most likely, the arithmetic teacher twisted everything around to make me look like a real troublemaker. My only comfort was that someday he would kick the bucket. None of us last forever.

Dear Harold,   *April 22, 1934*
  I guess yer wonderin why I'm sending ya another letter so quickly, when I jus finished writing the last one. Well, it's cause I want to warn ya about all the trouble yer gonna git into when yer thirteen which is jus about now. Don't let them ship ya out like they did me. Make sure yer Dad keeps his barbershop going in Junction and not git fancy ideas bout maybe starting up a shop in a foreign

country. If I were ya I would stay in the clubhouse as much as possible.

I hope ya guys have started the collecshun to git me out of here. I was thinking that maybe yer mom could talk to the preacher of our church if theres a new one and ask him if they could take up a collecshun in church fer me. They have these collecshuns every Sunday after the prayer about all the people in trouble. I am sure when the congregashun hears that it is the former preacher's son who is in trouble they'll really shell out the money. Tell yer mom to tell the preacher that I'll pay em back later with beanfield earnings so its not like they ain't gonna git it back. Usually when they pass the plate around and have collecshuns in church the congregashun never git a cent back, so in my case its a good deal.

Things are gittin worser and worser here all the time. I can tell ya, if I warn't a preachers son I'd wring that awful rithmatik teachers neck until he choked. I know he hates me cause when we gotta do rithmatik problems, he walks down the aisle with his stick behind his back stopping at kids desks to see if they're doing the problems right. When he comes to my desk I can feel him hanging over me like a big dark cloud. His eyes always seem to have an angry glow in them and seem to sort of drill right into me. It makes me shudder jus to look at him. Well, when he stops at my desk I don't dare look up or move cause I can't stand the sight of his long needle-point nose and I'm afraid he might grab me and do something awful. He's always yelling and hollering. It's enough to wake up the dead. I know he hates rithmatik as much as we do. We all hate it. Cursed is the man who invented it in the first place giving birth to the threatening beam thats aimed directly at my worry department.

A few days ago I was moved to a different classroom but still with small kids and fer a moment I thought the awful rithmatik teacher would finally leave me alone and disappear, but he's still around. Tomorrow we gotta have another torture seshun with him. I would give anything to have him shipped in a box to Junction where we could tar and feather him and chase him out of town. This guy's name is Mikkelsen - and he's mad!

Well, in this different classroom I sit next to a gal. She warn't bad looking when they moved me there and she is still okay to look at and the boys in the class don't tease me about sitting next to a gal cause they all got to do it to prevent wispering. I don't have to do any work in the classroom, except for that rithmatik stuff, so I jus sit there and theres not much to do. I'm supposed to pay attenshun but I don't, cause I don't know what they're talking about so I jus pretend I'm intrested. Most of the teachers don't bother me and since I sit near the back of the room, I kin mind my own bizness and nobody notices nothing. So today I spent my time drawing pictures when the teachers wern't lookin. It didn't take long before the gal sitting next to me noticed what I was doing and she wispered to me that she would give me a piece of chewing gum or licorish (it depended on which I wanted) fer every picture I drew fer her. I didn't understand what she was saying in Danish but figured it out to be something like that. She had lots of that stuff. It was against the law to wisper in the classroom but we did it anyways. Well, that was a bargin so I drawed a picture of a couple of warships and got two pieces of licorish (one fer each warship) and then while I ate them I drawed an airplane and got a piece of chewing gum and while I chewed that I drawed a tank with lots of smoke coming out of the gun. She liked that and gave me two more pieces of licorish. Then I drawed an American freight train with 100 boxcars. That was worth three pieces of chewing gum.

Finally she said she reckoned she had enough, so I stopped drawing and took an American book out of my school bag called 'Oliver Twist' which I had sort of smuggled into school and I read some of that fer awhile jus to have something to do. But then I got tired of that so I started yawning. Every time a kid yawns in the classroom the teacher say 'Good morning' in Danish so as to stop the yawning. But I find everything so boring that I jus git plain doggone tired and worn out doing nothing. How much can I guy take?

All this boredom almost makes me fall asleep and I don't know what the teacher is jabbering about so I jus git more tired and have to yawn and yawn all the time, so every time I have to yawn, I pull out my blowrag and pretend to blow my nose and then yawn under the blowrag. Since I yawn about 30 times an hour, I use a blowrag more than anyone else in the classroom. The gal next to me doesn't yawn at all, but thats cause she knows whats going on.

There's still trouble in the school yard. Nobody wants to play with me and I certainly don't wanna play with them. And they're always teasing and making fun of me. Everybody knows I'm dumb. Someday I'll git even with them. I usually stand alone in a corner of the schoolyard during recess cause then I can't be attacked from behind. Yesterday I really knocked the daylights out of a kid who thought he could push me around. The fights ain't noticed by the teachers no more cause so many things are going on in the schoolyard all the time so thats good, but I always have a lot of bruises. I don't like all this but its the way things are. The only kid in the whole school who I have talked to so far is that gal sitting next to me in the classroom. I don't think she knows I'm dumb and I'm not gonna tell her. I'll draw her some more warships and then she'll never know.

I've ben thinking, Harold. It's about our gang and the night when Merle Burton and Jimmy Hansen came to git the hinges off the door of our club house. Ya jus can't seem to trust no one no more - not even members of our gang. I've ben thinkin what a nut I was fer storming out of the back door of our house to scare them away. Jus think, Harold, instead of coming out of the back door which was in plain sight, I could have run out of the front door where the rockerys were and out through the gate, across the lane and the lot where the house fire was and down to the corner on sixth near Freddie Millers house, cause it was there on the lawn where Burton laid down his bike. All I had to do was to grab the bike, take it back the way I came, hide it under our grapevines and then, last of all, charge forward and punture Burton and Jimmy with a volley of rocks and make them scatter. Then we could secretly paint his bike a diffrent color and sell it fer

50 dollars, when Burton and his family had given up hunting fer it and the thing had blowed over a little. Then we would be millionares! Would we be to blame if they found that it was the missing bike? No, of course not. The buyer would. Why in the nashun did he buy it if he didn't want to git himself into trouble? Well then they would can that gent in a jail fer a few months. Burton and his family would git the bike back and when the gent was out of jail he wouldn't be able to give us any trouble by telling the cops that we sold it to him, cause American police never bother to have a trial twice jus over an ol' wreck of a bicycle. Well after that everything would be fergotten and we would be rich and it wouldn't be stealing cause they got the bike back anyways. But I guessed I goofed a little and didn't use my brain much. Ya have a perfect right to curse me anytime ya want fer not having more sence that night. Jus think, Harold, ya might be having 50 dollars solid cash right at this very blasted moment - enough fer ya to buy a whole camping outfit and pay fer my trip back to Junction - if I had only used my brain a little more, but now the chance has gone ferever. Why in the world, did God create me if He knew I was gonna be such a fool? Why didn't He, at least help out that night, by putting the thought into my mind to take the bike? Why did He let those dern high-school kids tip over the first club house we had? Why in the tar nashun did He take me away from the only and best boy friend I got and dump me into this land of multiplying troubles and terrors?

Well, I guess ya guys must have got the tower finished by now. I'm sure a 100 foot tower is a lot better than the ol dinky 43 foot tower. Can ya see over the church roof? I really think we should make sure the tower has enough braces. When I get back, we can check it out together cause the higher we go up the more braces we need. I know that fer sure cause I saw a picture of a tower they got in Paris and they got braces all the way to the top. That one is made of steel. Hows the collecshun coming? I hain't seen a single envelope with money.

Yours till I rot. Visti.

CHAPTER THIRTEEN

Suddenly it was spring. It seemed to come overnight. It was May and the school was getting ready for the annual sports day. The school did not have a track or any outside facilities for sport activities and there was no training for any events. However, there was a certain degree of excitement and expectation as the day approached.

The school season was by no means over. It would continue right to the end of June, but at least for one day only, we would not have to sit in classrooms. It was hard getting used to the idea of going to school six days a week and with lots of homework on Sundays. It was, of course, easier for me than for others, because I was not expected to submit any homework for checking. The more I thought about it, the better I liked the idea. If I didn't learn Danish, I wouldn't be obliged to be an active pupil, burdened with rules, regulations and the tons of homework. As it was, I was so far behind in everything, that even with a crash program I could never catch up. I would always be called the 'dumb American,' but as soon as I got back to Junction City, I would be regarded as normal again. I decided to take one day at a time and not get too eager or let on that I knew more than they thought I knew.

May 15th was the big day. We all met at a small, local train station in the morning for a trip, which would take us to a large national park at the head of the fjord - a distance of about twenty kilometers. There must have been five hundred kids on the train, but only from our school. I stood in the corridor leaning out of a window. Nobody found any enjoyment in teasing me anymore, but I was still ignored by boys and girls of my age. However, I did have one friend. It was the little girl who sat next to me in the classroom. I found out her name was Lisbeth and that she was nine years old. She stood there at my side, also looking out of the train window.

It was a beautiful morning. The sun was shining and the beech trees were green. The little engine puffed its way along the side of the fjord pulling eight little railway cars with all windows open and packed with kids. The lilac bushes along the railway embankment were in full bloom and the water beyond in the fjord sparkled with whitecaps. It was almost enough to make me forget that I was a displaced person.

Although there were a number of teachers on board, there was no sign of the awful arithmetic teacher. He was probably at home, suffocating in cigarette smoke, devising new, insolvable arithmetic problems for his class - problems that would justify increased discipline, more punishment and greater use of his stick. He thrived on calamity.

Lisbeth offered me a stick of chewing gum. The train moved along at a slow pace due to the gradual climb in elevation. Farms passed by, telephone poles passed by, cows, pigs, sheep and chickens passed by - everything cradled in smoke from our struggling engine, which sounded like it was out of breath. The two of us, chewing gum, leaned out of the window with outstretched arms to feel the warm breeze and motion. It was the first time, since I left Junction City that I felt relaxed and relatively happy.

The park was situated high above the fjord overlooking the water and to an island beyond. We were at a place called Skamlingsbanken. The pupils spread out over a large grassy area and we ate the lunch we had brought with us. Everyone got a free bottle of lemon pop which tasted very good. Speeches were held by the school principal and two other teachers - about what, I do not know. The Danish flag was run up a flagpole while everyone stood at attention and sang the national anthem. It certainly didn't sound like the Star Spangled Banner, but it was okay. Following that, various classes were formed into groups for sport competition. It quickly became apparent to me that this was simply an internal matter, with classes A, B and C competing against each other in each grade. There were no other schools present.

Since I was three years older than all the others in my class, I was excused from the events. The exhilaration I experienced earlier in the day evaporated, as I was more or less obliged to sit on the grass off to one side, to watch the activities as a spectator. But there were many others who were not actively participating, so I was not alone. Various markings were set up for running and jumping events. For a while there was a lot of commotion as teachers and students alike, attempted to organize something that resembled an official track meet.

The events finally got under way, first with the younger classes, boys and girls separately. There was the high jump, the 100 meter dash, relay and obstacle races and even such a non-Olympic event as sack races! This was definitely not the big league. A baseball game at the diamond at Laurel and 12th in Junction City had more credibility. But it was entertainment and it was a sunny day.

The view over the fjord from our location was magnificent. Being right at the entrance to the fjord, I imagined that in the days of the Vikings this must have been an important observation post. There was a tall stone monument in the park. Maybe that had something to do with the Vikings. A vessel with sails entered the fjord and I found this momentarily, of greater interest than watching the games. I imagined myself as the spotter and the boat as the intruder - in the days of the Vikings. I wondered how the spotter could signal ahead to the town at the other end of the fjord. Smoke signals like the Indians used would be out of the question on account of the wind. Signals with mirrors probably wouldn't work, because the mirror was yet to be invented and often it was not sunny. It probably all had to be done on a horse like Paul Revere. I spent the next half hour analyzing the situation. Yes, a horse would be the only way to beat the boat.

One of the teachers tapped me on the shoulder and asked in English,

"Would you like to take part in the games?"

"I dunno," I replied, "I'm too big for my class."

"Yes, that is true, but I was thinking you could compete with the boys of your own age."

"I don't know any of them. They don't like me."

"That's nonsense. This is a good opportunity to get to know them."

"Well, what would I take part in?"

"Anything you want. Well, let's see, much of it is already over, but there's the 100 meter race coming up. That would be good for you to try."

"Well, what am I to do? Do I just walk over there without permission?"

"You have my permission. Here, I'll take you over and tell the boys that you will be participating in the race together with them."

I felt most uncomfortable about it all. I felt much better when I was lying in the grass looking at the sailboat. Reluctantly, I followed him around the edge of the track over to where the older boys and girls were gathered. As he approached them, he raised his voice and said something in Danish and the kids looked at me. Most of them were surprised, but accepted my presence. However, a couple of the boys I recently had been in scraps with in the schoolyard, snickered and visibly indicated their disapproval. To them, this intrusion into their territory was revolting. I stood by myself, a little off to one side and waited.

The girls were lining up to run first. I was surprised that no one wore sport or gym clothes for the events. The dresswear and atmosphere was that of a school picnic, rather than that of a sports day. Twelve girls, at the sound of the starting pistol, ran like fluttering butterflies down the grass track to the ribbon a hundred meters away, midst shouts and squeals of encouragement from all the other girls. There was no doubt, that their skirts hampered them, making it impossible to break any world records. A blue ribbon was given to the winner and there was lots of clapping.

It was now the boys turn - four from each of the classes A, B and C - the grade I should have been in, if I was 'normal.' The teacher beckoned me to join them for this race and I walked over and took a place at the left end of the starting line, keeping my distance from the rest of them. There was a great deal of shouting and cheering from all the other kids. I wondered why they were not in the race, but found out later that they were in previous races and had been eliminated from the finals. All this had gone on while I was watching the sail-boat and solving the problems of the Vikings.

The school principal put a cap in the starting pistol and motioned for all runners to get ready. A great silence fell over the crowd as though the volume control on a radio had been turned off. We all crouched like coiled springs ready to pop open. The principal, standing at the side raised his pistol toward the sky, said something that sounded like it could be 'On your mark,' followed by a single word that probably meant 'Get set' - and then a moment of suspense with the whole world waiting.

A second passed. And another and another. Some of the runners dashed forward, but the shot was not heard. Something was wrong. The noise level of the crowd went up again as the principal fiddled with the pistol, trying to figure out why it didn't fire. Everyone stood around waiting.

After a ten minute delay with teachers in a huddle, a shot was heard and we knew that we were ready once more. Again the principal pointed the pistol towards the sky and we crouched in position. This time it worked. At the sound of the shot I bolted forward and ran with the same intensity and speed as I used to do in Junction when we got into trouble. It was all over in a flash. I actually got to the ribbon first! I could hardly believe it.

For the very first time in this foreign country, I had achieved something. There was a lot of clapping and cheering from the crowd and disbelief among the other runners. It was a wonderful feeling to suddenly find myself the center of positive, instead of negative, attention.

We all trotted back to the starting line where I received a blue ribbon from the principal. He shook my hand and I bowed as one is supposed to do. I went back to my class and all the kids cheered, obviously impressed that one of their class could beat the bigger kids. I was their hero. Lisbeth came running up, very happy and excited and said a lot of stuff to me in Danish. I could feel she was proud of me and for the first time I wished I could understand the language.

I might just have to do something to get out of the rut I seemed to be in. Maybe if I stopped reading 'Oliver Twist' during class hours, it might help - and no more drawings of warships in exchange for chewing gum and licorish. However, this proposed change of attitude was by no means an indication that I was about to resign myself to my fate. I was just a visitor to this country and still determined to get back to Oregon as soon as possible.

I felt real good on the train as we all returned to Kolding. It was a feeling of confidence and I hoped that the bothersome kids at school now would treat me with more respect.

At home, Daddy, Mom and the kids were delighted that I won a race and we all looked at the ribbon that had *Nr. 1* printed in gold plus the date. Not much, but nevertheless, the winner's ribbon and mine. For Daddy and Mom, this event was a relief, because for a long time they could feel that I was downhearted and unhappy. They knew I needed something to cheer me up. Winning a race wouldn't resolve any of the problems regarding education and adjustment, but just for a brief moment it provided stimulation. It was a good day.

Dear Harold   *May 20, 1934*

I guess yer wondering how yer gitting another letter so quickly when yer still reading the last one. Well, its cause I got good news. Nope, it warn't in the noospaper, but alot of kids know about it and now they gotta look at me with respect. I won the 100 yard dash on the school sports day. I beat everyone else and got an award ribbon that says No 1. So I've decided that I'm gonna train fer the olympics. I won't be able to git into the next one which is gonna be in Berlin cause I'll only be 16, but the one after that will be jus right. I hope that one will be in Oregon. The world record fer the 100 yard dash is 10.3 seconds and I am sure I'm very close to that. I'm trying to figure out how in the dickens they measure that. I've been looking all over the place to see how they do it and the whole dingozzled works leaves me flabbergasted.

I got loads of plans of what I'm gonna do in the future if I kin jus git rid of the burden of school that rests on my shoulders and is jus about crushing me as flat as a pancake. I'm gonna make a racebug only one foot high with ball bearing wheels that kin wizz under furniture and things and then in the winter jus take the wheels off and use it as a toboggan. I'm gonna call it 'The Wild Western Rattletrap' The only problem is I aint got no money right now cause I'm saving it all fer my return to Junction, but its a good invenshun.

Do ya remember, Harold, the time in Junction when a bakery somewhere invented a loaf of bread where half was white and half was brown and then they had a competishun to find a name fer the bread and some brainy nut down in Eugene came up with the name 'half an half' and won a big prize. Well, I aint seen that bread here. So I've ben a-thinking maybe I should go to a bakery here and sell the idea to them and then the money they give me will pay fer making the rattletrap. I don't think that a bakery way out in Oregon is gonna find out that a foreign bakery in another country is stealing their invenshun, cause first of all its gonna have a diffrent name in danish and a guy's gotta be here along time to understand what these foreigners are saying. Danish aint easy. Speshully here in Jutland where they talk like they got something stuck in their throat. And if they decide to come over in investigate ya kin always warn me and I kin tell the baker to git rid of the stuff until the storm blows over. Well, this an awful short letter but I jus thought ya should know bout my plans.

Yours till I rot. Visti

June, the last month of school, came very quickly. I felt a little more comfortable in the classroom. Everybody got tired of giving me a hard time. I still found it extremely difficult to understand any of the subjects except for arithmetic, gymnastics, drawing and English. The English class was a breeze. Everything was conducted in English from the moment the teacher walked in the classroom until she left an hour later. There was nothing for me to think about, nothing to worry about and nothing to do. It was total relaxation.

The teacher, Mrs. Petersen, a middle aged lady, who liked to convey the impression that she was more English than Danish, decided one day that I might serve a useful purpose in the classroom. Addressing me, she said,

"Visti, I wonder if I could ask you to come up here to the front and read a paragraph or two from this book for the class?"

"Yes, Mrs. Petersen," I replied, feeling suddenly quite important.

I walked up to the front and she gave me the book, pointing to where I was supposed to start. Clearing my throat, I read,

Where am I going? I don't know.
Down by the stream where the king-cups grow.
Up on the hill where the pine-trees blow.
Anywhere, anywhere. I don't know.

Actually I knew very well where I was going. It was back to Junction City.

"Thank you, Visti. Just pause right there before we go on to the next verse"
The teacher faced the class and asked,

"Now, can any of you tell me what is wrong with this poem?"

There was dead silence. Nobody knew. Maybe they didn't even understand what she was saying in English. Standing there, holding the book open, I couldn't figure out what was wrong. I didn't know what a king-cup was, but other than that it sounded okay.

"Do any of you know?"

She looked about the room in search of just a spark of intelligence. There was no response.

"Well, I must tell you that the word *don't* is not proper English. It should be *do not*. Is that understood?"

"Yes, Mrs. Petersen." Twenty-six voices filled the classroom in unison. Mrs. Petersen was indeed an authority. She turned to me.

"Visti, you may continue."

Where am I going? The clouds sail by,
Little ones, baby ones, over the sky.
Where am I going? The shadows pass,
Little ones, baby ones, over the grass.

I stopped momentarily, looking at Mrs. Petersen to see if she wanted to say something about this baby stuff, but she nodded for me to continue.

If you were a cloud, and sailed up there,
You'd sail on water as blue as air,
And you'd see me here in the fields and say:
"Doesn't the sky look green today?"

"Thank you, Visti. We will pause here for a moment."
Again, addressing the class, she came up with a new problem,
"Is there anything wrong in these two verses?"
All the kids looked at her, waiting for her to figure it out. Standing at her side, I almost felt like I also was an authority of the English language, but glancing at the verses a second time I couldn't find anything. Since there was no response, she decided to reveal the flaw, but not without a lengthy pause to build up tension and anticipation. There was total silence in the classroom and one could almost feel the humming of two dozen brains hard at work. Suddenly she made the revealing announcement.

"There is no such word as *you'd*." She looked over the class and singled out a girl. "Inge, do you know what *you'd* means?"
Inge immediately stood up and said,
"No, Mrs. Petersen."
"And how about you, Jens," she asked, pointing to a boy. "Do you know what *you'd* means?"
Jens jumped to attention.
"No, Mrs. Petersen."
It seemed to me as long as the kids agreed with her all the time, they had no problem. I doubted whether they understood very much of what she was saying. They just looked at her, waiting to be enlightened. After a rather lengthy pause where it was hoped that some bright kid in the room would resolve the issue, Mrs. Petersen gave up and spilled the beans.
"*You'd* should be *you would*!"
Great relief everywhere. We could all relax now. It was quite evident that Mrs. Petersen was able to keep a tight rein on the English language to prevent misuse and deterioration. The kids in the classroom looked at her in awe and she looked upon them as a necessary audience for her uncanny revelations. English was her passion. I was sure that if it had been possible for her to change her name to Smith, it would have been done straight away.
"Visti, thank you. You may now go back to your seat."
The feeling I had of also being an authority of the English language, evaporated somewhat as I walked down the aisle, and was gone completely a moment later when, addressing the class, Mrs. Petersen said,
"Children, as you all know, Visti is American and does not speak proper English. His pronunciation is not correct. In this classroom we learn to speak the right way. Is that understood?"
"Yes, Mrs. Petersen," they all shouted in unison.
Had I had a slingshot at that moment, Mrs. Petersen would have been in serious trouble.

CHAPTER FOURTEEN

Xenia started to reveal unusual musical talent and our big upright piano from Boston was in use many hours a day. She could sight-read any music and play it with ease. At other times she had the asthma attacks, which were always traumatic and of concern to Mom. Xenia was often compelled to take a rest during the daytime and always after an attack, which could happen any time of the day or night. We had no feather pillows or flowers in the house and doctor visits were frequent. The cabinet in the bathroom was full of prescription medicine bottles and tablets that didn't work.

One solid hour of piano scales followed by three hours of sonatas was quite normal for Xenia. This background music became a way of life for all of us, but it was the scales that almost drove us mad. First the C scale major, left and right hand together - four octaves up and four octaves down - about ten times. Then the same thing in minor. Next would be the C sharp major scale - four octaves up and four octaves down - ten times. Then the same in minor. Next would be D major and so on and so on - until we could hardly stand it anymore. It was a form of musical torture.

Sometimes the scales or sonatas would stop in the middle of it all and Xenia would cross the floor, open the door and shout,

"I can't practise with all this noise going on!"

Then she would slam the door shut so the whole house vibrated and return to the piano, playing even more vigorously than before. We were cautioned against starting an argument with Xenia about too much music or whatever, in case it might cause an asthma attack.

It was understandable that Daddy was unable to prepare any sermons under these conditions, even with the study door closed. So he moved his work to the church office where there was peace and quiet. One would think that stirring music could be inspiring for the preparation of sermons about hope and salvation, but it didn't work in this case, even though it was classical music.

Like the others, I was always at home after school. I spent most of my free time drawing pictures. I could make all kind of things happen in the form of cartoon series. There was no limit to my imagination. Also, being so much alone without friends, I also started reading books. Daddy had a large library of English and American books in the study that he had collected over the years, which now for the first time, I was beginning to discover.

The constant background piano playing didn't really bother me. Actually I was able to play piano a little bit myself, having taken piano lessons at the age of nine and ten, but when we arrived in Junction City there was no time for music. The activities of the Hornibrook Gang was a full time job. I remember clearly how my fingers used to hurt after each music lesson - not from playing, but from being whacked with a bamboo cane by the music teacher. Every time I looked at my fingers instead of the sheet music there would be another whack across my fingers. I think the music teacher enjoyed this more than the music itself.

I liked to assume that the reason my music lessons stopped was due to our gang activities, but as my mother later told me it was due to economics. Daddy could simply not afford to pay for lessons in Junction City. In Xenia's case it was different. Her music teacher gave music lessons free of charge, because it was felt that Xenia had unusual potential. And with all the musical racket going on, we were now experiencing the consequences of that potential.

While Daddy was out trying to save the world, Mom had all she could handle - such as buying food, preparing meals, cleaning house, washing and ironing clothes, sewing, taking care of colds and sickness, helping us with our homework and our problems. Her daily life was the same as in Junction City - seven days a week. It made no difference what country she was in. When Daddy came home from the church around supper time, the table was set and all was peaceful. After supper only quiet activities were allowed, because Daddy had to spend the evenings in the study preparing for next days schedule, which could be anything from weddings to funerals. In the case of funerals, a bit of research was required to find out if there was something good the minister could say about the deceased. It was comforting for the relatives to have a sympathetic and understanding pastor who appeared to know the deceased well. In the case of weddings, no research was required since no one required comfort. At least not from the minister.

Funerals were both time consuming and demanding. Both the minister and the attending family or friends of the deceased had to be in good physical condition. Following the funeral service at the church, the flower-decorated coffin was placed in an open funeral carriage, a bizarre looking, black wagon with four wooden sculptured columns and a flat roof, pulled by two black horses draped in black cloth with holes for their eyes.

Perched on top of the wagon roof was the driver, dressed in black, wearing a top hat and holding a whip and the reins. It was all designed to look as grim and morbid as possible - something out of Dante's Inferno. I had difficulty in understanding why images had to be made so intensely unpleasant and ghastly for someone who was about to enter paradise - an event, all churchgoers continuously prayed would also happen to them. Instead of rejoicing in celebration, the whole scene was one of defeat and sorrow.

The minister, dressed in his black church gown with the white collar and black top hat, led the procession from the church to the cemetery. He was followed by the horses and carriage and the church janitor who, dressed in his Sunday best, walked behind the carriage with a small shovel and pail in case it was needed. Then came the bereaved, all dressed in black, followed by relatives and friends - wearing black armbands, the symbol of sorrow and sympathy.

With the church bells ringing to create the appropriate atmosphere and with the rain pouring down, (it always rained when there was a funeral), the procession slowly moved through city streets under black umbrellas to the cemetery on the far side of town. Along the way, people and traffic stopped as the black carriage with the coffin passed by. It was traditional to do so and also for men to remove their hats, and in respect, stand motionless on the sidewalk and face the passing procession.

Following the burial ceremony at the grave, everyone, cold and wet, would walk all the way back to town to attend a reception at a local tavern or hotel where everybody would console everybody over a cup of coffee in the hope of quick recovery. It was usually a very sad occasion and nobody jumped up and down in glee that the deceased was now happy in heaven enjoying an everlasting life. These funerals lasted all afternoon and it was no wonder that Daddy used to come home like a tired, wet dog, completely exhausted.

Out in the country surrounding the towns, everything was more practical. The graveyard was next to the church and the tavern was next to the graveyard. Since the tavern could not financially survive on the prospect of only an occasional funeral reception, they stayed open all the time to serve the general public, and also the church congregation if they were so inclined. It was all very conveniently planned, except for the noise problem in the summertime when all windows were open. The singing of church hymns could be heard in the tavern and the drinking songs in the tavern could be heard in the church.

School exams suddenly loomed up. Everyone was busy trying to catch up on what they neglected to do during the year. I floundered along helplessly, not knowing what would happen. All these subjects - what did I know? Most of them I couldn't grasp at all. I was never encouraged or guided along by any teachers, and there was no such thing as a school counselor. They were not needed, as everyone was obedient, and the school strap in the principal's office took care of any problems that might arise.

One thing was clear. I would have to take the exams. It was decision time. As a registered pupil, I could not get to the next grade without oral and written examinations. My only salvation was a Danish-English dictionary that was given to me by the school and which I was permitted to use at the exams. Nevertheless, a nightmare stared me right in the face.

I started to size up the situation. German and French would be losers. That was for sure, but English would be a winner. Arithmetic and geometry would probably be about average, but mathematics would be a total disaster. There was no exam in religion which, of course, was too bad, since I knew a lot of stuff the teacher didn't know. Natural science, chemistry and physics were new subjects and pretty basic, but I had only been a spectator in the classes and there was the constant language problem to cope with. I would certainly fail in these.

History was going to be another disaster. Much time had been spent on memorizing the names and birthdates of the Vikings and all the battles they fought and very little about all the action in the United States. Not a single word about Custer's Last Stand or Jesse James. Geography would be okay if I could figure out what the questions were. Drawing would be a winner. That was the one subject I really liked at school and I could do anything the teacher could do, although it wasn't noticed or appreciated.

There seemed to be so little time to prepare for this day of reckoning. Since it all was so confusing, I hardly knew what to concentrate on. It was almost impossible for me to figure out the meaning of words on a page, let alone the topic. Whereas others only had one problem to solve at a time, I had two - first solving the meaning of the question and then what the question asked me to solve. I guess the school figured the only way I was going to learn anything, was for total absorption into the school program and activities. It was total, all right. I was practically drowning.

The last two weeks of school were like a bad dream. The written exams took place in the gymnasium hall where rows and rows of desks and chairs were set up for the pupils. The distance between each row of desks was about six feet - enough to completely prevent any form of communication with others. Grim looking teachers were standing at strategic locations in the gym to watch for cheaters. The whole place was ready for a test of nerves. We all filed in at the stroke of eight, tired and exhausted from studying all night.

As we sat at the desks waiting for torture to begin, papers and pencils were handed out at each desk by teachers, who with great authority, relished in this manufactured environment of tension and fear. A great silence descended on the hall as the test papers were being distributed. This was it!

I stared at the page. The subject was German. It seemed to start off with a statement followed by a couple of more lines. Then below that was a blank line where the answer would go - probably in German. I opened my dictionary to start translating the Danish words to English. After a bit of frustration and searching around, I got the introduction to read,

Please write the following sentences in German:

Then came the subject which in Danish, *Jeg er meget syg.*

I figured this out to be 'I am much sick.' They certainly weren't kidding. I felt very much sick! Well, then I had to get this into German. I knew the word for sickness was 'crank,' because when the teacher explained that word to us the first time, I noticed that she looked sick and cranky herself. In an attempt to remember words, I found it easier if a word registered as something visual in my mind. So I figured it out and wrote,

Ich bin ser crank.

Not bad, I thought. I'll get through this stuff somehow. There were six sentences to be translated to German and unfortunately six sentences from German to Danish. Somehow I got bogged down with the translation in the next two sentences and didn't know the German words, so I gave up completely.

This struggle repeated itself for other subjects as the week wore on. I was spending too much time trying to figure out what the Danish meant without getting around to the questions.

But then the day came for the English tests, and that day I was morning fresh, ready to tackle anything before me. I went through the procedure of

translating the Danish to English and wrote the first sentence as follows:
The family went on vacashun.
The next one was even easier. I wrote,
The tayler opened his store for bizness.
Everything went smoothly until I got to the sentences where it was from English to Danish. It was curtains. I gave up.

I found it difficult to sleep at night with all this pressure and knowing that I was losing ground. And when I did sleep, I seemed to have bad dreams about having to explain to the principal why I didn't learn anything. Daddy and Mom sympathized with me, but admitted there was not much they could do until it was all over. They tried to help me each evening with homework but it only amounted to comfort.

The oral examinations were even worse than the written exams. I was excused from most of them when it was discovered how little Danish I knew or could understand. I found it very humiliating and embarrassing to be called into a room for the oral examination only to return to the school corridor less than a minute later. The other kids noticed this and it simply confirmed their opinion of me - not only that I was dumb, but maybe also a little retarded. Only Lisbeth believed in me. She often defended me when others said unpleasant things about me - saying that I was okay.

Eventually, the nightmare was over and the day arrived for the verdict - the last day of school. It was the end of June. We were all at our desks in our classrooms and one by one, we were called to the front to receive our report cards. Practically all the kids, opening their report cards on the way back to their desks, looked very happy. For them it was a good day.

My name was called and I went to the front. The teacher handed me my report card and I returned to my desk and sat down before opening it. I could see at a glance that there was trouble. The marks were terrible! There was something written at the bottom of the page.

I couldn't read it so I took out my dictionary to check it out, but Lisbeth, sitting next to me, saw what it said, burst into tears and ran out of the classroom. The commotion created a slight disturbance in the proceedings, but the teacher then resumed the issuing of cards. It took me a little while to figure out what the word *dumpe* was. It sure sounded like 'dumb.' It couldn't be 'dumplings.' I moved my finger down the page under the D's. Here it was: *Dumpe* - fall, defeat, drop down, fail.

This was it. I had failed! I just sat there in the back row in silence. Nobody knew about this yet. Only Lisbeth. I would have to keep it a secret. Moments later we were all out in the school corridor. Kids were running all over the place, yelling and shouting - their wooden shoes making the whole floor vibrate. Freedom was here at last. I walked by myself down the stairs, out through the doors, across the school yard towards the portal - feeling more alone and isolated than ever before.

In the portal I stopped and decided to take another look at my report card.

Let's see, a B in drawing. Not bad, but I should have received an A. Here was a C for geography. I would go along with that. What's this? C in English! Surely they goofed here. That's absolutely impossible when it's my language. That must have been Mrs. Petersen. What reason was there for revenge? I didn't like her, but I never bothered her. Well, one thing was for sure. No one would ever get to know that I flunked in my own language. That would be a secret I would carry to the grave.

I put the report card back in my pocket. It began to dawn upon me that, having failed, I would have to take the same grade all over again the next school season - which was only six weeks away. This was tough going. It would be another year of ridicule. I would definitely have to get back to Junction City before that. Maybe Daddy and Mom would help me. That was the only solution.

Just as I started walking out of the portal, Lisbeth came running up to me. I could feel she was still disturbed by it all - just like myself.

"I am so sorry," she said in English, looking at me as if I had been wounded in a battle.

"I'm sorry, too," I replied.

We didn't really know what else to say. We stood there for a few moments and then we parted. I liked her very much.

CHAPTER FIFTEEN

Dear Harold,   *August 3, 1934*

Today is my birthday and I am fourteen years old. I am very, very, very, extremely, awful, powerful glad to get over the terrors of my thirteenth year. Its been a nightmare and I sure do hope you get through yer thirteenth year without terror. I sure do pity you. And now I'm in my fourteenth year and there ain't a single drop of hope fer me cause I gotta go to school real soon. I'll let you in on an awful, dismal, horrible secret if you promise not to tell a single soul - cross yer heart and hope to die, if it leaks out. Nobody knows about it here except my family and the little gal named Lisbeth who gives me chewing gum once in while. I reckon you kin hardly wait to hear what the awful secret is.

Well, here goes.------------ I FLUNKED!

This is not due to lack of intelligense but only cause I don't understand the foreign language they got here. I can't understand why people want to talk foreign languages when American is the best and so easy to understand. I gotta go in the same grade again when school starts and fer a whole year. It ain't fair cause I know fer sure they were all ganging up on me. All the teachers and all the kids except that little gal Lisbeth. Anyways, like I told ya when they had the annual races, I won that 100 yard dash. I beat the first kid at about ten feet. So that will always be remembered but it won't help me now cause school starts in twelve days! Think of it, Harold - in only twelve days. I almost wish I could die before it starts.

My dad said that maybe I might be going to another school instead of the place I went to, but it warn't settled yet. Xenia, Vita and Ben all passed in school and unless we can figure out how to get me on track, they'll be way ahead of me.

My mom and dad didn't go fer my plan to return to Junction right now on account of school, so theres nothing I can do bout that. After school finished, I met a kid my age on the street from same school and he said that I was a good runner. It was kinda hard to talk to him cause my Danish ain't no good, but its getting a bit better now. His name is Hans Holm and he's kinda fat. Well anyways he said he had a speshal watch that can count seconds and if I was intrested we could test my running speed with it. The reason he had a speshal watch was cause he's a bankers son and bankers have loads of money. So I says okay. Well, jus when I was gonna see this kid, my dad and mom decided that it was time to go to my uncle Anders farm fer vacashun and thats where I am now. Maybe I'll see this kid when we get back to Kolding. I'm not particularly intrested in this kid cause he might be a sissy, but I would like to see the speshal watch.

Well, anyways here I am on my uncle's farm with Xenia, Vita, Ben, Sonya and David. My uncle has woods on his on his property and also a beach. He says that every summer lots of people come and camp in their tents in the woods at the beach and stay the whole summer. He doesn't like it and says that no trespassing signs don't work.

So I'm now gonna help him and chase the whole rotten bunch out of the woods and here's the way I'm gonna do it: ----- first of all, I'll write a warning on a piece of paper that they'll have to get out before a certain moonless night at midnight or else something very, very, very rottenly, exceedingly terrible AWFUL will happen and I don't mean maybe ---- I

will do that AWFUL thing the next night. I'll tack that paper to their tent and it will be covered with drawings of skulls and skeletons and rotted coffins with the dead climbing out of them and knives with stale blood dropping gently to earth and secret signatures written in blood that will come from me and a drawing of an old rotten graveyard with gravestones covered with blood, sunken half way down into the cold solemn, uninviting earth and some horrid, deathlike shrieking voices floating up to heaven from the dead ----! Well, if they stay then I will do the AWFUL thing which is this:

I'll smother warnings and notices all over the place and pull up all the tent stakes and alot of other junk that might scare 'em. And if they still refuse to get out, I'll steal all their pots and pans and things and hide them under a rock a couple of blocks away along the beach and use a slingshot. All this terrible stuff will be done at night and all the warning signs will be in American except the important ones which I'm sorry to say will have to be done in Danish.

Unfortunately I can only go to the woods in the afternoons cause in the mornings I gotta do garden work. That is something my dad decided so I wouldn't get into the habit of laziness. Everyone is busy milking cows when I come back to the farm. There are two farmhands and a fat woman. They all wear wooden shoes and the woman has a dull blue cloth wrapped around her hair to keep it from getting tangled up in the milk. She is powerful kind to us kids, cause today she gave Sonya a bag of choclates and the other day she gave Vita a box of candy. Theres lots of cats in the cow stalls and they drink milk out of old wooden shoes.

At night time I sleep in a feather bed. Its the same bed I slept in when we came to Denmark. That was in the winter and it was very comfortable although it made me feel like a pancake. But now its awful. A feather bed has three pillows. Two of em are mighty big ones cause ones a matress and the other is the cover. The third pillow is jus an everyday pillow that goes under a guys head. Well, Harold, you wouldn't believe this but in the summer this bed is like a herd of ovens. All a guy can do in bed

is sweat and sweat and SWEAT! What do people go to bed fer? Just one thing. They go to bed to get some sleep. What do I go to bed fer? I go to bed to sweat and thats all I can do in this bed. Its real awful - something I'll never ferget.

I also got to read a little in the bible every night cause my dad says I must do it every day, but I ferget to do it all the time cause things in it are so dry and unintresting. Well anyways, last night in the sweatbox which I call my bed, I read about how God made the world and the stars and the moon in a single week and how He said 'Let there be land and water and fishes and animals' and so on.

I think thats a lot of silly bunk what He said. How in the blooming nation do they know what He said when there warn't a blasted soul living at that time to witness it. One time I asked my mother bout that and she said that was the way they supposed it happened. But jiminy Xmas - if they supposed that then they might as well suppose that the moon is made of petrified milk and is inhabited by a herd of hogs made out of glue and arabian dish-rags and they eat a kind of a plant made out of sour gasoline and rotten strawberry-shortcakes and that the dark spots on the moon are some kind of swamps full of stale vinegar and they are inhabited by a herd of mosquitoes which are made out of dish water and buttermilk grinded up with glass and chewing-gum.

There's one thing funny that ain't in America and that is the "light nights.' In
the summer time the nights are almost as light as day fer some reason or other.
It doesn't get dark till midnight and then only fer a couple of hours. It's cause
we're close to the North Pole.

Jus think, Harold, Xenia can ride a bike now and it only took her five minutes
to learn. Now she can knit, play a piano (very good), roller-skate, nearly talk to
languages, juggle three balls at once, is very good in school and rides a bike and
jus think, she can do all that and she's only 11 and a half years old and is sick
nearly all the time.

I think I have found the perfeck branch to make the perfeck slingshot out of
for the AWFUL thing I gotta do. It's an oak tree in the woods and close to the
beach. It's real hard to cut through oak wood and I dunno if I'll be finished in
time. I would have had it finished if it wern't fer three gals who were swimming
in the water jus near the oak tree. I was up in the tree working and they were in
the nude in the water making an awful racket screaming so much I thought they
were drowning. How can a guy make a perfeck slingshot, with gals making so
much noise, speshally when oak wood is so hard to cut through. Gals always
make so much noise. They are a real bother. All that sqawking really gets to me.

Harold, how's the collecshun going? I hain't heard from you fer a long time.
Every day I expect the postman to come with some money but so far I ain't seen
a cent. I was jus a-thinking, if they make a collecshun at the church fer me, get
it changed to bills before you send it cause you can't send coins in an envelope.
They never give bills in church cause they don't make any noise when they pass
around the tin plate and then when nobody can't hear nothing they might be
cheating. I know this fer sure.

I also wanna know whats happened on the tower, whats happened on the
tank and what youve done bout the secret drawings I sent you. Please write,
Harold. From a friend in a rotten lot of trouble which is twelve days away!

Yours till I rot. Visti

The return to Kolding brought us all together again. Mom spent a couple of
days at the farm, but the six of us were mostly cared for by Uncle Anders and his
wife, who also had to care for 28 cows, 5 calves, a black bull, 4 horses, 19 pigs,
60 chickens, 1 dog, 14 cats, their own kids, two farmhands and the fat woman.
Our holiday on the farm allowed Mom to enjoy freedom and peace for awhile.

Daddy had good news for me. I would not have to go back to that horrible
school. I would now be going to a boys' school and in a class with boys my own
age. This was a relief, as a return to Latin School would have been a nightmare.

Auntie Annie and our grandmother then came over from England and stayed
with us for a week. They had presents for all of us and paid for expenses during
their stay. It was a good time. In the evenings when we were sitting around the
table, they told us exciting stories about the insane in England. Auntie Annie
described how they would test their intelligence by asking a simple question,
such as: 'The man walked to the top of the hill. He then turned around and walked
---- the hill?' They were unable to figure out the word 'down.' I began to think

of myself - having experienced the same sort of problems this last year in school, and wondered if I was insane without knowing it. The more Auntie Annie talked, the more concerned I became. I decided to keep this newly discovered problem to myself.

Dear Visti   *September 10, 1934*
   I got your walloper of a letter yesterday and I hate to tell you this but the tower ain't no more. And neither is the clubhouse or the tank. It was all torn down months ago when the new preacher came to town. I was gonna write you a letter about this a long time ago but then I fergot about it. And then when I remembered again I fergot whether I had told you or not. Lewis and Junior helped me tear it down. My dad used some of the lumber to build a new outhouse because the old one we had was sort of on a slant and ready to cave in.
   We got rid of Hornibrook and got the Black Band going, but there ain't much to do anymore, because we all gotta go to high school. Nobody is interested in the collection. I got a dime from Freddie and Burton gave me a nickel so I dunno. I guess you're stuck there. But I sure like your letters.
   Yours truely - Harold

The school season began the fifteenth of August. The only reason I could come up with for such an early date - right in the middle of summer, was that they were trying to learn too much and needed all the time they could get. I don't think anyone was happy about it. They were much happier in Junction City where vacations were longer and where they eased up on education.
   I decided that I would go by myself to school on the first day. I didn't want any of the kids there to see me, at my age, escorted by my father. The school, called *Drengeskolen,* was in the same downtown area as the other school. Early on the fatal morning, I registered at the school office and found myself an hour later sitting in a classroom with about two dozen boys my age. They looked like a rough bunch, as do all boys at the age of fourteen.
   I was introduced to the class as a new pupil by a teacher who seemed to be very calm and polite. There wasn't any snickering by the other kids, but they didn't smile either. I was simply regarded as another pupil. I figured as long as I didn't have to say anything or I wasn't called upon, everything would be okay. There was no English here. Everything was in Danish. I understood some of the classroom instruction, but not much.
   My attitude on this first school day was somewhat a state of appeasement, rather than that of anger or concern. I had been through a rough time and almost had the feeling I had now graduated - being with classmates of my own age for the first time in this disturbing country. This feeling of hope and tranquility didn't last long, however. During the first recess in the school yard I was approached by one of the kids in my new class.
   "Did you used to go to Latin School?" he asked in Danish.
   I understood quite well what he said and replied,
   "Yes."

"Then you must be the Dumb American!" he exclaimed excitedly.

He had made a major discovery and raised the alarm, shouting to the other kids. A number of them gathered around and eyed me with curiosity. It would have been wonderful if I had been looked upon as a celebrity and was about to sign autographs. However, adverse publicity obviously leaked from one school to the other, resulting in me being labeled as some sort of a freak. This was disturbing.

Nothing makes fourteen-year-olds happier than self-initiated confrontation with excitement. Amid a lot of shouting, yelling and encouragement from the others, the kid who had made the discovery, gave me a shove. I kicked him in the shins. He responded and a moment later we were both on the ground engaged in 'mortal' battle. It was the Latin School syndrome all over again. And as in the past, my opponent was saved by the school bell - or so I liked to think. The truth of the matter was, that I was badly shaken and again felt compelled to be on the defensive.

The rest of the day was nothing but problems. I went home feeling very unhappy and somewhat angry. The only comfort in this new dilemma was that I was not on public display surrounded by small kids, so at least the matter of embarrassment was not there.

Daddy and Mom were a bit disturbed as to what had happened, but it was decided after some discussion that we would just continue - in the hope that the other boys would eventually get tired of their games and normal school activities would prevail. Although Daddy never had much time to be with me to provide confidence, on account of all the funeral ordeals, sermons and weddings, he was concerned, and in his peculiar way attempted to remedy the situation.

On the wall in my bedroom a picture frame suddenly appeared. It was a poem. Daddy said it would do me good to read it every morning before I went to school. The poem, called *If*, by Rudyard Kipling consisted of four verses and started off with,

If you can keep your head when all about you
Are losing theirs and blaming it on you,
If you can trust yourself when all men doubt you,
But make allowance for their doubting too;

And so on. The last two lines were the clincher:

Yours is the Earth and everything that's in it,
And - which is more - you'll be a Man, my son!

With prayers at bedtime and the poem at the crack of dawn, I should be able to develop into a young man, morally strong with lots of confidence and appreciation for the fortunate situation God so graciously had blessed us with. I failed to see anything gracious about being beaten up everyday, but Daddy pointed out to me that it was the broader picture we should be looking at. As far as I could see the broader picture just meant more fights. My negative attitude disturbed him somewhat, but in the end I said I would try to do my best and read the poem every morning. He created more interest, when he offered to pay me two kroner if I would try to learn it by heart.

So with this stimulation and a full breakfast each morning, I was ready to face the world, but each day I returned home with bruises, scratches and dirty clothes. The kids at the boys' school were giving me a rough time. The fighting simply did not stop. Even after school on the way home, I was compelled to watch for ambushes. I would choose different streets to go to and from school day by day to avoid planned attacks. The boys seemed to work in groups. I considered carrying my slingshot to school as a concealed weapon.

Daddy got in touch with the school principal to discuss the situation and as usual, part of the blame was said to be mine.

"You must try to not let them antagonize you, Visti," he said.

" But they're after me all the time."

"That's because you provoke them by fighting back."

"Well, what am I supposed to do - just get beaten up?"

"No, Visti, just turn the other cheek. We must follow the teachings of the Bible. I'm sure you understand that."

"I dunno."

No, I definitely did not know. If they hit me on one side of the face and I offered them to do it on the other side - well, it would be double damage. I might be known as the Dumb American, but I wasn't that dumb and certainly would not allow myself as to be known as a coward or a sissy.

After three weeks of bedlam and frustration, the principal, the teachers, the kids, Daddy and Mom all gave up and I was removed from the school - not by force, but by admittance by all parties, that a mistake had been made. It was the wrong choice of school, Daddy said. I could have told him that all schools are the wrong choice.

Dear Harold, *November 3, 1934*

I got your letter this morning, but I didn't read it until this afternoon cause I wanted to try to keep it as a suprise as long as possible. But I was awful sorry that there warn't no money fer my trip. I think your mom could have least tried to talk to the preacher. They do help the needy, you know. Thats what churches are all about. Maybe I'll have to write to the minister myself. Do you think you can get his name fer me? Maybe someone out on Dane Lane might know.

I jus bout fell off my chair when you said that the tower and the clubhouse and the tank are all gone. I know it was on the parsonage property but what kinda guy is this darn preacher anyway. Preachers are supposed to show compashun. And heres something else. Whats this idea of using the lumber from our clubhouse to build an outhouse. Thats the most shameful thing Ive ever heard. Boy, if that ever leaks out and the Moore gang hears bout it we will have to hang our heads in shame fer evermore. In your letter you menshun a kid named Lewis and another one named Junior. I don't remember any nuts of those names, so I reckon they must be a pair of new runts in town. I hope you ain't letting them join the gang until we check up on them. You never know. They could be spies. School is dragging along the same as usual and by that I mean ROTTEN! It gives me headaches and worrys by the dozen and makes me feel sick all the time. At this very, very moment I got an awful thundering headache and a hunk of a bellyache - all on account of school. If this keeps up I might have to see a doctor. After the summer vacashun I had to go to a boys school that was another nightmare. I had fights with the brats there every single day fer weeks and they always lay in ambush ready to pounce on me when I went home from school, but I went home a different way each day so they got all confused.

I didn't learn nothing and those dern Danish kids gave me the creeps. So my dad and me decided that theres only so much hassle a guy can take, so we threw in the towel and now I go to a little dinky private school only a block away from those other two awful schools I went to. This time there ain't no trouble with kids and I don't have to be with little tiny kids no more, but there's far too much homework and all I learn here is how to get sick and increase the size of my worry department. This school is called Realskolen. It's real, alright! My worry department is jus jammed with all kinds of rotten worrys from school but the worst worrys are German and French. I don't make no progress in either language although I sweat and work as hard as I can. It takes me two hours to learn 20 words in German and the lo and behold, the next morning I find out I've fergotten it all. It takes me a week or two to learn jus a few words in French and the sight of a French word makes me vomit. Everything I learn I ferget. I hain't got no idea why I have to learn that silly French. Why in the heck would I wanna go to France? What good will that crazy language be to me when I'm gonna go straight to America anyways. My mom says it's a beautiful language, but I don't see nothing more beautiful about it than the hind end of a cow. And who needs french in Junction? It won't happen in a million years.

My aunt in England runs cookoo house over there and gets just loads of money cause there's so many cookoo people in the district where she lives. Each summer she goes to foreign countries and this year she was here in our foreign country. She gave us all nifty presents. There was a 300 page book about Robin Hood and his gang fer Ben and Grims Fairy Tales fer Sonya and a book called the Magic Walking Stick fer Vita. Xenia got the book she was always craving fer - Little Women and my aunt gave me two books: Daddy- Long- Legs and Dear Enemy. They were intresting, except that there was too much stuff about gals, dancing and love and that sort of hogwash to suit me. Maybe you'd like them better cause you once said that books where gals get into trouble makes better books. The thing is that in these books they don't really get into much trouble so I yawned most of the time. It's certainly swell to have a rich aunt like we got and good-lookin' to boot, speshually when we are poor. It's a bloomin' shame you ain't got such a one. Every poor family should have a rich aunt.

I hate to talk bout school again, but it's important you get to know all the trouble I got. It's hard to believe, Harold, but the blackboard in our room is an old board jus painted black and most of the paint is worn off. Some school, this is. They have dishrags fer erasers and chalk in the form of a hunk of dough. Most of the brain-buster teachers who operate this place are very old and are living on borrowed time and should be in their graves. Everything's falling apart.

And that's not all, either. In our worrying room we got an ol' wreck of a stove which burns fuel we gotta pay fer. I mean us kids! The bill is bout a dollar a month fer heat. I sit on the left side of the worrying room by the window. Well,

it's a dinky room which we're packed into and it gets stuffy in no time, so the brain buster opens all the windows to let the stuffy air go out, but then all the heat goes out too and a cold wind comes a-tearing in and makes the worrying room as cold as an icebox. And just think, Harold, we have to pay fer the heat that disappeared and then we have to sit there with our coats on to keep warm. They're plum crazy.

This private school is very small and is run by a family. It's got eight little classrooms and each of 'em are in separate one storey buildings that are white with red tile roofs. The whole place is surrounded by a wall and a high wooden gate so as to trap kids inside when school starts. I think they even lock it when school starts to prevent anyone from escaping. And another thing. The school yard is so bloomin' dinky that I first took it fer a chicken coop with the roof blown off. They got the craziest rules fer it that ever entered a human brain - fer instance: we ain't allowed to run in the school yard, or throw a snowball, or kick a rock around, or ride a bike, or play with a ball, or tackle a guy. That's jus some of the rules. There's herds more. The whole schoolyard is made of cement, so if you fall down you might be a goner. This afternoon I fell down and it made my hand so battered and torn up, that it feels and looks like a piece of tissue paper, saying nothing of the amount of blood that leaked out.

Well, Harold, heres some news you won't believe. I met a boy my age whose name is Hans Holm and who has a speshal watch which can tell how fast you can run. I can talk quite a bit of Danish now but I mix American words in when I talk but its all right. When I first met him, I thought he might be okay, but lo and behold, he ain't. No-sir-ee. Now I've found out this kid is an honest-to-goodness sissy! And heres the true story what happened:

About a week ago he invited me to his house to see the speshal watch. Its a heck of a long way out of town. It took me half an hour to get there cause I ain't got no bike yet and I was nearly frozen to death cause it was a ripping cold day. It was about twelve o'clock at noon so his mom gave us a dinner and then after that we loafed around and he showed me the speshal watch. It had a hand that moved counting seconds which is jus what you need fer running and you can stop the hand by pressing a button. He said it was a brand new invenshun and cost a lot of money. Well, after we looked at that there wasn't anymore to do so he took me up to his room. It contained a desk, a couple of chairs and two bunks built over each other. One is for his brother, Jens - a fifteen year old kid I can lick. On the desk was a row of school books, a lamp and several mounted photographs of SOME GAL FRIENDS OF HIS!

Well, it struck me like a devastating thunderbolt and I almost fell off my rocker - to think that he had gal friends! What a shock!

And it struck him like a thunderbolt when he found out that I didn't have any. He said,

"Haven't you got a single one?"

And I says, "Of course not. What in the world would a gal friend be of use to me?"

And then he bursted out, "TO DANCE WITH, of course!"

Well, I almost exploded with the devastating shock. Jus think, Harold Frode Bruce, - a kid ONLY FOURTEEN YEARS OLD dancing with a gal! Don'cha think thats disgusting. I didn't believe it but then he showed me some cards which ran something like this:

"Will you (Hans Holm) be so kind as to come on such and such a date to Mrs so an so's house fer a dance. Miss so and so and Miss so and so will be there, so there will be enough to dance with. Your brother is also invited."

All the cards were similar to that one. I told Hans if I ever got such a card I would pretend to be sick or invent a mashine I could dance with instead. So you see what I mean when I say he's a sissy. But you needn't get hysterical, Harold, cause I ain't finished yet.

Han's brother, Jens is more crazy over gals than Hans himself is. He keeps a photo album full of pictures of his gal friends. His gal friends send him presents and they usually are packets of cigarettes. They both smoke and their room stinks. All they think about is cigarettes, gals and dancing. Jens kept peppering me with questshuns bout a gal in my class at school.

"You know the one I mean," he says, "the one in the yellow raincoat. Well, what do you think, is she the prettiest gal you've ever seen?"

"I s'pose so," I said . Then he asked me what her name was, but jiminy crickets, how was I to know. I told him I had no idea and then he says,

"Well, haven't you ever spoken to her?"

I said I hadn't, but I believe she said 'Good morning' to me once, but it could jus as well ben said to a desk which was in front of her cause it's very unusual fer a gal to say 'good morning' to such an awful-looking runt like me. Well, he kept peppering me with lots of other questshuns and finally at last he says that the gal in the yellow raincoat is the one he likes best of all the gals he knows. Well, fer crying out loud, why didn't he say so right off the bat. Ain't this terrible. I wonder what makes kids be like this. Both Hans and Jens take dancing lessons so that proves they're real sissys. Well, by gum, but I nearly fergot - I can dance too - I mean the kind you do when ya chop yer finger half off. Finally I got fed up with all this gal stuff and decided to head fer home, but I took one last look at the speshal watch before I left.

When I was walking home I remembered I fergot to tell them that I knew a gal named Lisbeth from that terrible school I used to go to. But she was only nine years old or maybe ten now, and they were only intrested in older gals the same size as themselves. Besides, Lisbeth ain't around no more.

Well, I hain't got much more to write, so you can now ofishally sigh a long forlorn sigh of relief. I agree with you, Harold, all this jabber about school and gals gives me the shivers. I jus gotta say one thing more. Today it is exactly a year since I last saw you and Junction City. I am still as homesick as ever and I will never get to like Denmark and so that's that. If I write a letter to the church minister in Junction, will you deliver it to him, Harold? It's not like you have to go to church or anything like that. Just give it to him on the street before the service starts. And make sure you don't menshun that I had anything to do with the tower or clubhouse. Jus act nutral and keep your mouth shut. I'm getting to the stage where I reckon the church is my only hope.

Yours till I rot - Visti

As I entered my second year of exile, the cookie jar with coins remained static. With no income except one krone per allowance I was unable to save up enough money for my return trip to Junction. It was depressing. And other things were also depressing. With only four hours of daylight we went to school in the dark and came home in the dark. Add to this the biting cold, winter winds and a flood of homework, and it became a perfect recipe for misery and gloom. I could see now why the Vikings turned out to be such a tough breed. If they were not battling the enemy, they were battling the elements. In our case, the enemy was our homework.

It was a great comfort for me to be in a class with kids my age and no longer the object of ridicule. Also, I had two things going for me. I was at the top of the class in drawing, and my knowledge of English was appreciated. My ability to draw developed as a result of my isolation. There had been little else I could do in my spare time. I was always at home with the family, and apart from that peculiar afternoon at Hans Holm's house, I went nowhere.

I would spend hours drawing cartoon series, frame after frame, where I could stir my imagination and make things happen. There was no limit to the exciting disasters I could create. The subject was always our gang, battling floods, hurricanes, fires, thunder and lightning - and the terrible enemy. Needless to say, the gang was armed with slingshots for self defense at all times. These 'masterpieces' were in sequel and much of the daily required material for the series was generated in my mind as I walked in darkness to and from school.

Another series was the detailed construction of our lookout tower, step by step - definitely confidential information. I found comfort in drawing. It was no longer important to me, whether or not I had other boy friends.

There was the possibility that I might get acquainted with other boys in my class, although up till now there had been no breakthrough. They all had their group of friends and I was an outsider who didn't fit in anywhere. After school they all left in various groups, talking, laughing and playing around, while I alone, went straight home. My inability to speak proper Danish and the fact that I was 'different' put me in a classification all by myself. Being a preacher's son didn't help. It would be revolting for any kid in the school to be observed being too friendly with me for fear of ridicule by his classmates. So far in Denmark, I had passed the period of rejection by others and entered the period of tolerance. But there was a long way yet to acceptance. To make my life more exciting and interesting, Daddy decided that I should have music lessons. It would complement one of my school subjects which was music theory. What Daddy didn't know was, that it gave me less time for drawing my cartoon series, which was my only recreational activity. It also reduced the opportunity after school hours to meet or be with other kids. Now I had to practise piano every day and once a week endure criticism by an old, nerve-wracked music teacher. So the workload increased, but Daddy was convinced it was for the best.

The teachers at school were all relics. With the exception of the music teacher and the history teacher, nobody was under seventy. But at the rate the school music teacher was going, being as high-strung as his violin, he would reach seventy long before the set calendar date. The violin had a lot to do with it. The only thing that came out of the violin were squeaky, sour notes. During class when he played, I would inconspicuously put my fingers in my ears, close my eyes and whisper 'Heaven help us.' I figured there could be a number of reasons for this sad state of affairs. To start with, the violin could be out of tune, or it could be very old, or maybe simply poor quality. Perhaps it was the bow - which seemed to have a lot of loose hairs dangling from it and was used to whack kids with. Maybe the poor quality of music was because the music teacher was faking it and really didn't know how to play the violin. For awhile, I considered reporting him to the school principal as being an imposter, but looking at the violin bow, which looked like a whip, I decided against it.

The English teacher, a middle-aged, bosomy lady with grey hair shaped into a bun that looked like a potential beehive, also taught history and her favorite subject was the French Revolution. This significant event occupied all her thoughts night and day. It was the only part of history worth talking about. Her description of the Reign of Terror period in France had everybody in the classroom on the edge of their seats. She knew all the gory facts about the beheading of Marie Antoinette and 1400 others and described it all in great detail. She relished the morbid satisfaction of seeing her class totally shocked. On one occasion she even had me come up to the blackboard and draw a picture for the class, of a guillotine complete with the victim in place. She simply could not get off the subject and the class was enthralled with the horror of it all. It was the school's most fascinating hour and we enjoyed it twice a week. Her name was Miss Gertrude Gerslund, but we called her Guillotine Gerslund.

Dear Church Minister, Junction City   *December 2, 1934*

I kinda reckon you don't know me but my dad ran yer church fer a number of years until we headed fer Denmark. The reason I'm writing is cause I'm stuck in this foreign country and want to get back to Junction City where I belong. My dad is to busy with stuff going on at the church over here to help me and my mom has got so many kids to take care of and we are kinda poor so it ain't easy to get back on my own. I am what you might call one of those unfortunate souls in a faraway place that needs help like the ones menshuned in church prayers. I kinda thought that maybe one Sunday a collecshun could be made to kinda help pay fer my trip back. You don't have to say much to the congregashun. I don't want this to be a sob story but at any rate jus tell them that I intend to pay them back as soon as I earn some money in the beanfields. I will work real hard and maybe even earn a bit extra so the congregashun will get more dough back than they put in the collecshun plate. Thats a good deal cause they usually don't get any back. I know this fer sure.

My friend Harold will give you this letter or maybe his mother if Harold ain't got time. And when you get the money, give it to Harold's mother and they will send it to me. Her name is Mary Bruce and she lives over on Washburne.

Remember, this is a speshal case and the first time I've ever asked fer help.

Yours truely - Visti Favrholdt

At home all was going well. A highlight that brightened up my life was that I could play 'Sweet Sue' on the piano. This was a revolting piece of music as far as my nerve-wracked music teacher was concerned, and for Daddy, who heard it only once, it was sinful. If I wanted to become frivolous in my music, 'The Teddy Bear's Picnic' would be more appropriate.

As we approached the Christmas season, a re-occurrence of the pain Daddy experienced many months ago, came back. For a period of about four days he was not well, but then the pain went away. We figured it was due to the heavy workload. He seemed to be getting all the funerals in pouring rain while the other minister, Dean Rosen conducted the weddings. Mom suggested Daddy have a talk with the other minister about sharing church work more equally. Dean Rosen seemed to have a very snobbish opinion in general, putting himself in the position of a religious advisor, apart from the normal church duties. There was a certain amount of friction between him and Daddy. The fact that Daddy completed his theological training in the United States instead of in Denmark, put Daddy in an inferior position. Much emphasis was put on a person's education and standing in the community - especially by peers and snobs. Dean Rosen, would have liked to have been looked upon as a saint. However, in this world there was little hope for that.

Xenia continued to have asthma attacks now and then and there was very little we could do about it. We often had a doctor come around who would go through the same routine every time. He would place his black medical suitcase on the chair in her bedroom and look at her in a very concerned, professional way for a few moments. He would then hold her wrist with one hand and his big gold watch in the other to check her heartbeat. Following that, he would open his suitcase which was full of medical things and take out a hearing aid contraption to hear if anything mysterious was going on inside Xenia's chest. Then her temperature would be taken, and he would tell my mother that she did not have a fever - something we knew all along. The final step was to again look at Xenia in a very concerned, professional way and then write out a prescription for a bottle of medicine. There was hardly room for any more bottles in our cabinet.

Vita, Ben and Sonya were gradually becoming totally submerged into the

Danish way of life. It was surprising how quickly they were forgetting their past. They would mix Danish and American together when they were out with their playmates, but at home we all spoke only American - except Mom, who was from England. David was still too small to comprehend what had taken place in his short life. He would grow up to be totally Danish, but being born in Junction City, his birthplace could only be an asset. Not everyone enjoyed the privilege of starting life in such a beautiful place. We others had to settle for locations of birth that were less inspiring.

CHAPTER SIXTEEN

Dear Harold,   *January 15, 1935*
I blooming sorry I hain't written you fer a heck of a long time, but I've ben so rotten busy I hain't had no time to write. Now I reckon youve noticed that in this envelope is a speshal letter for the minister of our church in Junction. I want you or your mom to handed it to the preacher and we will see what happens. I figure he will find it a pretty good deal. Its not like I'm starving or something but I do need help from outside cause otherwise I might be stuck here forevermore and its so dark and dismal.

About a month ago it got around in school that I could draw pretty good. It started with a drawing I had to do fer our history teacher Gertie Gerslund, on the blackboard and it was a drawing of a French guillotine and I made it look real horrible with a guy laying there ready to have his head chopped off and I showed a lot of blood all over the place from other victims. It was real gory and the teacher

Guillotine Gerslund

and all the kids thought I did a real good job, so now every time a teachers want something drawn on the blackboard, I am called upon to do it cause they know it's gonna be good. Yesterday I drawed a rabbit for another teacher.

Lots of kids and teachers say that I am the best drawer in the whole, rotten school except one teacher who is our art teacher. He still thinks he's the best. One kid asked him if he could draw guillotines but it looks like he can't. There were a lot of kids who were able to hold up their heads with the thought that they were the best drawers in school before I came but after I was dumped there and started drawing guillotines all over the place, their fame went down to a million degrees below zero with the force and speed of a  *thunderbolt!. Yes-sir-ee, thats the truthfullest truth I know of. In fact some kids paid me money fer guillotine pictures. I charged 2 cents fer jus the guillotine and 5 cents if they wanted one with a guy laying there ready and 10 cents fer the completed job, but of course it was in Danish money. Not many could afford the completed job.*

Well, things went on like that fer about a week or two and then all of a sudden my mother showed a lady a few of my drawings and that lady said they were perfectly, unbelievable marvelous and she'd buy about 25 Xmas cards. I charged 10 ore per card (2 cent in American money). Well, that lady went and jaw-waggled it to her friends and so by an' by orders came pouring in like pudding and I was so rotten busy that I didn't even have time to breathe. There were some nights when I stayed up until eleven o'clock just drawing and drawing until I thought my heart was at the busting point. Well it all stopped dead in its tracks when Xmas came cause nobody needs Xmas cards after Xmas, but it didn't matter cause I had earned 8 krone which is 2 dollars in American money. Next year I'm gonna start earlier so that I can earn more money.

There are two show- houses here in town - and rotten ones at that. They only hold about a hundred people each. In one of 'em the floor slants downward so that the guy who sits in front of you won't block your view, just like in Junction, but in the other place they made a  *horrible mistake and everything is perfectly rotton cause the floor slants upward instead of downwards and so you don't see nothing 'cept the guy's noodle in front of you. I think what happened, they turned the seats the wrong way or the screen was supposed to be at the other end.*

Both show-houses have the dizzyest and crazyest rules in the world. If you got a kids ticket you gotta sit in the first three rows. I think thats pretty mean. They jus like to git all the kids pushed up as far as possible near the front to git 'em out of the way so that the grown-ups can have the best seats. And the front rows ain't 20 ft back so you can see the film properly. No-sir-ee. They're tucked away up as near to the screen as possible so you gotta bend your head way back if you wanna see the picture and get a terrible strain on your neck so that when the show is over you feel more dead than alive and can hardly crawl out on the street. I've seen lots of kids who jus stare at the wall below the screen when they have to sit in the front row cause they can't bend their neck back far enough to see the picture and I've seen kids come out of that place who got their necks all twisted and ready fer hospital. And that ain't all. Theres another rotten thing about these show-houses and that's that nine out of ten shows have that dreadful and horrible sign outside that says "Children not permitted". They tack that up cause they think kids are gonna make too much noise and also cause some shows ain't good fer kids to see on account it might make em git nightmares or make em cry. If a show has got too much shooting in it, they tack up that dirty sign. About 100 shots is okay but if things get out of hand and theres more than 200 shots then they gotta put up the sign. Its the law. If they think that's gonna scare kids then they hain't got no more sence than a herd of hogs.

In the show-house where the floor slants downwards they only show films from America so I always go to that one cause I can understand every single word. Well, it jus so happens that I've jus come home from a show at that show-house one hour ago and it sure was a wallopper! It was American and a cowboy show at that. It was called "The Rider of Death Valley" and Tom Mix and his hoss was in it. There was also an extra film about "Mickey Mouse" which is made by a man named Walt Disney. And another walloper of a film is coming soon called "Treasure Island" which is made after a book written by a pirate named John Silver. I think they call him Long John Silver cause one of his legs is longer than the other on account of one got shot off in a battle at sea. My dad only allows me to go to a show if I do all my homework.

I hain't got a bike yet and I ain't looking forward very much to the time when I will get one, cause I'm quite sure that time will never come. Jus think, Harold, I've never had a bike in my whole darn life. I had the one in Junction, but that doesn't count cause it only had one wheel on account I couldn't afford to finish making it.

I can talk pretty good Danish now - anyways good enough to answer the telephone, but I don't like to get entangled in a conversashun cause I couldn't tackle it. I have decided after pondering fer many, many days, that when I git to be a man I'm gonna be a cartoonist or an author or both and I'm gonna be a bachelor cause then I don't have to be bothered by gals with all their continuous squawking and noise. I notice that here at home Xenia makes so much racket playing the piano and Vita and Sonya make so much racket quarreling that its impossible to get anything done like making my drawings. Ben and David don't quarrel cause they're boys. So I had to make up my mind about my future and that's what I did.

I'll be finished being a boy in April cause that's when I gotta be confermed. My dad says I gotta start bible lessons at the church next month. I don't know what it's all about but every kid gets confermed here when they are 14 years old and then after that they are grown-ups and can smoke and swear and see all the films they want and don't have to pay attenshun to the sign outside the show-house. When you are confermed they call you "Young man". So, Harold that's the way it is here and there's absolutely nothing I can do about it cause it's the law of the land. Yer lucky to be in Junction where you can be a kid as long as you want.

I started to write this letter centurys ago, but I had to wait fer my mom to scribble to your mother and thats taken two weeks and she ain't finished yet - but anyways, us men and boys will have to put up with such things, cause women and gals always are that way. They hain't got the slightest idea why it is so praktical and wonderful to rush and tear around and get things done in a hurry.

I don't know when I am gonna make it back to Junction. Everytime when I think I'm ready something pops up - like this confermashun thing. But I can tell you, Harold, if I was in Junction right now I would cause a serious disturbance, cause I would start a gang that would be a million times better than Donald Dill's Gang, The Silver Flash, The Rinydink Gang, the Hornibrook Gang and the Black Band. The reason it would be a million times better is cause I got more sence now than I used to have. The purpose of the gang would be to lay an extra lot of destrucshun around about on Halloween night. The name of the band would be "Devastashun."

Jus think, Harold, I've ben here over a year and I hain't tasted any of the following things since I left Junction: watermelon, pumpkin, lemon, cherry and

apple pies, blackberries, Coca Cola, coconut, purple grapes, peanut butter or bubblegum. I kinda smuggled the letter to the preacher in this letter. My mom and dad don't know that I am doing this but I'll tell em when the money starts pouring in. The letter to the preacher is important. Remember what I said about keeping mum about the tower. The church is my only salvashun, thats fer sure.
   From your very best friend. Visti

Many days passed but finally Mom finished her letter. It started to snow and my hope was that it would continue, so that they would have to close the schools. When I took the letter to the mailbox it was already six inches deep. I reckoned it would take about a foot before they would surrender.

Dear Mrs Bruce,   *February 3, 1935*
   Everyday Visti is asking me to write to you so that he can get his letter off. Outside it is real wintry - white crispy snow and clear snappy air - we haven't seen such lovely snow since we were in Michigan. The children are delighted and tomorrow we will buy a sled. We are fortunate in having a warm flat - that is the advantage of living on the second floor.
   It was very interesting what you told me about aluminum mines, etc., but I really doubt if aluminum has anything to do with cancer, because that metal is hardly used in Denmark- most people having the heavy iron pans lined with enamel. Yet cancer increases with enormous rapidity just as in other countries. It is no doubt due to our different way of living and hopefully some day some clever person will find the cause.
   As for Xenia - she is much better this winter but is still as thin as a pole. When school examinations are over she is going to spend a month in hospital to be lazy and get fattened up. That can be done in a little country like Denmark at a cost of only 10 cents (50 ore) a day (the government controlled insurance company paying the remainder) and that includes violet rays and X ray where necessary. She is getting on well in school - is nearly at the top in the class and speaks Danish without an accent.
   Visti finds school much more difficult but it does not seem so easy for boys to apply themselves as for girls. By the time he is through with this school we hope he will like Denmark better - at present he can only see it's bad sides and only the good sides from the life in Junction. When he thinks of bean-picking it seems nothing short of paradise, and I remember how he hated the job and complained about the beans making him sick, etc. He is very clever at drawing and makes pocket money all the time by making sketches for the children at school. His music lessons had to be dropped, because he has so much homework to do and 3 languages to learn including Danish. It is school 6 days a week and it starts at 8 o'clock each morning. To a person like me who hates to get up in the morning on cold, dark winter days, it feels like getting up in the middle of the night to get the children off so early. The children certainly have to use their brains over here. You should see the music studies Xenia has to do in a week - it would make pupils over there faint. She is studying the old masters now and has to learn and

memorize two of these big pieces a week - also she has to play with much style and perfect technique. She is real quick, but even so she has to put in much concentrated study.

This letter has been lying around for a week to be finished. In the meantime we bought a nice big sled and the following day a nice warm rain began to fall and washed all the ice and snow away - now the sled is tucked away in the basement, Such is life!

While I think of it, I must give you a couple of funny incidents from school. The other day a girl in the fifth grade came to school with some lip-stick on, so the teacher sent her in the kitchens to get a bowl of water, soap and a scrubbing brush and made her sit before the whole class and scrub it off, - If any of the girls have nail lac on their nails, the teacher scrapes it off with a pocket knife, making the nails very rough and unpleasant. They just wouldn't stand for that treatment in America, would they? - Over here there is great respect for teachers. - As for cosmetics - one rarely sees it on anyone but "doubtful" persons. Permanent waves is as far as a respectable person can go.

In your last letter you say nothing about the new Sunday school classes or the new choir the church has formed. But we are so glad you have a nice minister at the church. I presume Harold is doing well in high school. Visti is to be confirmed on April 14 - my husband has ninety-one confirmants to confirm on that day. Well this is where I wind up.

Kind regards to all our friends.   Bertha Favrholdt

The confirmation classes were held at the church twice a week after normal school hours. With daily homework from school, and now the time spent at the church, there was little time for my latest project - making wooden guns that could fire rubber bands.

In Daddy's confirmation class were fifty-five girls and thirty-six boys. I found the lessons to be difficult as it entailed memorizing passages from the Bible in Danish and being asked questions about various things in the Old and New Testament. I didn't do very well. Now, had I been asked how many ceiling tiles or how many light bulbs or window panes there were in the church, I would have had all the answers and been classified as a winner.

In preparation for this serious, upcoming event which would catapult me into manhood overnight, I would have to have a black suit. An appointment with a tailor was made and I spent an hour in his little downtown shop being measured up for my transformation. Somehow I didn't feel I was ready for all this. The Hornibrook gang certainly wouldn't approve of such revolting stuff happening to one of their members. But you can't turn the clock back and as Daddy always said, the writing is on the wall.

I felt rather silly the day I stood in the living room with my new, black suit on for the family to see and for Mom to check.

"I think the waist measurement is a bit too loose," she remarked.

"I'm sure there's time to get that adjusted," Daddy replied.

All the kids stood around as if I was being packaged and going to be sold somewhere. Xenia could hardly contain her concern and embarrassment.

"You look like an undertaker," she said, holding her hands to her face.

"Xenia! Shame on you!" Mom looked at her. "Visti looks just fine. He looks like a fine young man."

"Mom, is Visti gonna leave us?" Vita asked.

"Of course not. What makes you think of a thing like that?"

" 'cause he's all dressed up. He must be going somewhere."

"As we have told you before, it's for his confirmation. It is a very important occasion. Your turn will come some day."

It was agreed a few adjustments were to be made to the pants. A pair of brown shoes I had were dyed black. A white shirt and a funny looking black bow tie that looked like a propeller, completed the transformation. Visually, I was now ready to leave childhood.

The confirmation service at the church was a very formal affair, with the boys looking very uncomfortable in their new black suits, and the girls, dressed in white, floor-length gowns, white gloves, jewelery and fancy hairdos, looking like ladies at the King's ball. Chairs had been placed down the center aisle for us all. We were too important to sit in ordinary pews. We had to be on display. The church was packed with relatives and daffodils. There were daffodils around the altar, all up and down the center aisle and in the window alcoves on each side. Soft organ music created the proper atmosphere, as Daddy, in his formal black church gown with the white pie-shaped collar, entered the church.

He walked down the center aisle to the altar, kneeled on the cushioned step in solitary, silent prayer for a few moments and then rose, facing the congregation. A blessing was bestowed upon us all as we opened the psalm books to sing the first hymn. After a fair amount of singing and ritual passages from the Lutheran church book which I understood very little of, Daddy left the altar, went out through a side door and moments later, parted the black curtains and appeared in the pulpit.

For the next hour we were given the sermon of our lives, so to speak. Being directed toward the young confirmation class, rather than the aging general congregation, we were told of the blessing of innocence and happiness that is the rightful environment of being a child - surrounded by the loving care of parents and the church. But today, as we stood on the threshold of adulthood, we were also blessed with many virtues bestowed upon us by the Lord. However, with these blessings came responsiblities and obligations which was part of being an adult. We must constantly appreciate and be aware of all the good things we have been blessed with, and our new role in society. Today as adults, we entered a new world and a new stage in our life. Our obligation to society, our parents and relatives, our future family and to the Lord would always be of paramount importance. To emphasize the importance and credibility of the religious obligation, various passages were quoted from the Bible throughout the sermon. Although intended as enlightening spiritual insight, these references also brought about the fear of guilt and damnation, should we waver in any way.

After the sermon, there was the lengthy prayer, directed towards suffering humanity and sinners everywhere, similar to the way it was in Junction City. A couple more hymns were sung by the congregation and then, with the appropriate background organ music, each confirmation pupil was individually blessed and presented with a Bible with the church seal stamped on the first page. Another hymn was sung, followed by the closing prayer. The service was over. After a lot of handshaking and congratulations all around, out of the church appeared ninety-one new adults, groomed and ready to meet the responsibilities and obligations now placed upon them. The total transformation from child to adult took two hours.

It was shortly after my confirmation that the good news came. Daddy and Mom had bought a house for 17,200 kroner with a down payment of 2,000 kroner. It was located, just a five minute walk from the church, in a newly developed area overlooking the town called 'Skovhoj,' meaning Forest Hill - but that must have been during the days of the Vikings because there was no forest there anymore. The house was new, had electricity, central heating, hardwood floors and double glazing. The bathroom was 'a perfect darling' as Mom described it. It took us two weeks to complete the move. Xenia, Vita and Sonya shared a room. Ben and David shared another room and, because I was now a 'Young man,' I got a room for myself downstairs in the basement.

The big upright piano from Boston looked very good in the new living room. Next to the piano was a window that had a view of the church. On top of the piano were the three small, bronze monkeys that seemed to have always been on the piano - ever since we lived in Michigan. One monkey covered his eyes with his hands, the second one covered his ears and the third one covered his mouth. This meant 'see no evil, hear no evil, speak no evil.' The problem was that they couldn't see, hear or speak anything good either - being in those positions.

Next to the piano on a high pedestal was a white statue, about twelve inches high - another item that had always been in the house. It was of three women in the nude, standing in a group as if they were waiting for a train or something. I was told that it was a replica of a very famous sculpture and it was called the 'Three Virgins.' I reckoned they must be from the Virgin Islands and why they were standing around without any clothes on, was more than I could figure out. Maybe this had something to do with religion and they were on their way to heaven - like the nude baby angels in our Bible books - the ones with the wings.

Dear Harold,   *September 8, 1935*
I reckon you figured I was dead since I ain't written fer such a long time. Well, its getting close to that. This darn school has started up again, extinguishing the flame of freedom and its a pain in the neck, but this time they moved me up a grade even though I failed again cause I can't stay in the same grade forever. Ain't it strange that I can't make no headway. I'm so powerful, doggoned tired of going to school that I feel like a sawed off, hammered down, southwest end of a lob-sided rotten spud - sprinkled with salt 'an pepper to boot. All the stinky, cockeyed tests they have all the time jus drive me up the wall. I ain't the

cleverest in my class and I ain't the dumbest. Me and my great talent kinda seem to hover midways, undecided which way to go. Sometimes when the teacher scolds me (the teacher ALWAYS scolds me), I feel like wringing her dinky neck. But nine times out of ten it dumps me into an unhappy mood an' kinda makes me think how blooming dumb I am and how clever all the rest of the kids are. But then later on it usually pops into my head that I got my rights fer saying that I'm clever cause I can speak two languages almost and draw kinda good, and I'll be doggoned if that ain't more than anyone of the other kids in my class can do.

Can you believe it, Harold, they say I got almost two more years to go in this prison and if I fail it will be three years. They were nice to me this year to let me pass, but I've been warned that I better smarten up or I'll be in big trouble!

Certain things have attracted my attenshun lately and occupied all the space in my day-dreaming department. One of these things is the building of a streamlined racebug which will beat Campbells "Bluebird" all to hollow. It's gonna be made of a few sheets of flexible, three-ply wood with a steering wheel from a car. The length will be about seven ft. and the width will be fourteen inches. It will be silver and black and christianed "Bullet." I've already got some of the framework done, but it's slow work cause school is always trying to get smart and interfere with the building of my future, fissilless record-smasher. Anyways, I gotta stop talking bout school cause I'm almost ready to vomit. Excuse me while I dash to the bathroom.

I don't know if you know this, but I ain't a kid no more. The big change came last April when I was confermed. All kids over here get finished being a kid when they get to be fourteen. It all happened at my dads church and it took two hours. Now people are supposed to say 'Young man' when the talk to me, but nobody's said it yet and it's probably cause they don't know I'm confermed. You're lucky that you ain't confermed cause then you can be a kid as long as you want. But I must say there are some advantages cause kids who are confermed can do the same things grown-ups do. Now if I want to I could smoke, drink wine and swear and lots of other things and nobody could say I can't do it. All the kids in my class smoke and lots of 'em swear. So that shows they're confermed. But I can't swear cause I'm a preacher's son and I don't want to anyways.

Well, I won't bother you with too many details bout the confermashun since you ain't no "detail collector" but we had a big dinner and all our relatives were there, also Uncle Magnus and Agnes who both looked much older now and I got a lot of presents such as books, a pot of flowers, a keen, dandy drawing set and lo and behold - a real honest to goodness, well blow-me-down bike! The very first one in my whole life. I also got a lot of money so I bought a safety lock and a light fer my bike which both amounted to 10 Kroner. My new bike is black. They only make black bikes here and thats cause you can hardly see them at night in the dark cause they're black, and that prevents them from being stolen. In a way it's kinda nice to get confermed cause you get an awful lot of presents.

Well, you won't believe it, but a circus came to Kolding in July. It costed two bits and it was worth it too. It was the best one I ever saw, except fer the three ring circus I saw in Michigan as a kid. It was in a monstrous tent and there must have been more than a hundred guys that took part in putting up the tent. This was the first Danish circus I had ever seen and really something.

I think I'll draw the circus tent and ring instead of telling about all the details

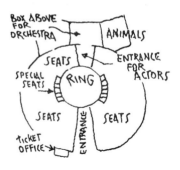

cause it will save paper. Well, first of all a curly headed guy that looked like ol' Kelso came in the ring that was all lit up with big spotlights. He started out juggling some balls - about four of them. Then he juggled a dagger, a cup, a ball, a stick of wood and a bottle - all at the same time. Then he did a lot more junk and then he was out of the ring in a wink. The band played some jazz music during that performance and fer most of the following.

Well, before a guy could even think of yanking his blowrag out of his trash-holder and wiping his sneezer, a long line of horses came tearing in and went racing around the ring, one behind the other. There must have ben a dozen or more and before I could blink, a ringmaster came in and stood in the middle of the ring. He was a long lanky man with a mustash and he wore a black stove pipe hat and a black suit with coat-tails that went as low as his knees and he had a shirt on as white as an eggshell and as shiny as a mirror. He had a long, long whip which he cracked at the horses heels. By and by the horses went a-tearing around the ring so fast that I wondered why they didn't all churn to butter. All of a sudden the ring master gave an order and the horses teared around in couples - one couple after the other and then he said something else and they went around in triples and so on. They did a lot more junk such as standing on their hind hoofs and bowing to the audience. Then the ring master gave another signal and the horses went sailing off the ring in a wink. Then the ring master made a low bow and took off his lid to the audience and was out of the ring in another wink. Those horses were all brown.

Next some clowns came in on roller-skates. They were awfully funny and were supposed to be the best in Denmark and then three black horses came a-tearing in with a man on each. They did barrels of stunts on them such as turning summersalts on one horse and then landing on the next while the horses were going full speed ahead.

Next a horse came in as white as snow with a dancing gal on it. She did a lot of stunts and acrobatic tricks and then that horse went out. And jus as we were getting tired of horses all the time, in comes three men with a ladder apiece. The stood them upright in the ring and climbed up them and they warn't leaning against a thing. They could stand on top of them and play a violin, flute or anything. It was perfectly amazing. After that a couple of gals came sailing in with hardly anything on. A person had to look twice to make sure, but there wasn't time for that, cause they did a lot of stuff straight away like balancing on each others head and other daring, amazing feats and then they rushed out before you could say "six thick thistlesticks."

Well then came the scary stuff. There were tigers that jumped through rings of fire and lions that did alot of daring feats and then there was a black panther which wrestled with a man - but the panther finally got a death-grip on the man, so the guards that were standing around incase of an emergency made the panther stop cause the guy was almost a goner. But they still called the guy the winner although any dumb nut could see that it was the panther who won. The crowd booed cause they knew that it was the panther who should have been declared the winner, but anyways, the panther didn't mind a bit. It was probably planning to finish the guy off in the next show. Then there wouldn't be any mistake who was the winner.

This circus was a million times better than that ol' rotten tent show that came to Junction City, where all there was to see was that guy stick pins through his shriveled-up jaw and boast about that rotten medicine he had and jabber to the crowd about that blamed ol' dollar-baby.

This summer I went to my uncle's farm again fer two weeks with the rest of the kids. The rest of the vacashun I didn't do much. But I did draw the best cartoon series I have ever made and it was about us and a secret gang and a hideout we would have out in the woods - a kind of a dugout with dirt and leaves on top and with a long tunnel entrance leading to it. It was all about what you and me would do. The object of the gang would be only to go out of the woods at night into Junction and wreck and tear up all the dinky, flimsy ol' clubhouses all over town. A kid would wake up gayly one fine morning - and lo and behold, looking out the window he would find his dear beloved club house laying a piece down the alley - nothing but a heap of smoking ruins, with a flag on a pole sticking out of the middle, waving gallantly with our gang's coat of arms on it. Well, then most likely the kid would exclaim,

"Wal, fer crying out loud, who in the stinky tar nashun ben monkeying around here. I'll be a catapolted, sawed off, lob-sided son of a two-sided squash if I'm gonna stand fer this here, believe me!"

Well Harold, thats how things would go and then he'd most likely run and tell all the other kids in town and get busy rigginghis gang together to track down the unknown enemy - which of course, would always remain unknown as long as all the guys on our gang would hold their mugs and keep mum. Our gang would only be ten kids and they would be choice kids. I jus about got this cartoon serie finished and when its ready I'll send it to you, cause then you can go out and find choice kids and start making the dugout. I got a lot more money in my cookie jar than I used to have so I expect to return to Junction pretty soon now. I've given up on the preacher in Junction. You can tell the gang to get ready fer my homecoming and put out a red carpet at the train stashun. I'll let you know the exact date. I might have to wait a little while cause my dad had to go to hospital when I went to my uncle's farm and I can't leave until he gets better which will probably be pretty soon. I'm fifteen now.

Your very best friend. Visti

CHAPTER SEVENTEEN

It was during the summer that Daddy took ill. A visit at the doctor's office revealed that there was something wrong. I had noticed for quite some time that Mom was rather quiet. She always sang while she worked and had a beautiful voice. She also sang in the church choir every Sunday. To me, the change was somewhat like a bird singing in the morning sun and then not quite so much when the day turns to rain - and unfortunately, that was the way it looked now. Mom and Daddy had obviously known about this situation for some time. A more thorough examination then revealed that Daddy had cancer. This came as a shock to us all. How could it happen? And why him, with such a large family to care for and so much to do at the church? We actually did not believe the doctor. However, arrangements were made that he would have to go to hospital in Kolding. Further tests were conducted and as it looked as though radiation treatments might be required, it was decided that he should be in a special hospital in Odense - a town, about two hours drive away on the island of Fyn. This was very hard for Daddy, because not only did he have periods of severe pain, but also the anxiety of not being able to care for his family, who depended so much on him. Friends of ours were helpful in providing assistance and transportation to Odense. Mom accompanied Daddy, where she stayed with acquaintances for two weeks, while the six of us were sent to my uncle's farm for the same period of time.

It was a shake-up for the family. The eight of us had always been together. It was hard to imagine that it could ever be different. Our boat had always managed to stay afloat with all of us together on board. We seemed able to weather any storm. Now suddenly, we temporarily lost the captain.

Two weeks later Mom returned and so did we. The daily life resumed and I was surprised to see how Mom handled the situation. She was completely back to normal, cheerful and singing, which in turn, made us feel likewise. It was almost as though Daddy was on a vacation, getting a well earned rest. That would have been a blessing. He did get rest, but not peace of mind. It was determined that he would have to remain in hospital for an extended period of time. Fortunately there were no financial problems, as under the Danish system, hospital care was paid for by the government. Also Daddy's salary would continue indefinitely. But we all missed him so much.

During the fall a few things changed in the absence of Daddy. It was possible to make more noise in the house without creating a disturbance and I could play 'Sweet Sue' on the piano without a feeling of guilt. The kids brought in their friends more frequently for fun and games, now that the sacred section of the house, the study, no longer required an aura of religious peace and tranquility around it. But the study looked uncomfortably empty and things were not right.

Without Daddy at the helm, we all felt that we should stay closer together, supporting each other as much as we could. We helped Mom with the daily chores and tried to be obedient, doing our homework on time, making our beds and always being home in time for supper. Needless to say, I was always at home, except when there was a show that I could see.

It was planned that if Daddy had to remain in hospital in Odense longer than expected, we would try to visit him once in awhile, although we had no idea how we would get there - unless someone helped us. We could never afford the train or bus trip for all of us. Well, hopefully he would be home soon.

It was a day in September, cold and windy as usual. I had left school for home and was passing the bus station, which was just across the street from the horrible Latin School. As a rule, I avoided walking this way home. I didn't want to be confronted by any kids from that school after my dismal downfall. Suddenly there she was - Lisbeth! We almost bumped into each other. I hardly recognized her. She had grown so much.

"Oh, I haven't seen you for a long time," she exclaimed, "where have you been?"

She looked so happy, all bundled up in overcoat, scarf and wooden clogs.

"I go to a different school now."

"Say, that's pretty good," she said, "you can talk Danish!"

"Yes, I guess so - a little bit."

"My, you've grown a lot. I can hardly believe it. What school do you go to?"

"It's Realskolen."

"Oh, I know the place. That's only for big kids. Gee, I can't get over you talking Danish. It sounds funny."

"I know. Not very good." The cold wind was a bit too much. I suggested we go into the bus station where it was warm.

She agreed and I pulled open the door for her. Looking at her, I still found her to be just a child. She looked like eleven or twelve and I was now fifteen. She barely came up to my shoulder. But there was something very nice about her that made me feel comfortable. Maybe it was because she was on my side all the time. We put our school books on a bench and stood near the window.

"How's things with you?" I asked.

"Fine. I'm fine. Here, do you want a piece of chewing gum?"

"Gee, you still got that stuff. Sure, I'll have some."

We looked out of the window, chewing for a while.

"It sure has been a long time since you've been around?" She said.

"I just couldn't go near that school - after what happened. You know that."

"Yes, I know. It's a bad school. I'm glad I don't have to go there much longer. In a couple of days it will be over."

"Why, what happens then?"

"We're moving to Roskilde next week," she said.

"Really. Then I won't see you anymore."

"No, I guess not." We chewed some more.

"Can you draw animals?" she suddenly asked.

"I can draw a horse or a cow."

"No, I was thinking of a giraffe. Can you draw a giraffe?"

"Maybe."

"I still got your drawings, you know. The warship you did was nice but, I like giraffes better than warships."

"Okay, I'll draw you one."

Her face beamed. She looked so happy. "A real big one, - one which I can take to Roskilde with me?"

"Sure, I'll do that. It might take a few days"

"That's okay. You know, I still can't get over that I can talk to you like this. I mean, you talking Danish. You have a funny accent. And you're so big. You've changed, you know."

"I guess so - and so have you."

We decided to meet again here in the bus station the following Monday. We picked up our school books and went out on the windy street. She looked very happy, as we parted - and so was I.

It was Saturday afternoon, with two days to go. All week I had tried to get a giraffe to look like giraffe. I just couldn't get it right. There were no giraffes in Junction City or in Denmark, so I had to draw from memory. Why couldn't she have settled for a cow? I was an expert on cows. I decided to go to the library to see if they had a picture I could copy.

The lady at the front library desk looked perplexed for a moment. She referred me to the books in the children's section. I went through the shelves, took out a few illustrated books and sat at a library table. I had pencil and paper ready. After going through a couple of books, I suddenly found the perfect specimen. It was in a book called ABC. There was a big letter on each page and as to be expected, for G was a picture of a giraffe.

Two boys from my class at school entered the library. I knew them fairly well, but apart from selling a guillotine drawing to one of them a long time ago, I didn't associate myself with them. They were heading for the technical book section of the library, when one of them noticed me, said something to the other and then they disappeared from my view. I did some sketching and soon had all

 the details I needed for a perfect giraffe. After that, I leafed through the other books again to make sure I hadn't missed anything, when suddenly the two boys passed by my table to see what was going on. They 'caught' me looking at a picture of a bunny rabbit with two big ears, surrounded by Easter eggs. I guess it must have looked a bit silly. They didn't say anything, but I got the impression they were laughing as they left the library.

Very quickly the news spread through the school for those who might be interested - which seemed to be everyone. Not only was I at the bottom of my class, which was known to all, but it appeared that I read kindergarten books in my spare time at the library. This was the first disturbance I had encountered at this school and I felt bothered by it. There was not much I could do.

Lisbeth appeared right on time at the bus station the following Monday afternoon. It was another windy day. She had a couple of girl friends with her, who I seemed to remember from the time I was in their class. I had the giraffe drawing rolled up, neatly wrapped with paper and string. She beckoned her friends to walk along and she would catch up with them.

"Oh, I can hardly wait to see what you have made. Is it good?"

"Yes, I think so." I gave her the roll.

"Should I open it now?"

"If you want to."

"Well," she hesitated, "maybe I'll wait till I get home. It's so nicely wrapped. It's also so windy here. Is that okay?"

"Sure, that's fine."

I thought it would be nice if she did open it, because then I could see the happy reaction to my drawing. On the other hand, if she didn't think it was good, then it was best we let it remain in the roll. It was hard to know.

"I got something for you," she said, reaching into her coat pocket. "Close your eyes and hold out your hand."

I did as I was told. I felt a coin placed in my hand, It was an American two bits - a quarter!

"Gee, where in the world did you get that?"

"My uncle gave it to me a long time ago. Do you like it?"

"Oh, I sure do. Do you know how much this is worth in America?"

"No. How much?"

"It's worth plenty. You can buy twenty-five packs of licorish cigarettes. There's four in a pack, so that's a hundred in all."

She was impressed. "But I want you to keep it."

"I will. Thanks, Lisbeth."

Her girl friends down the street were calling her.

"Well, I guess I got to go," she said, holding the roll close to her.

We stood there for a moment silently, both wondering how to say goodbye. The wind was blowing her hair.

"Maybe I'll see you again - some day," I ventured.

We touched hands. Then she left, waving goodbye. I had the feeling that I had lost something. This, I thought was a bit strange, because I hadn't seen her for well over a year - and now only briefly. But she was still my only real friend.

By the time October came around, the dreadful, long winter season was upon us for good. Even in September one could feel the change. The days were now getting darker and gloom filled the air. Maybe others didn't feel that way, but the monotony of the six-day-a-week tread mill at school with all the homework was getting to me. Last year was bad, but this fall, things seemed to go on and on without end. If they only had a spooky Halloween or something for excitement, it would help.

They did give the pupils one week off in the late autumn, which, when you looked at the calendar definitely was autumn, but looking out of the window, was winter. It was called the 'Potato' holiday. It was an annual thing, dating back a hundred years when there were only farms, and when all hands were needed to dig up potatoes like mad before the winter frost appeared. Since that was no longer the case, and since nobody wanted the holiday cancelled, the schools cunningly replaced potato work with homework.

Not being the type to plunge into homework on the first day of the Potato Holiday, I decided to cycle down to the harbor and take a look at a large Greek ship that had docked overnight. It's cargo was corn. There was an item in the newspaper about it being the largest vessel ever to have entered Kolding fjord, and that it would be open to the public while docked.

Dear Harold,   *October 24, 1935*

Well, you won't believe it but in this letter I ain't gonna jabber bout school cause I don't wanna get depressed. But I jus gotta say that being at the bottom of my class I can't sink any lower so thats a comfort. And when I get back to Junction it will all be a faint distant memory like a nightmare long long ago in a different century like something I read in a dusty old book from a library. I think a real good thing bout Junction City is that you don't need an education to live there and everyone is happy to have it that way. And its good not too many people know bout Junction cause they would pour in by the carloads and the whole place would be overcrowded. But if that ever happened we would put them to work in the beanfields.

Jus recently there was a big Greek ship down at the harbor here in Kolding and naturally I went a board jus to look around. Some of the other kids from my class at school were also there. Well, when I was in the middle of a conversashun with a burly sailor who was busy oiling mashinery, I noticed a long, thin sleeky-looking sailor coming down towards us from the forecastle. He wore a dinky old slouch of a hat like a Robin Hood cap and he carried a pail of water in one hand and a dirty mop in the other. Well, he came a-walking along the deck and was jus passing by us, when all of a sudden he sneezed so bloomin' loud and terrible that I nearly thought the ship was sinking. I got a tiny bit scared and was about to asked the other sailor what the matter was, when suddenly he put down the mop and pail, took hold of my left arm, lifted it up and began smelling it with all his might. I began to think he was crazy, when he jumped back a step or two and exclaimed,

"Ah ha! Jus as I thought. I hain't made a mistake yet."

I kinda wondered what in the stinkin' tar nashun he was a-squawking about, when he sneezed perfectly awful again and then he turned to the sailor who was oiling the mashinery and said,

"Say, do you know what. This kid here is a preacher's son."

Then he took his pail and mop and continued his errand, blowing his nose so loud, that I kinda imagined the deck was shaking. Now, how in the woosily wheezers did he know I was a preacher's son? Jus think, he was jus a plain common sailer who had never seen me before in his whole life and yet he knew I was a preacher's son. I wonder if preacher kids smell different? I hain't figured it out yet.

Well, then we went to the gallery and lo and behold, I met an American. He was the ship's cook and was the very first American I have seen since we left USA. He was from New York and told me lots of things. The other school kids didn't understand what he was saying cause there was alot of American slang so I translated the important stuff. He said the boat was called the mystery ship cause they never knew where they were going. Only the greek captain knew and he warn't telling nobody. He had been to almost every port on the face of this earth and sometimes they were at sea fer fifty days without seeing a single speck of land. He said the rest of the crew were a bunch of nuts cause they always complained bout the food he was making. It was real intresting to meet a real American and I told him I was heading back to Junction City at the earliest possible moment, but he said he had never heard of the place. I can't understand that when Junction is so important.

Do you know we still got a bottle of rootbeer extract from Petes grocery in Junction. I thought we had used it all but theres still some left. My mom says next summer we can make rootbeer. I can hardly wait until that day dawns.

This confermashun thing I went through didn't do me no harm but it sure has made most of the kids at school into a bunch of noodleless brats. Every single kid I know swears like the dickens and that ain't all - 99% of the kids smoke stinky cigarettes. Infact there ain't a blamed kid I know who doesn't smoke. Holy smoke and stewed taters, but the awful stink of those blooming cigarettes certainly is rotton when a guy gets in the vicinity of such dumb kids. I really think the church should be more careful when they conferm kids cause all this smoking and swearing is jus too much to handle. I know they don't think its gonna work out that way, but when ya try to make an adult out of a kid in two hours theres bound to be trouble. Well, I guess I gotta quit now cause I'm supposed to be doing my homework.

Your best friend. Visti

Back at school I noticed that I was treated with more respect following the meeting with the American cook. The school kids who happened to be with me on the ship were really impressed with my ability to translate what the American had to say. This was a real breakthrough. For the first time since coming to Denmark I was appreciated by my classmates. In the days ahead I felt the change. I was no longer shunned. I was respected. Boys began to talk to me during the recesses and after school. I began to feel equal to them. It was as though a burden had been removed from my back - just like it happened to that funny little figure, Christian on his way to Celestial City.

However, the other burden was still there - that of learning. I was still at the bottom of the class in most subjects. I had to work harder than the rest, not only to keep pace, but simply to catch up. To be in a class with classmates my own age only came about, because I was permitted to jump up three grades. This was unheard of in the school system and normally only granted to geniuses. I don't think anyone expected me to be on a level with others my age, but I was encouraged by my peers to do my best.

The tests before Christmas and exams in the spring would most certainly reveal the truth of the matter. It would take a miracle to pass at the end of the school term. During the periods of schooling in Denmark, I had so far gone through various stages from rejection to tolerance and finally to acceptance by others. What was still lacking on my part was not intelligence, but knowledge.

One dark, winter afternoon as I was leaving school I saw, much to my surprise, Hans Holm's brother, Jens standing near a street lamp in front of the school wall entrance. I went over to him and asked what brought him to this neighborhood. He said he was waiting for the girl in the yellow raincoat.

"She doesn't wear the yellow raincoat anymore," I said.

"Well, I know what she looks like."

"Do you know her?" I asked.

"Not yet, but today I will."

"How are you going to do that?"

"That's easy. I'll just go up to her, say hello and invite her to a show or something."

He seemed so sure of himself. Then he asked,

"How about you - have you been with any girls lately?"

"No."

"You seem kind of funny. Hans thinks so too. Didn't your dad tell you anything?"

"About what?"

"You know, - things."

"I don't think so." I was trying to figure out what he was talking about.

"Well, he probably will one of these days. It's called the father-son talk."

This kid, Jens was really mixed up. I couldn't figure head or tail what he was driving at. Daddy and I had talked many times - mostly about my school grades.

Suddenly, I saw his dream girl walking down the street with other girls.

"I think that's the girl you want to see," I remarked.

"Gee, you're right. Well, I'll see you around."

He left, running down the street in the darkness.

Daddy came home at Christmas time from hospital. He looked tired and weak and the treatments at the Odense hospital were by no means over. He had to return to hospital, but for a few days we were all together. This year we all decorated the Christmas tree for him. He was too weak to attend any church service, let alone preach. During his absence, a substitute minister had taken his place at the church and it looked like that would have to continue for a while yet. Also during Daddy's absence, we had not been attending the Sunday church service. We did not know the new minister and we didn't want to see someone else in the pulpit, reminding us of Daddy's plight. Mom, however, continued to sing in the choir.

There was much to talk about while Daddy was with us. We didn't have to return to our schools until Monday, January the sixth, so the eight of us were together most of the time. It could hardly be called a holiday for Daddy, but for the first time ever as minister, he could relax without having to think of church duties. He and I had games of chess together in the afternoons. In the evenings the eight of us sat at the dining room table playing dominos and a brand new game, called 'Monopoly,' which was a Christmas present from Auntie Annie.

As always, the subject came up as to how I was getting along. I was the only 'problem' child in the family because, for some reason or other, I had difficulty in learning and adjusting. This observation by Daddy was nothing new to me. It had been going on now for almost two and a half years. But he had a remedy now which might help part of the problem.

He called me into the study one afternoon for the 'father-son' talk. At least, that was what I felt it was at the time.

"Do you have many friends, Visti?"

"I know a kid name Hans, but I don't like him much. Then there's a kid named Ilias I just met, but that's all."

"How about at school? Do they treat you alright?"

"It's okay."

"I really think you should be more active and meet others. Mom says you spend far too much time in your room."

"That's because I got so much homework an' stuff to do."

"Yes, I know, but you should get out. I suggest that you might go down to the YMCA once or twice a week in the evenings - just for an hour or so. It will give you the opportunity to meet some fine young men your age in a good Christian environment. You realize, Visti, that you are growing. You will soon be sixteen."

I was very much aware of it.

"Someday, Visti," he continued, "you will find that it's time for courtship."

"What's courtship?" It sounded like something from the middle ages in England. Maybe King Arthur stuff.

"It's the choice of selecting a girl for marriage - the time of falling in love."

"Oh."

"Meeting a girl, with marriage in mind might not come about for many years. You must first grow up, Visti. But your interest in girls could happen before then. It is only natural."

"I guess so." I wondered if he could read my thoughts.

"So, I must ask you always to respect girls and endeavour to be kind and polite at all times. Always be a gentleman."

"I will."

"And never, ever look upon a girl with lust in mind. That is evil. Spiritual desire and understanding should be the first foremost attraction, followed by the desire to love and care for the girl you choose to marry. Remember that marriage is a holy ceremony and is a commitment for life. You choose only one girl and only after marriage is the expression of physical love for each other permitted. I am sure you will understand this more clearly as you grow up."

"I guess so."

I really didn't know what this word 'lust' was, except maybe it meant 'loving a girl like crazy.' Also, this matter of 'physical love.' I guess he was referring to a kiss. Well, I saw that kind of stuff in a Tom Mix film, and the cowboy and the pretty girl were definitely not married - and they were not struck by a thunderbolt from heaven or anything like that.

"I am very sorry, Visti, that I have to return to hospital, but I know you will do your part to help Mom."

"Yes, I sure will. I hope you come home real soon. You are getting better, arn't you, Daddy?"

"I would like to think so. We must all pray that all will be well again. Will you promise to do that?"

"Yes."

"And Visti, remember you are the eldest, so you must be a good example to the others."

After the lovely Christmas with all of us together, Daddy, assisted by friends of ours, returned to the hospital in Odense, A few days later, the seven of us visited him there. He had books to read and had started to put photos into our family album. He was also able to write letters. There were flowers on the side table. It all looked peaceful, but there were more radiation treatments ahead and we had no idea when he would get well and leave the hospital for good.

There was no shortage of activity at home. With school, music, homework and the childrens' friends dropping in all the time, the house was like a beehive. Mom always had more than enough to do, holding everything together. Xenia was forever at the piano, if she wasn't resting in her room after an asthma attack. Vita seemed to be invited out to birthday parties almost all the time. Ben was getting himself more and more involved with arithmetic and mathematics. He couldn't get enough of it. Sonya was always out playing with her friends, coming home late for supper, and David spent his time playing with his lead soldiers on the living room floor - his last fling of total freedom before the school grabbed him like the rest of us.

CHAPTER EIGHTEEN

Dear Harold   *December 28, 1935*

Just think, the last time I wrote to you was way back in October. That's a long time ago. I ain't got no excuses fer not writing except that I only write when I take a noshun to, so you got to wait until that happens. Holy Smoke, but have I been a-longing to see you! Just think, Harold,- I've lived here in Dinky Denmark now fer more than two years and not a single dingbusted thing has happened in all that time except piles and piles and piles of homework. That stuff never stops. When will they realize that a guy can only take so much? It's enough to have to go to school from 8:00 in the morning to 2:30 in the afternoon, six days a week, but then they dump all this homework on you - so when I get home at 3:00, all I can do is sit down and ponder over it all, wondering where to start and that takes up most of the afternoon. Then at 6:00 o'clock or somewheres around there I naturally take a bite to eat and then the rest of the evening is spent trying to recover from the awful, bloomin' shock of the thought that my homework is still laying around only half done or maybe less than that, and then - I'm sorry to say, there ain't nothing else to do but play hookey the next day. That's the only way out of the horrible mess, but since that's against the law, there's no hope. Yup, to tell you the truth, Harold, I just hate this kind of life with the whole of my dinky heart - and always will.

Harold, in my last letter I fergot to tell you that we bought a house fer a lot of money - 17200 kroner to be exact. It did cost 25000 kroner but the guy who owned the joint softened up a bit when we put the pressure on. But anyways, we had to pay 2000 raw cash. Remember that it's kroner I'm jaw-waggling about and not smackers. I got a room for myself cause I'm no longer a kid anymore.

Well, dead loads of things have happened recently and most of them are very important things. During the last few days I've decided to save up fer a movie mashine that I saw in a store window which cost 8 kroner. That's about 2 dollars. It's a perfect dandy thing - heavy and strongly made. Here in Denmark you can buy old films and parts of cartoon films fer hardly nothing. I'm planning to buy a monstrous, powerful lot of them and rig up a little show-house here at home just fer the kids in the family. And I've ben a-thinking of building a walloper of a toboggen fer next winter, about 8 or 9 feet long, but of course, it's only a thought yet. But maybe some fine day I'll have my thoughts manufactured into reality.

I'm fifteen and a half years old now and the strongest kid in my class at school. I hain't got no special friend yet and I don't s'pose I ever will. Things of that sort are exactly the same as it was two years ago. Nope, I hain't got no close friend which I can tell my inner most thoughts to, except you, - but I mean here in Dinky Denmark.

I don't see that kid Hans Holm very often because he and his brother only want to go out with gals now. But I just met another kid named Ilia who lives in the place where we used to live. He might be okay. I don't know yet, but he wears breeches and long pants like me and not those sissy-looking knickerbockers that all the other kids wear. My motto is: If it's not American I don't like it.

Ilia's noodle is thatched with a forest of light colored hair and his hands are always where they belong - in his pockets. He ain't a coward and he's kinda strong. He looks exactly like you from the rear, infact many's ben the time since I met him when I called him Harold by mistake. I like him because he doesn't laugh when I make a mistake now and then in Danish and because he likes to hear about the things we did in Junction and all about the Hornibrook gang. He doesn't smoke or swear like all the other kids so that proves he's got alot of sence if he's got any. Ilias and me are pretty good friends but I don't think we'll ever become pards. Anyways, I like him alot more than that brat, Hans Holm who I hardly ever see anymore and when I do, he's nothing but a rotten noosance full of slush, hogwash and humbug.

When I get more grown up, I'm gonna be a film cartoon drawer. I mean a guy who draws films such as Walt Disney does. Of course, I might start out like *a common guy and draw junk for the noospapers in the beginning, but believe me, I certainly am gonna end up to something of a drawer - anyways, that's what I hope. I've ben a-drawing a heck of a lot in this last month. Nearly an average of three hours a day, cause I got so many card orders. In all, I did 200 Christmas cards and earned 20 kroner. This warn't so bad, considering that I'm only a kind of beginner. In the month of October some important shots came to the house and asked me if I would draw a bunch of drawings fer a certain Christmas noospaper. Of course, I told them I would, considering I got decently payed fer them. So I drew them and they were printed in that noospaper and a few weeks ago the papers were dished out here in town by the thousands. Well, now all of a sudden, I've become so blamin,' rotten popular that I can hardly stand up. Even the kids at school and on the street now say "Howdy, Visti" when they see me which is kinda nice. It's also because I'm a good translater in case they want Danish changed to American.*

Well, now I got something to write about, which in a way I don't want to, but since it's you, Harold, that I'm a-scribbling to, I'll do it. But you must promise to keep it a secret forever and ever, cross your heart and hope to die cause I wouldn't want the gang in Junction to know.

It's something which has been my inner most thoughts fer more than a year and nobody has ever known my inner most thoughts. It's about a gal! Yup, to tell the most honest-to-goodness truth, it's about nothing else, but a gal. No it's not about that gal Lisbeth. She was nice because she looked like Shirley Temple and she never teased, squawked, screamed or carried on like other gals do. She thought I was okay and gave me two bits American which I always have in my pocket. But she's left town.

No, this is a different gal. I hardly know how to say it, Harold, but here goes - I've been in love with this gal fer more than a year! I never told nobody. Now I know you have just fallen off your chair, thunderstruck and crushed, wondering how the leader of the Hornibrook gang could betray his forces. I know, Harold, we promised never to have anything to do with gals, but this is different and I am not crazy. I am as clear thinking as ever. The only reason I allowed this to happen is simply that since I can't find a boy to be my pardner in this rotten country like you was in Junction, I've shifted over to a gal. This gal I'm talking about, ain't one of the common sex - I mean them which are so sassy. Oh no, I should say not. This one ain't silly like other gals and one thing I know, she sure suits me.

The very, very, very first time I ever saw her was in November 1934. That was the time I got dumped over to that third school I told you about in one of my former letters. The very first moment I layed my eyes on her, that was it! - I knew I was in love. It didn't take more than thirty-five seconds and I've been in love with her now fer almost one and a half years. She somewheres around fourteen or fifteen years of age and about the same height as I am. She's awfully, awfully good-lookin' and dresses as pretty and neat as salad-dressing. She's got long, curly, dark brown hair, which comes down to the shoulders and she's got dark eyes with long eyelashes, kind of high cheekbones and a good complexion. She goes in the same grade as I do, but not in the same class. I know her well - I mean

I've seen her every single day of the year, except during vacashun, but I've never ever spoken a word to her. I kinda consider her too sacred for that.

I reckon she knows me as well as I do her, because I am popular at school now on account of the guillotines, Christmas cards and noospaper stuff I drawed and also because I'm a good translator from Danish to American, but as far as I can figure out she doesn't care a cent fer me. I mean she doesn't take any more interest in me than any other kid. She's a kind of quiet sort of gal and doesn't talk much. I don't know quite how in the heck, I can get acquainted with her. Loads of times I've thought of buying a present and then sending it to her, but I haven't dared yet. I think if she ever, ever said a single word to me, I would faint immediately.

By the way, I hain't told you her name yet. Well, it's a perfectly beautiful name - probably the most beautiful name in the whole world. Her full name is Ellen Skafte! Doesn't that sound absolutely perfect!? I dream about her all the time - also during school hours and wish the class period would hurry up and end so that I can get just a glance at her when she comes out of her classroom. Every day is the same. I'm not interested in school any more. I just want to dream of her. If I were her and she were me, I certainly would take the chance and ask if she'd marry me, because, Harold I ain't just a common kid. I can talk, read and write two languages and can draw kinda good and I'll be a doggoned hunk of a squashed, rotton lob-sided hamburger if that ain't more than these cockeyed, cussing, cigarette smoking Danish kids can do and I'm a real American and they're scarce in this country. But I gotta remember, that gals don't go much fer talent and wisdom. They go mostly fer looks and sorry to say, that's a thing I lack like thunder.

I ain't quite as gal crazy as you think I am as you read this, cause I wouldn't care a blooming cent if all the rest of the gals in the world were dead, but not Ellen - No-sir-ee. I'd drather die like they do in fairytales than lose her. Jumping flappy doodler, my heart just pounds away when I see her. This is the honest-to-goodness, hunky-dory truth. I know it all sounds loco and I guess you're wondering when all this slushy stuff is gonna stop. Well, when she's mine, I won't bother you no more with details after that, but anyways, darn it all, I hain't got her yet.

I have no idea how to get to know a gal. It was different with that kid Lisbeth because we sat next to each other in school. Can you imagine what it would be like to sit next to Ellen Skafte in school! I bet'cha you'd go right through the roof! I just can't bear the thought of what that would be like. It would be like an electric shock.

Don't cha think in a way it's kinda early to start talking about this stuff? They usually start at about twenty years of age, but anyways, I don't care. I'll just keep it a secret until then. I'm a-lookin' forward to the day, when my house will be occupied (of course, I'll design and build it myself), by me and my future wife - Ellen! I think I said in one of my former letters that I was gonna be a bachelor, but since I might be able to afford to have a wife, I might as well have one. Naturally the house will be speshal and the most modern contrapshun on earth,

with the doors all sliding into the walls by a gentle push of a button, to save space.
Well, I'll be sure to tell you next time I write, if any part of my dream has come
true, and if you have any ideas how to get to know a gal maybe you could rush
a letter to me. I was thinking maybe there might be a clue in one of your Zane Grey
cowboy books.

That brat Hans Holm has a brother who says all you gotta do is walk up to
a gal and say howdy and invite her to a show, but I couldn't do that. I'd rather
sink through the floor because I know I would faint. And what if the gal says no.
It would be the end and the whole world would collapse.

Just think, Harold, you are the only living soul in the whole, rotten world I
have told this to, so please don't regard it as some slush or humbug - and DON'T
tell nobody.

Your friend ferever more. - Visti

The YMCA was downtown on the main shopping street, a quaint, narrow thoroughfare with three-storey buildings all tight together on both sides. It was just a couple of rooms on the second floor above a store across the street from the theater. At least, that's what it looked like, when I was standing in the queue to see the Tom Mix film. YMCA was printed on the second storey windows.

It was with some reluctance that I went down there one dark, windy Saturday evening on my bicycle. But I was told by Mom that Daddy would appreciate if I would give it a try - but that she would like me to be home not later than ten o'clock. I didn't know what to expect as I went up the dark narrow stairs from the street.

An elderly man, sitting in a small office at the top of the stairs, greeted me. I thought of telling him I was here to 'size up the joint' - or maybe as Daddy would have preferred - 'to meet some fine, young men.' Instead, I put it to him plainly,

"My name is Visti. I just happened to be passing by and I thought I would drop in and look around."

"Very good, very good. You are most welcome," the elderly man said, getting up out of his chair, "Here, let me take your coat."

He hung it up on a coat rack and showed me the way into the main room.

"See, we have everything here - a chess table, a piano, ping pong table and over there," he said, pointing with his hand, "are many books in the cabinet for your reading pleasure."

There were other things; a lot of chairs stacked up in one corner, an old sofa against one wall, a horrible looking coffee table with stains all over it and a sign on the back wall saying 'This way to washroom.' Two skinny kids were playing ping pong and a kid who looked retarded and with an awfully big head, was rocking on a chair and staring into space.

"Oh yes, I should introduce you to your new friends. Ole, Peter and Frederick, I would like you to meet - er - what did you say your name was?"

The ping pong game and the rocking chair stopped for a brief moment.

"Visti."

"Oh, yes, Visti. I would like you to meet Visti, who was just passing by."
We all said hello and the ping pong game resumed. Frederick, the one who was retarded, started rocking once more. That was all. The elderly man went back to his small office and I stood there wondering what I should do next. Maybe I should go home. I walked up to the large front windows and gazed down on the cozy well lit street. There was a line-up at the show house across the street. This place was the dumps, I thought. What a way to spend a Saturday evening. It was much better at home where I could do so many things.

As I stood there, leaning against the window frame with ping pong ball sounds in the background, I suddenly experienced a jolt - because right down there on the other side of the narrow street, standing in the queue, was my dream girl, Ellen! I was suddenly wide awake. Was she alone? No, it looked like she was with three other girls. What was the film they were lining up to see? On the billboard it said 'Little Women' with Katharine Hepburn. I watched her every movement - the way she smiled, the way she moved - everything was flawless. Unfortunately, the only things I shared with her were school and the air we breathed.

After about ten minutes during which I experienced total bliss, the queue moved forward and they all disappeared into the theater. Almost immediately, I came up with a sound decision. I must get into that place. With luck, I might get a seat right next to her or close behind her. I walked across the room, grabbed my coat, passed the man sitting at his desk, ran down the stairs, crossed the street and stood at the ticket office window.

"I would like one, please," I said, feeling in my pocket for money. This was the chance of a lifetime - if I could get a seat close to her. What's this? .... No money? I had none! This was a moment of despair. But then I felt the quarter. I always had that in my pocket. I wondered if they would accept American money.

"Here is your ticket," the lady said, "That will be 15 ore."

I hesitated, and it was just long enough to recover from insanity. I couldn't sacrifice the coin Lisbeth gave me. I walked slowly back across the street, grabbed my bike and started to cycle home - thinking of so many things. Then a new brainwave popped up. I suddenly realized that when the show was over, my dream girl would be coming out of the theater. That's when I could see her. I would be casually walking along the street and she would see me and she might just stop and say hello. I made a U-turn and headed back to the YMCA.

"Oh, you are back. I thought you had left for the evening. I should remind you that we close at eleven - but the boys are still here."

The elderly man seemed happy to see me again. The ping pong was still going on and Frederick was still rocking and staring into space. I got a chair from the stack in the corner, placed it at the window and decided to wait right there with an eye on the theater entrance, no matter how long it would be.

At quarter passed ten the phone rang. The elderly man came and said the call was for me. I went with him back to the office and picked up the phone. It was Mom.

"Visti, it is late. Don't you think it's time to come home."

"Yeah, I guess so. Okay, I'll be on my way now."

Darn it all. As I cycled home in the dark, I felt kind of mixed up. I was supposed to do one thing and then I did another and then nothing worked out. Mom had tea ready when I came in the door. She was always about to make tea, or had tea ready or had just finished tea and ready for another cup. That's how you were when you grew up in England. The kids were in bed. It was late.

"Well, Visti dear, you must have really enjoyed yourself since you stayed there so long. Did you meet some fine, young men?"

"Nope, just a couple of skinny kids and another one who looked crazy."

"Oh dear. Well, I won't bother you for details. You look tired. I guess it's bedtime for us all."

Later as I lay in bed, I wondered what 'fine, young men' looked like and if I was such a person.

It was two weeks later that I read in our daily newspaper that a retarded young man, staying at YMCA had committed suicide. It was sad. I never went down to that place again.

Dear Visti   *January 6, 1936*

I don't know much about this conformation stuff you wrote about but I guess when you are a preachers son you gotta go through with it. Nobody in Oregon gets confirmed and they can smoke anyways. I sure liked your letter about the circus you went to. I ain't ever been to a real big circus. The ones that come here might have a horse or two but no panthers. I'm starting to make a radio so my dad and me went down to a store in Eugene where they got all kinds of parts for making radios. I used some of my bean money for parts. We learnt some stuff about radio waves in highschool and thats what got me interested. I also want to make a model of the warship Old Ironsides like what we saw in Portland but thats a lot of work and I dont like work very much. Well I guess things have changed and youre stuck over there. Sure sounds like it.

Truely Yours - Harold

In my spare time, which was almost nonexistent due to homework, I started practising piano daily on my own. Having been saturated with Xenia's classical music over the years, it was time to turn to jazz. Now and then we would hear about the latest tunes. Not having the sheet music, I had to fake it on the piano. After many days of practice, I was able to play 'Dinah' and 'Ain't She Sweet.' Now I knew three tunes, including 'Sweet Sue' - all in the key of C, unfortunately, but at least, the beginning of a new era.

Xenia, however, was not impressed with my piano playing. She said I had the chords all wrong and there was more to life than just the key of C. The tune 'Ain't She Sweet' should be played in the key of E flat to sound right and 'Dinah' should be played in the key of G. But the black notes on the keyboard were still somewhat beyond familiar territory for me, especially since I was playing by ear and faking it. In time things would get better.

Dear Harold,   *February 16, 1936*

Holy Smoke! Wotta Suprise! To tell the honest-to-goodness truth, I thought you was dead. You see, its ben such a dirty, blooming long time since you've written and so of course, you can't really blame me for taking you for a corpse. You don't write nothing about our gang so I wonder what's going on.

This Xmas we didn't have any snow and everybody was so awful sorry about it, but they didn't have to be sorry very long, because a few weeks later the sky suddenly darkened up and the sun plopped down behind a terrible lookin' cloud. Everything became so still and solemn and it got colder and colder.

Well, then all of a sudden, disaster struck! A storm came a-rumbling in from Russia. It sounds kinda everyday-and-common like, but it wasn't. No-sir-ee, you can bet yer boots it wasn't. There was a wind so strong that we had to hang on to things for dear life. It was screeching and a-whistling through telephone wires and through the branches of trees. The windows were rattling and everything was howling, making a marvelous racket. And then it snowed and snowed and snowed. It was worser than a blizzard in Colorado. Of course we didn't go to school that day, nor the next, nor the next. The busses, trains and ferries all got stuck dead in their tracks and our fjord began to freeze. The moat around the castle here in town was already frozen and hundreds of people were skating as if the whole dingozzled works was only gonna last a day.

By and by things got worser and worser. I saw two wallopers of trees ripped up by the roots and laying dead and sound as a log in a big snowdrift - the wind did that! Telephone poles lay around about like nine pins. Windows were smashed and tiles tumbled off the roofs of houses. Lots of damage was done and it was said to have ben 240,000 kroner. That storm wasn't just in Denmark. It was all over Europe and many ships sank in the North Sea.

Say whats the big idea in writing "truly yours" at the end of your letters. That blooming kind of hogwash and milksop certainly does get on a guy's nerves, when you really come to think of it. Hain't we ever ben friends before? Of course we have. So remember that next time. It was interesting to read about your radio and things, but in your next letter, tell me more about life in Junction.

This gal I told you about - well I still don't know how to get to know her. I had hoped you would have told me the best way to start talking to a gal without scaring her away, but you didn't menshun a darn thing. Maybe you didnt get my last letter in time. I know you said once that the girls in Zane Grey books are always in trouble and have to be rescued and maybe thats a good way to get to know a gal cause then she would have to thank you for rescuing her and then you could talk to her some more about taking care of each other.

The only problem here is that I am the one who has got to be rescued before I die from lonesomeness but I dont dare go up to her and tell her that. She would think I was some kind of a nut if I got to be rescued. Imagine if I went up to her and said, "please rescue me." She would think I was crazy. Well, maybe someday I might just go crazy if nothing happens. By the way, her name is Ellen Skafte. I think I menshuned that in my last letter. Ain't that a perfect name.

Your best friend. - Visti

CHAPTER NINETEEN

During the school Easter break, we all went to Odense to see Daddy. Again friends helped us with the transportation. Daddy was very happy to see us and we had much to talk about, but it was apparent he was tired. The good news was that maybe he might be able to return home in a month or two. We all hoped and prayed that this would come about.

In the field of film entertainment, much was coming from America. There were films such as 'A Midsummer Night's Dream' 'Tarzan and the Apes,' 'Les Miserables' and 'Modern Times' with Charlie Chaplin. We saw them all.

Much to our delight, Auntie Annie started sending us piano sheet music from England of up-to-date tunes such as 'Lambeth Walk' and 'I get a Kick out of You'. Xenia started to tackle the original version of Gershwin's 'Rhapsody in Blue.' Apart from the music, I even had my list of favorite film stars - Mickey Rooney, Jackie Cooper, Jane Withers, Joe E. Brown, Wallace Berry and Tom Mix. But other than the American films, sheet music from England, and a little bit of jazz on the radio, there was no entertainment of any sort in Kolding. The two show houses - the one where the floor sloped up and the other where the floor sloped down plus the YMCA place, was about all I could think of.

Ilias,who was aware of my interest in jazz, said that he knew a kid who played drums. Maybe it would be a good idea to start a band. It certainly was. I had never thought of that before. One afternoon, Ilias took me over to this kid's place to meet him. He looked Italian and very much like a professional musician. I told him I could play Sweet Sue and Dinah.

He seemed to be impressed. Then Ilias asked him about the drums. He led us into a backroom and there it was - a huge drum that had 'Kolding Fire Department' printed on it - the kind you carry with straps over your shoulders.

"Is this all you got?" Ilias asked.

"No, my dad has one more. It's at the fire station, because they use it in the parades every week"

We stood in silence, looking at this monstrosity. It was awfully big. How this could do anything for Sweet Sue or Dinah was beyond me.

Dear Harold   *May 24, 1936*

This is an important letter because the day of doom is just ahead and just a month away. I am getting so powerful, doggoned sick and tired of school that even to menshun the word gives me the creeps. I doubt very much if I'll pass the awful exams next month. Music theory, drawing and English are not enough to pull me through. There's only one thing that cheers me up and makes school a little bit easier to look upon and that is the thought of getting to see that walloper of a gal, of whom I scribbled about in my one of my last letters.

Since I'm gonna fail, I've decided to tell them after it's over, that I'm fed up being kicked around and they can all go and jump in a lake and then I'm gonna be a cartoonist like I told you before, because I've noticed that my style of drawing is very slowly, but surely changing to that of the Mickey Mouse type. I've also come to the stage in my drawing where I can draw pictures without having to make a pencil sketch first. Last week I earned around a dollar just selling drawings to kids at school. Another thing that I've started to make money at is little wooden pistols that can fire rubber bands. All the kids want them and I've sold ten so far. I make them in the basement at home and my mom doesn't mind as long as I do my homework - but she says she doesn't think my dad would approve of guns being manufactured in a church minister's house.

Well, now as to the girl of my melancholy thoughts. A couple of weeks ago I went to the show house and saw the film 'David Copperfield.' My mom gave me permishun because she said it was probably a good film. But that wasn't the reason I wanted to see it. No-sir-ee. It was because I knew that Ellen Skafte (don't cha think that is the most perfectly, lovliest name you've ever heard) would be there. I got wind of this, because I heard her talking to her girl friends about it and I knew what night they were going. So I went there and lo and behold, there she was a few rows in front of me, chewing gum. Well, all during the whole film I kept on a-looking at her and devouring her beauty - two solid hours of it! To tell the honest truth, I didn't see any of the film, but she was worth it!

About a week later on a certain Saturday afternoon during the last school period of the day something happened. The gals in both of the eighth grade classes had gymnasium in that period, but Ellen got excused from such rot, because she said to the teacher that she had sprained her arm. So, while the rest of the gals were in another building having gym, she sat alone in her classroom and waited for her gal friends. A kid at school named Bent and me usually hang around school when the gals have gym, because then we can go tearing around in the empty classroom, walking all over the desks as if they were the floor and scribble all over the blackboard and all kinds of things that you can't do when the teachers are there. Well, it happened this time that we galloped into the classroom where Ellen was sitting! There she was - IN PERSON! - her beauty radiating in all directions.

The first thing you know was we got a-talking. I mean this kid Bent and Ellen. I didn't say nothing because I didn't know her and had never, ever said a single word to her. But she knew Bent because they go in the same class at school. I don't reckon I'll squawk any about the details of the jaw-waggling Bent did, except to say that it was about one of Ellen's gal friends who was supposed to have gotten powerfully drunk on New Years eve at a party. He said it was the honest-to-goodness truth and that he got to know all about it from so and so. Well, did that ever make Ellen mad!

She got up and said that it ain't nothing but a big lie and that he should be doggoned ashamed of himself for saying such rot and that if it happened to be the truth she would cut the bond of friendship between herself and her gal friend on the spot. Yup, she said that the whole works was a real disgrace. It was perfectly beautiful to see her like this, all fired up. She has such a marvellous voice. She really scolded that kid Bent and he sure deserved it.

Well, by and by the talk died down and the subject grew stale. All this time I had been a-sitting quietly on a desk in the background, admiring Ellen's looks to my forlorn, broken heart's content but she seemed wholly unconsious of my being in the room. Can you imagine that, Harold? Well I can tell ya, I sure knew SHE was there. I could feel it all over. It was a scary feeling but I sure liked it. Suddenly, out of the clear blue sky, she says .... to me!, "Visti, what did you think of that David Copperfield film?"

I was so nervous and shy that for a moment I wondered if this was the middle of the night and maybe I was dreaming. Just think, Harold, these were the very first words between us - although I had been there almost a year and a half. This was an important moment of my life and I had to say the right thing. I felt as if my brain warn't working and I was about to faint, but I managed to say "I liked it very much."

She said it was the same with her and that she kinda wished she could get hold of the book cause she wanted awfully bad to read it. Well, then Bent starts butting in and says that she'd most likely break down and cry while reading it. Doggone this kid. He spoiled everything. Bent's squawk put a damper on everything and my lovely conversashun with my dream girl died down much to my sorrow. Then Bent left, saying he was going home.

This was it! I was actually ALONE in this room with Ellen Skafte! Never in my wildest dream did I ever, ever, ever think that this was possible in my life time. I didn't know what to do or say. It was scary!

Well, then she asked me if I'd draw something on the blackboard. Of course I said I would and so I got up and drew a two-gun cowboy from the wild west coming out of a saloon door with guns a-blazing, using up the whole blackboard and all my blessed talent. And then she and I got a-talking. I could hardly believe this was happening to me - talking to ELLEN SKAFTE IN PERSON! I was very nervous, Harold. I don't know if you've ever talked to a girl the same size as yourself that you are intrested in. It's a strange, pleasant feeling but it sure makes you nervous. Anyways, I began to tell her about some of our famous gangs we had in America, about you and about Junction City. She seemed awfully intrested - speshally about Junction City and when she looked at me it kinda sent an electrical feeling or something through me.

But, all of a sudden - there was a yell - a gal's voice at that from out in the corridor and Ellen sets up an answering yell and leaves the classroom in an awful hurry, leaving me to talk to the desks and furniture. I sat there alone for awhile and then went home as melancholy as ever. And that night I lay restless in bed, burdened with the awful thought - does she love me or does she not? I pondered over that earthshaking queschun until one-thirty when I think I fell asleep, entering a dismal dreamland as a poor shattered, defeated hero.

I ain't finished yet, so don't get nervous. Say by the way, if you don't take no stock in reading this kind of stuff, just write and say so, but I certainly honest-to-goodness wish you'd say yes because it certainly is a powerful great relief to have somebody to write or talk to about this and to relieve me of it's worrys. It's not slush I'm writing about. It's the real thing.

Well, all that happened about ten days ago now and I ain't had a spoken a word to Ellen since because she doesn't notice me more than anybody else and I am afraid to talk to her. I wonder if I said something to her that she didn't like. I don't know how gals think. Now I noticed she's got a boy friend - something I never knew before! He's much smarter than I am and he's got expensive clothes and knows how to do magic tricks and things which girls like. Well, a couple of days ago I made an important, sorryful discovery. I saw Ellen a-talking to this kid alone in the hall. I kinda past by as if I was unconsious of their being there. Luckily I overheard a line or two of their (most likely) lovetalk. The kid, Kaj by name, said to Ellen at that moment that he'd see her that evening at eight. That got me a-wondering and so I reckoned I'd shadow those two fer a while.

That evening a little before eight I was down in the neighbourhood of Ellen Skafte's place waiting to see what might happen and sure enough, suddenly there came a dark shadow a-gliding up the street and the light from a rusty old lamppost in front of Ellen Skafte's house presently revealed it to be no one else but that kid Kaj. He stopped by the lamppost and whistled a few notes - a signal, I figured out. And so it was, cause a minute or two later out came Ellen wearing a hat and coat (she seems to have at least a half a dozen different coats from what I've noticed). Then she and Kaj went down the street together and of course I follered them at a distance.

Suddenly I got an awful suprise cause I saw them go into the showhouse to see a German film - and Kaj paying for both Ellen and hisself at that. The showhouse is the only place you can go in the evening cause theres nothing else in town. I kinda felt a bit sick and jibbed after that event and felt more melancholy than ever. Well things passed on like this for awhile and I can tell ya, Harold it ain't much fun going around shadowing others in the dark of the night. But then I made another important discovery. I found out that this kid Kaj doesn't love Ellen a blooming bit! Nope, it's her girl-pardner he's so rotten crazy about. Well blow me down, but to tell the honest-to-goodness flappydoodle naked truth, I was powerful glad when I discovered that. So now lately I've ben a-watching Ellen mighty closely to see if she took any special interest in any other boys - and thank goodness, not a one. So maybe I have a chance after all. I'm gonna have to do some careful planning.

Ellen Skafte lives in a big apartment house on the first floor and her father is a shoemaker. Ellen's girlfriend lives on the second floor and she's got a brother my age who I know well. His name is Andrew but he doesn't take much interest in Ellen cause he's got a wolloper of a sweetheart down in Hamburg in Germany and he says they often write long letters to each other. He showed me a photograph of her and I must say, she warn't bad looking. Doggone it all, I certainly wish I had a girl friend. I kinda think that being a preacher's son and an outsider scares girls away. I'm sure there's a reason.

I had started to draw a lot of pictures for Ellen which I was gonna give her someday when maybe I would know her better, but now they're all stuffed in a drawer in my room - forever more. I don't feel good. I hate to ask you this, Harold, but since you are my best friend maybe you know. Tell me, how do ya get a girl

to be intrested when she ain't? That's something I really want to know. I asked
you this before.

I really can't come back to Junction until I have solved this problem. I worry

about it night and day. It's just too bad I gotta
end this letter on a sour note. Actually it's two
sour notes - one is the loss of her - my dream
and hope, and the other is the upcoming dark
cloud of looming disaster that is about to
crash in on me with it's deadly force and blow
everything to smithereens! And that's
SCHOOL! *I almost know for sure that the exams will finish me off for good.*
Your best friend. - Visti

As predicted and as expected, the month of June was my downfall. The exams were a torture from beginning to end. I got an A in drawing, which of course, I expected. In English, History and Geography I got a C. These were Guillotine Gerslund's subjects and I felt she was kind to me. Music was also a C, but all the other subjects - about eight in all, went right down the drain. So when the verdict came, it was no surprise that again I had failed. I was getting so used to failing that the shock no longer bothered me. The only uncomfortable thing about it all was embarrassment. Very quickly, everybody knew about it at school, including Ellen.

That was the hard part. I really wanted to make a good impression at all times as far as Ellen was concerned - hoping, of course, for a breakthrough in our 'relationship.' One brief conversation could hardly be called a relationship - especially when the beautiful creature didn't show the slightest interest, but now with failure in exams I had nothing to show.

The thought that I would have to go through another school year in the same grade was terrible depressing. I would definitely be out of the ballpark as far as Ellen was concerned. Actually I was already, but didn't believe it. I went straight home when the last school day was over. Perhaps there were school parties and celebrations going on somewhere, but I didn't know about them. I wasn't invited nor did I care.

As to be expected, Xenia, Vita, Ben and Sonya all passed, and as usual they and Mom were sorry I didn't make it. But they knew I could do other things, and Mom in particular, was always optimistic. The best news of the day was that Daddy was coming home in a weeks time. It seemed his cancer was in remission. Mom said that she spoke with him on the phone and he said he felt much better. There was even talk that he might resume part of his church work. For the next few days we all found ourselves busy cleaning the house and tidying up, getting ready for his homecoming. Arrangements were made with friends within the church congregation to bring him home from the hospital in Odense. We were all so excited and happy.

The Danish flag, with the white cross on a red field, conveys the feeling of peace, happiness and celebration. This was in contrast to the Star Spangled

Banner, that we pledged allegiance to every morning in Junction City. The American flag stirs up feelings of patriotism, liberty, loyalty and even memories of the Civil War. Somehow a picture of the Star Spangled Banner never looks right unless there is gun smoke in the background. The most natural background for the Danish flag is the blue sky. Always mounted on a white flagpole and always flowing gently in the wind, one can only think of serenity. Almost every villa had a white flagpole. The flag is not only raised for Danish national holidays and the King or Queen's birthday, but also for family events such as birthdays, anniversaries - and homecomings. And so it was with Daddy's return. Unfortunately, we did not have a flagpole or large flag, but in his study window which faced the street, we displayed a smaller flag and I made a sign that said 'Welcome home, Daddy.'

Daddy came home on a Friday afternoon, but being rather tired after the trip, had to go straight to bed. However, the next day things were much better and we were all together at the breakfast table. After the grace and a prayer by Daddy giving thanks for our good fortune, we talked together for over an hour. He did not have too much to tell us, since not much happened in the hospital, but we did, and eventually the subject came around to that of our school and exams - and eventually it came around to my personal misfortune. There was a moment of silence, but happiness and gaiety were quickly restored by Mom, who managed to change the subject.

Daddy spent the next few days resting in the garden and reading books. It was warm and there was sunshine. Friends dropped in to see him all the time and Mom found herself continuously making tea. He frequently had to take a nap and each evening went early to bed. Having visitors was very tiring for him.

A week later, we all attended the Sunday church service, with Daddy sitting with us in the pews. After the sermon by Dean Rosen, and when the minister turns himself into a bulletin board to make all the announcements about birth of babies and upcoming events, Rosen mentioned that Pastor Favrholdt was back among us, for which we were most grateful. This was followed by a prayer of thanks. Many of the congregation greeted him after the service, welcoming him back and we all stood around feeling very good and happy. We had a lot of kind friends. Two weeks later he was back in the church as minister, but only for conducting the weekly church service and baptisms.

The summer vacation was relatively carefree. This year I did not have to spend time at my uncle's farm. I had my friend Ilias to be with now and then, and a couple of times Hans Holm turned up with his special watch. I seriously thought of training for the Olympics in the 100 meter dash and we used the watch for timing my run - which at the moment was 12.5 seconds. Not bad, considering I had to shave off only two seconds to break the record. I still had melancholy periods thinking about Ellen. I knew that it was all over, but the memory of the one episode in the classroom made me feel very good, because I was floating in a dreamy state at the time and it was an experience to remember. The memory would be with me always.

But in the horizon were the dark clouds of another dismal school term ahead. Both Daddy and Mom were aware of my situation and together we had talks as to what alternatives there were. It was a fantastic relief when Daddy suggested that perhaps it was time I learned a trade instead of continuing school. I could hardly believe that this could suddenly come about.

"What do you think you would like to be?" Daddy asked.

"I wanna be a cartoonist and draw Mickey Mouse stuff."

Daddy and Mom looked at each other, thinking deeply.

"I don't really think there is anything in that line around here, and besides I feel we should be looking at a more dignified profession for you - like, er - painting or sculpture."

"I dunno."

"Yes that would be real good, Visti dear," Mom pitched in, "because they both involve drawing, which is your speciality."

"You see, Visti," Daddy said, "we have to think of a profession or trade that will provide you with a living for many years to come. Such a thing as Mickey Mouse is probably a fad that will be gone next year. Never put all your eggs in one basket on a sinking ship."

I didn't quite follow him there.

"There is a sculptor here in town," Mom suggested, "let's see ...... what is his name? .... Oh, yes, I have it now.... Kristoffersen. ..... Gustav Kristoffersen, that's it. Maybe you could make an appointment and take Visti to see him."

"What do you think, Visti? Would sculpture interest you?" Daddy asked.

I didn't have any idea. The only sculptures I knew anything about were the three nude women from the Virgin Islands in our living room and the statue of Jesus at the church.

"I really don't know."

"That's understandable. But I'll tell you what. Let me make an appointment to see Mr. Kristoffersen. You never know, there just might be the chance that he is looking for an apprentice at this time. At the very least, you will be able see what sculpture is all about."

"Okay," I replied, not really knowing what to expect.

Mom spent all week trying to fix up my old confirmation suit, so that I could be presentable when we were to visit Sculptor Mr. Gustav Kristoffersen. Mom said he was quite well known and a very respected citizen in town. She managed to lengthen the pant legs of the suit so that I looked somewhat normal, but the jacket sleeves were a bit short. However, being the born optimist, she said that as long as I stood up straight and did not bend over, I would look all right. I didn't really care about details. The main thing was that, with luck I wouldn't have to go to school anymore - ever.

Mr. Gustav Kristoffersen knew Daddy well, although they had never spoken to each other, because Daddy was also a respected citizen and well known. As soon as my confirmation suit was ready, Daddy arranged for the appointment. He suggested I take a few of my best drawings with me to display my talent. He saw what I had and he said it was fine. So, dressed in my black confirmation suit with a white shirt, blue bow tie, my hair combed, shoes polished and finger nails clean, I was ready to apply for my first job.

We drove to Mr. Kristoffersen's residence by taxi, because Daddy still was unable to walk long distances. The villa looked much like all the other villas on the street - red brick facade and red tile roof. Mr. Kristoffersen greeted us at the door. He was a large, elderly man with a stern appearance and wore a white shop coat. The top of his head was bald, but the back was thick with cascading hair to make up for what wasn't on top. It looked as though it had all slid out of place. Daddy introduced me to him, and bowing, I shook his hand. We were then ushered into his atelier, which was flooded with daylight from the large skylight above. There were plaster of paris molds everywhere, wire and clay sculpture pieces in progress, rolls of sketches and drawings on the table - probably of future masterpieces and shelves on the side wall with finished objects ready for admiration or sale. There were also paintings, with and without frames, brushes in jars and an easel with a half finished canvas showing two seagulls flying up a cliff face.

Daddy and Mr. Kristoffersen started off by talking about the weather and then the conversation switched to his work, which we politely admired. That in turn, made Kristoffersen proud and conceited and put him into our ballpark. Then Daddy brought me into the picture, by saying that I was interested in becoming a sculptor.

"Visti has shown interest in this type of work and I believe he has talent."

"Very good," Kristoffersen said, "it is not often these days to find young people interested in this noble art form."

"My son and I have been discussing sculpture as a possible profession and were wondering if an opening for apprenticeship might come about."

Mr. Kristoffersen looked at me and did some thinking.

"Well, this is not a cut and dry profession like being a bricklayer. I am sure you understand that. There are techniques that can be learned at art school, but unless there is a natural talent to start with, it would not be worth while."

"Oh, I do believe Visti has the talent," Daddy stressed.

"Mind you, there are times when I could use an assistant. That happens quite often, but as I said, there has to be a background of natural talent and also a feeling for this type of artform - almost a dedication."

"Would you like to see samples of my son's work? We have it here."

"That would be fine."

I gave the folder to Daddy. He carefully opened it and presented the first drawing to Kristoffersen, who put it on the easel. It was a picture of Popeye. The three of us looked at it in silence.

"What else do you have?" Kristoffersen asked.

Daddy placed the next drawing on the easel. It was the Portland Rose - the train that took us away from Junction City. Daddy and I stood to one side and waited in anticipation. Again more silence. And then my last drawing - the Hornibrook clubhouse under construction. There wasn't much to say. The artwork was self-explanatory.

Mr. Kristoffersen looked like he was deep in thought. So were we. It was a tough decision for us all. After he finished thinking, he said,

"Perhaps your son should consider another profession. I am afraid this is not inspiring to my particular type of work, but do not be discouraged. I am sure things will work out for you."

He gave me back the drawings and patted me reassuringly on the back. We shook hands, bowed and departed. On the way home Daddy said he was sorry it didn't work out, but I replied, saying that I really wasn't interested in that type of work. All I wanted was to become a Mickey Mouse cartoonist.

"I really don't feel that would be reliable enough," he said, "and where would you find such a job?"

"In America, of course."

"Next week you will be sixteen. You are still young. I think you should learn a trade first and then you can do other things later."

"Well, I don't know what trade I want."

"It should be a trade that you will enjoy. How about carpentry?"

"I dunno."

"It is a respectable trade. As you know, Jesus was a carpenter. I think for a minister's son that would be the very best. There are many fine people who choose that particular trade, because it has biblical significance."

"I guess so."

"Well, Visti, I can look into this, if you wish? I could make enquiries."

"Okay."

It was either this or school. However, sooner or later I was determined to be a Mickey Mouse cartoonist.

Mom made a nice cake with candles for my sixteenth birthday and I received sensible presents such as socks and handkerchiefs. With eight of us all in one house, birthdays were commonplace. We seldom invited anyone to a birthday party at our house, because being so many, we formed our own party.

It was just one week before school was to start, that a local construction firm by the name of Bondesen accepted my application to serve as carpenter apprentice with them for the next five years! A terrible long time. Actually I didn't have anything to do with it. Daddy arranged everything. So to avoid two years of schooling, I would be signing up for five years of carpentry. I didn't know which was the best deal. Of course, school could be more than two years if I continued to fail, so perhaps carpentry was the best.

The hard part in not returning to school,was that I no longer would see Ellen. However, I started to linger near the building where she lived, hoping to catch a glimpse of her. I didn't really know what I intended to do if I did see her. I would certainly be too bashful just to walk up and talk to her without a purpose. She might get suspicious - wondering what the reason was behind it all.

After about three days of this, I suddenly got a good idea. All the drawings I had made for her, which were stuffed in my desk drawer, had been there for months. I would simply walk up to her and say that I just happened to have these drawings laying around and thought she might like to have them. Very simple. No reason to be shy and no reason for her to feel threatened in any way. What would happen after that would be up to her. Hopefully she would say 'I love your drawings, Visti. Do you think there is some place where we can be alone so I can see some more of your drawings?' And then after all that, I would sum up enough courage to ask her to a show.

There were a dozen drawings in all. I put them in a flat envelope so that it would look casual. I would have preferred to give them to her wrapped as a gift, but again it was the question of suspicion. From then on, I spent a considerable time hanging around her place with the envelope in my hand - hoping that she, by chance would appear. So as not to be noticed, I stood down on the street corner about one hundred feet away from the entrance door of the apartment building where she lived. Sometimes it would be for an hour. At other times as much as three hours. Sometimes it would be in the afternoon. At other times it would be in the evening. Finally I gave up.

I figured she must be on a vacation somewhere. So I put the drawings back in the drawer. Mom was glad I had a good summer - visiting my friend Ilias all the time. At least, that is probably what she thought and I didn't want her to think differently. My difficulty in meeting a girl - any girl for that matter, was beginning to bother me very much, but it would always be something I would have to keep to myself.

CHAPTER TWENTY

I cycled into the lumberyard early in the morning. It was dark and windy. There were lights in all the windows of the office building and the carpentry shop at the back of the yard. The noise of machines operating in the shop could be heard over the whole yard and also in the office building, where I had an appointment regarding my apprenticeship. In the corridor, I took off my wooden clogs and placed them along side all the other pairs lined up on the floor. I had been wearing clogs ever since my American shoes wore out. It was standard footwear almost everywhere, and it was customary to remove them when entering a home or office.

After explaining my presence to the office girl at the front desk, I was introduced to the manager - who would be my boss for the next five years. He welcomed me and talked to me for awhile, saying that if I worked hard, I would become a good carpenter and an asset to Bondesen Incorporated. He said there were fifty-two carpenters and six young apprentices in the company and my first assignment would be to work in the machine shop for a year. Following that, I would be working on construction jobs around town. He told me to report to Mr. Christensen in the carpentry shop.

It was a nice feeling to suddenly have a place and purpose in this world, with no more homework - no more arithmetic, no more German, no more French, algebra, physics, chemistry and all the other unpleasant things of school. I was now entering a different world.

The carpentry shop was a terribly noisy place. There were six people working in the shop. One of them saw me and pointed to another - presumably the foreman, Mr. Christensen. I went up to him, bowed and shouted to him. He shouted back, but since we were unable to hear each other, he pointed to the door and we both went outside.

"What is it you want?" he asked, loudly.

"I am the new apprentice. I was told to report to you."

"Apprentice? How come nobody told me about this? I have no use for an apprentice in the shop. You should be on a jobsite."

I stood there feeling uncomfortable.

"Wait here," he said, "I'll check up on this."

Mr. Christensen then went over to the office building and disappeared inside the door. Ten minutes later he returned and said,

"I guess this is the way it will have to be. Well, follow me, but watch your step."

We went into the carpentry shop. Six machines were in operation, making the horrendous noise, spewing out sawdust everywhere. It was all on account of one machine in particular, called the 'planer.' The place was very much alive with fast moving drive belts on overhead wheels and processed wood spewing out of machines. Mr. Christensen led me into a little foreman's office in a corner of the shop and closed the door to cut down on the noise level.

"I really haven't got anything for you to do, but I'll give you a broom and you can sweep sawdust for awhile. We start here at seven in the morning. We have a break from eight-thirty to nine, lunch hour from twelve to one and we finish the day at five. On Saturdays we quit at two. You can start now."

Armed with the broom I thanked him, went out into the shop area and looked around. It was a question as to where to begin. There was sawdust everywhere. Mountains of it. I swept sawdust hour after hour. I lived and breathed sawdust. It never stopped coming. It was completely useless work and the accompanying whiny noise level made my ears ring. Finally after almost drowning in the stuff for a whole week, Mr. Christensen came to my rescue and gave me a 'promotion.' He said I could polish the windows. There were hundreds of small panes, so it was a major project, but like sweeping sawdust, the work was completely unnecessary and a waste of time, because an hour after the windows were cleaned, they were again covered with dust.

At the end of the second week, just as I was beginning to wonder if I had reached the peak of my career, I was assigned a more important job. It was to stand at the receiving end of the planer, take the boards as they came out of the machine and stack them. This job had it all - lots of flying sawdust, an extremely high whiny noise level at close range, and a large clock to tell the time, which just happened to be facing me on the wall behind the planer. It was though the clock hands never moved. Time went so slowly and the work was extremely boring. At the feeding end of the planer was a man facing me, who I was told, had the voice to become a potential opera singer. Although he continuously sang while he worked, I never heard a sound - on account of the planer. Every day was the same - just standing at the planer, looking at the clock, engulfed in sawdust and taking in that high pitched whiny noise that made me feel woozy. The days were long, the work was monotonous and I was tired all the time.

In the evenings during the week, I was always at home. Music, drawing and to be with the family was a comfortable state of affairs. But beneath it all, I was becoming increasingly desperate to get to know a girl. I had completely given up on Ellen, realizing I was no match for those brazen, smart aleck boys she was with every day. Being stuck in a noisy carpentry shop, didn't offer much hope and by the time I came home in the evenings, washed, changed clothes and had supper, there were only three hours until it was time to go to bed and sleep for the next day's ordeal. The idea of perhaps going out in the evening and maybe meeting a girl was so farfetched and remote, that I just couldn't imagine how it might happen. I wouldn't know where to go.

It was a short time later that Daddy took ill again and had to discontinue his work. He felt very tired. He rested at home for a few days, but then was advised by our doctor that he should be in hospital. It seemed that the cancer had returned. Again he was taken to Odense for radiation treatments and nursing care. We at home felt very sad. From then on, many of our daily activities were done without enthusiasm, or curtailed altogether. The kids didn't bring their friends in, as they otherwise did every day after school. I think we realized that this time he might not get well again.

After two weeks in the hospital, he was escorted home and placed in the study where we had arranged a bed for him. We were told by the hospital that his cancer was spreading and unfortunately, there was no more that could be done at this advanced stage - so it was best that he be with his family. Daddy slept a lot and the doctor came almost every day. There were periods, when everything appeared quite normal and we could all cheerfully talk together, but they did not last. Mom spent all her time with him.

It was after supper one evening, Mom told me that Daddy wanted me to come to his bedside. He looked thin and very tired. He told me that he was leaving us now and was sorry he could not stay. He said that he wanted me always to be good, helpful and understanding, supporting Mom as much as I could - and always be a good example to the rest of the children. He then blessed me just the way he did every night. I felt very sad and couldn't believe this was really happening. When I came out I told Xenia that Daddy would like to see her. Then the others went in by turn. We all felt the end was near.

The next day I stayed home from work to be with Mom and Daddy. It was in the afternoon that Mom came out in the backyard where I happened to be, and with tears in her eyes, said that Daddy was dying. We both rushed into the study and I could see that Daddy was sweating and delirious, unable to grasp what was going on. Mom immediately called the doctor, while I fanned his face, using a newspaper, in an attempt to cool him off. The doctor arrived an hour later, gave him an injection, but said there was little else he could do.

During the evening, Daddy quieted down and seemed to be resting comfortably. Mom suggested we all go to bed, as there was not any more we could do at the moment. It was a long time before I fell asleep. The next morning as we were getting up to start a new day, Mom told us that Daddy had died during the night.

The funeral, held at our church, had a very large attendance. There was no doubt my father was well liked - not just for his sermons, but also because he was very dedicated to his church work and the needs of the congregation. The fact he had been a Danish church minister abroad and had written books and articles about Danish immigrant life in North America, further enhanced his popularity. However, it seemed to me at the time that another reason for the large attendance was out of sympathy for the pastor's wife and her six children, who now were without a breadwinner.

At the church service, held by Dean Rosen, we all seven sat in the front row - side by side according to age - as we always did. All our relatives sat with us. There were many wreaths and flower arrangements surrounding the coffin, which was on display in front of the altar. Mr. Rosen praised Pastor Favrholdt as a kind person, for his work and for his dedicated, but unfortunately short service at the church. He said that he, as well as the congregation, friends and acquaintances would always remember Pastor Favrholdt and the few years they were able to share with him. It was very comforting.

After the emotional church service, the coffin was carried out by the pall bearers to the waiting flower-decorated black wagon at the side entrance to the church. It was raining lightly. We all took our positions in the procession for the long walk to the cemetery with Dean Rosen leading the way, followed by the horse-drawn wagon with the coffin. The seven of us and our relatives walked behind the wagon and behind us, the congregation and other friends. I noticed that many wore black armbands as we did ourselves. As the procession slowly moved through the streets under a sea of black umbrellas, the sound of the church bells filled the air. Onlookers on the sidewalks stood in silence as we passed by. At the cemetery the burial service was very emotional and a most difficult moment for all of us. Mom stood up to it all very well, but the sadness we felt was overwhelming. We had always been together - the eight of us.

I really don't know how we got through the next few days. We were all so sad and concerned. We endeavoured to help Mom with everything we could possibly think of. She quickly accepted the fact that Daddy was gone and that we must manage on our own. Friends dropped in to comfort her, there were many encouraging phone calls and she received letters of condolence. In less than two weeks she was her old self again - at least on the surface. But it became apparent that financially things could have been better.

The duration of Daddy's service with the church was not sufficient to qualify for a certain level of pension income. Mom now received only one third of Daddy's income, which in turn made it very difficult for her to make ends meet. But following the funeral, a collection was made within the congregation and the money, for which we were extremely grateful, went to make mortgage payments and also pay a number of accumulated bills.

Without Daddy, Christmas was not the same. We missed him very much. Also, all the religious details that were so much part of our daily life, were not there. There was no special grace at the table, no blessings in the evenings, no special Christmas prayers. He had led us in all these things. It was a quiet Christmas. All the presents from Auntie Annie and the dozens of Christmas cards we received from our family, relatives and friends made us very happy. Auntie Annie was a very strong support for us in many ways.

During those winter months we felt very lonely without Daddy. Knowing that he was not with us made us draw closer together. Perhaps we felt more vulnerable - not having the captain of the ship and our breadwinner. For a while Mom would be able to manage with the money that was given to us following the funeral, but eventually things would become more difficult. It was fortunate I was a carpenter apprentice. I received a weekly wage of twelve kroner. This was about a fifth of the normal carpenters' wages, but it was a help for Mom to have this every week.

That January we bought a radio. This was a very extravagant thing to do in light of our poverty, but Mom felt that it would cheer us up and provide us with a world of music. It was the first time we ever had one and we all just about went nuts over it. The kids would quarrel as to who should control the dials and what we should hear. It got so bad that Mom decided that we each would be allowed thirty minutes a day to sit at the radio and it would go by turn. I did my best, flickering across the scale, to find jazz, but it was mostly classical music. There seemed to be only two stations. Vita complained that when her turn came around, all she could get was Hitler - a madman, whose ranting speeches from next-door Germany, dominated the air waves. And Xenia seemed to be stuck with weather reports, so Mom had to reorganize it all.

Dear Harold   *February 12, 1937*
It's amazing how time flies. This year I'll be seventeen. I can't remember when I wrote to you last, but it must have been an awful long time ago. And how come you never write, Harold? I wonder if you've left town.

Well, things are a little different here than they used to be. My dad died a few months ago of cancer and he was only in his forties. For a long time we didn't feel good about it all, but I reckon things will get better. Our Auntie Annie in England has really helped us out, because we are still sort of poor. Do you remember what I told you about having a rich aunt. Well, this year it sure was good she was there.

You just won't believe this, Harold, but I don't go to school anymore which means in simple language - no more homework, ever! You're probably sitting there scratching your noodle and pondering, wondering how in blooming tar nation did he manage that and I don't blame you, because it wasn't easy. Last summer my dad and me figured that if the school wasn't gonna give me decent marks like all the other kids, then they could go and jump in a lake as far as we were concerned. The last school exam was a disaster. I figure it was rigged. One thing for sure, it was the final straw. Well, what happened after that, was that my dad wanted me to be a sculptor. That's a guy who makes statues. I don't think there ever was such a nut in Junction City who did that stuff. Well, the guy we went to for a job didn't like my kind of drawings so that didn't work out. I had a drawing of Popeye to show him, but he warn't intrested in making statues of Popeye. Over here they make statues of nude women - mostly from the Virgin Islands.

But then my dad got me a job as a carpenter apprentice which is a tough job and gonna take five years, so I'll be awful old by the time I'm finished. I just don't know when I'm ever gonna get back to Junction, with stuff coming in the way all the time, hindering my glorious return. I still dream about it all but it's like the dream is further away now. I'll never get used to Denmark. It will always be a foreign country to me, but I'm sort of stuck here. Also because I gotta help support my mom. The money I get as a carpenter apprentice is supposed to be used for buying carpenter tools but we need it at home. Right now I am borrowing tools from another guy on the job.

Well, this carpenter job is not for sissies. No-sir-ee. You gotta be tough! I was stuck in a machine shop for a heck of a long time and you wouldn't believe the racket and sawdust in that place. I thought it would never end. Now they got me working out in the yard just for a short while to help the carpenters chisel holes in heavy timbers they're gonna use on a building. This would be okay if it were summertime and nice and warm, but it's icy cold and freezing with snow and the wind that never stops blowing. I'm wrapped up in heavy winter clothes, scarf, knitted cap, earmuffs, mittens and thick socks and wooden shoes and I still feel like an iceberg. That's because I sit perfectly still hour after hour on the timbers, chisling holes in darkness with the icy wind blowing in from Russia. All the bad stuff comes from there. And this darkness is something else. I gotta be at work at seven in the morning and sit on those timbers covered with snow and ice in the yard till it's night time. My nose drips all the time and my breath is like white clouds. It doesn't get light until ten o'clock in the morning and then in the afternoon it gets dark at two o'clock. Every day is like this. It's a torture! Now I can hardly wait to get back in the warm carpentry shop.

Maybe someday it will be different, because I've noticed that next door to where we live is a guy who looks just like Wallace Berry and who works at a drawing board in his house. When I pass by his house feeling miserable, wet and cold and pushing my bicycle through the snow in the dark, I see the light shining through his window and he looks nice and warm in there making drawings. My mom says he's an architect. He's even got a motorcycle.

So I've decided that's what I want to be when I've finished with carpentry. It just so happens here in Denmark that if you want to become an architect you got to finish an apprenticeship first, in carpentry or as a bricklayer. I might as well go for the best, because I've figured out that even when I finish being an apprentice and become a carpenter I would still have to work out in the cold, snow and rain, so it's better to study to be an architect. Besides, they earn more dough. I always feel so tired and dirty. The only good thing right now is, that I have been given the job to go around on my bike to all the construction sites on Fridays with paycheck envelopes for the carpenters and that makes me feel important and keeps me warm. But that's the only good thing I can think of.

Another reason why I want to get out of this kind of work is because I never see a girl. There arn't any in the lumberyard or in the carpentry shop or at the construction sites - except one. That's a job we got down near the harbor. There's a girl, not bad looking who always seem to be hanging around the construction gate down there when I come around with the paychecks. I reckon she's just waiting for her husband to come out.

Well, one Friday she came up and said something to me that I just couldn't figure out at all. The foreman noticed her talking to me and later told me to stay away from her because she had something. I didn't really get what he said. It wasn't chicken pox or scarlet fever. It sounded more like prostitood. I've never heard of that before. It must be a Danish sickness or something. Oh, well, not to worry, because now I use the back construction gate when I see her hanging around. I don't want to catch anything.

All the rest of the kids are okay and they never think of Junction City anymore. Either does my mom. I got tired of looking at my Star Spangled Banner at half mast so pulled it up to the top of the pole. It's because now it will be five years before I will be able to get back to Junction on account of me being an apprentice. So I thought it was an insult to the American flag to have it flying at half mast for five years. And the money that was in the cookie jar is gone I am sorry to say. I gave it to my mom. But don't you worry, Harold, when I become an architect some day, I'll have piles of dough and then I'll return and look up the old places and see all you guys - so meanwhile just be patient.

Your best friend. Visti.

Nothing much happened until the month of May. Every day was the same. The kids had their school and homework, and I spent life in the carpentry shop. But it was then that Mom, who must have been concerned that her growing son had never met a girl, decided to do something about it. After all, in a couple of months I would be seventeen. So, one evening she said,

"Visti, I think you should take dancing lessons."

"What for?" I asked, completely surprised.

"It would do you good, you know. You would meet others and it is proper for a young man to learn dancing."

Immediately I figured out that although dancing wasn't something I was exactly crazy about, maybe this just might be the place to meet a girl. So, both she and I had the same idea, but we kept our thoughts to ourselves.

She made the preliminary enquiry and I followed up with making the appointment for six lessons, the first being a Thursday evening. This possible breakthrough occupied most of my thoughts right up to the important day. I had visions of the most beautiful girl waiting for me at the dance studio. And to actually dance with a girl where you have to hold her in your arms - well, that would be like going to heaven. This would be the very first time and I wondered if I would faint or something.

I never could figure out why it had to rain on days of utmost importance. The only way I could get to the dance studio, was to ride my bike and it was pouring down. I had spent considerable time polishing my shoes, because looking at each others' feet would undoubtedly be a vital part of ballroom dancing instruction. Also, in preparation for this occasion, I got a haircut, scrubbed my fingernails and wore a clean sweater. My friend Ilias had once told me that girls fall for guys in sweaters. I had never noticed that, but it was worth a try.

Like all other important businesses, the dance studio was located down town above a store, just like the YMCA. I arrived there feeling like a drowned rat. Shaking the rain off my umbrella, I was greeted at the top of the stairs by a lady who looked like a dance instructor. She remarked about the bad weather - all this rain. It was keeping people away, she said. I took off my dripping raincoat and tried to make myself look presentable. There were supposed to be fourteen here tonight, she said, but so far only five had arrived. I really didn't feel too good, because there was water in my shoes.

She led the way into a nice, well-lit room with a parquet floor and mirrors along the far wall. Chairs were along the nearest wall and two couples were sitting there, waiting for the class to begin. The instructor introduced me to them. The one couple was middle-aged and looked very much like husband and wife. The other couple was younger. Whether they were married or not, was hard to see. I sat down, a couple of chairs away from them, feeling very out of place. This wasn't exactly what I had envisioned. The five of us stared at our images in the mirror on the opposite wall - and waited.

The dance instructor went out to check if any others were about to arrive. Seeing no one, she returned and told us we might as well start, because it looked like the rain had kept the others at home. So she asked us to get up and come out to the middle of the room. We would start with the basic steps of the foxtrot. She went over to the gramophone player and was about to put a record on, when we heard someone coming up the stairs. The instructor went out to check. Then I heard a lady's voice say,

"What terrible weather we have tonight" and the instructor replied,

"Yes, isn't it awful. Here, let me help you with your coat."

Somehow, somewhere I had heard that voice before - especially the word 'terrible.' It was said in a dramatic way. Strange. Well, it wasn't strange very long, because in walked Miss Gertie Gerslund!

She was surprised to see me and needless to say, I was shocked.

"Hello, Visti," she exclaimed. "Imagine meeting you here! I haven't seen you for a long time." Then, turning to the dance instructor, she said,

"Visti was one of my students last year. He is such a clever artist."

They both looked at me admiringly. Gertie continued,

"I really expected you back this school term. What school do you go to now, if I may ask?"

"I don't go to any school," I replied. "I'm a carpenter apprentice."

"Well, well, that is a change."

The dance instructor decided to bring the class to order. Leading us out to the middle of the floor, she said,

"I am happy you two know each other. Now that we are three pairs we should begin. I suggest we start with the foxtrot and after that we will learn the quickstep."

She went to the gramophone and put a record on. I could hardly believe the crisis I suddenly found myself in. Dancing with a school teacher! And with someone so unthinkable as Guillotine Gerslund - who was old enough to be my mother!

"Now I want you all to start with your feet together, then take one side step sideways and then bring the other foot in ..... Visti, please hold your partner. Are we ready?"

There was only one way to get out of this confrontation and that was to fake sudden violent stomach cramps and crumple to the floor. Actually, looking at her almost made me feel that way. Feeling dazed, I put one arm around her waist and held her hand with the other - the way the others were doing. The music had lyrics like 'I'm in Heaven' and 'Dancing Cheek to Cheek.' Fortunately, there was no way of dancing cheek to cheek - on account of her large bust which was an obstruction in more ways than one. It was good for keeping my distance, but prevented me from seeing my feet. So I just shuffled around to the music.

How I got through the evening, I'll never know. Gertie Gerslund actually led me around on the floor, which was understandable, considering she had more bulk and I was only a lightweight. It would have been hard for me to steer such a large ship. She also knew the dance steps. I almost felt like her school pupil again. As a growing boy, there were times in my sleep when I experienced nightmares, but I would toss and turn and that would wake me up - thus escaping disaster. Well, here I had the nightmare, the tossing and turning and the disaster - but I was wide awake! I could hardly wait for the evening to come to an end.

As I cycled back home in the dark, I decided that dancing lessons were over as far as I was concerned. If I wanted to learn dancing, I could get it out of a book. I wondered what brought Gertie Gerslund to that place. Could it be that she, like myself, attended the class primarily in search of a companion?

When I attended her school, it was generally known that she was a spinster. In terms of today, she would be called a career woman. But at that time, being a spinster was recognized as someone who didn't make it - a women who failed to get married. Of course, it could be because she wore glasses. Girls who wore glasses, only had a slim chance of ever getting married.

When I arrived home, I told Mom about my 'initiation' into dancing school, stating that I had no desire to continue. She was sorry it didn't work out, but agreed with me that perhaps there were better places I could spend my time. I couldn't think of any.

On weekend afternoons, I would go for solitary walks in the woods, a place called 'Marielund' on the edge of town. It was dense with trees and there were trails that circled a small pond with ducks and swans. The occasional benches along the trails suggested a park-like environment, but other than that, nature had free rein.

Although I knew a few boys now, I still couldn't find a girl. It was becoming something that was constantly on my mind. But I had a lot of imagination and the walks in the woods allowed me to dream about girls - about what it would be like, if right now I was walking with one. We would walk side by side and I would tell her how pretty she was and about Junction City. And the walk would be a long one - maybe two hours or more. And hopefully, if she was tired, we could sit together on a bench. I had visions of what this special girl would look like. She would definitely have dark hair and brown eyes and would be the same height as me. She would be slim and wear the prettiest dresses and she would be happy all the time. And she would be very beautiful and only interested in me - and we might hold hands.

I found that, walking along the trails and going through the scenario of the romantic walk with the imaginary girl of my dreams, I actually felt a little better when I returned home. It was as though I had experienced something. It was also my secret. However, someday it would be for real, because I decided that sooner or later I would take the plunge. Somewhere on the street, I would select a girl that I liked, simply walk up to her and say, 'May I be your friend?' The only reason it had not happened yet was because it took a lot of courage.

Also, it was a question of what the first words should be. Perhaps I should say 'Let's be friends' - or I could say 'My name is Visti. What's yours?' or perhaps 'I like you. Do you like me?' A casual remark about the weather might be another way to get to know a girl - or maybe I should just walk up to a girl and say 'I would very much like to tell you something about Junction City.' There was enough to think about.

There were also other things to think about - such as my future. My plan to become an architect would cost a fortune. Where would the money come from to study? Who would I marry? Where would I live? Would I have a family? Although I was only seventeen, I knew that some day things would be different. Being the eldest, I would probably be the first one to leave home.

Hans Holm's brother, Jens, had already left home. He rented a basement room in the house just across the street from us. But he was a banker's son. They had lots of money. I most likely would have to stay home for many years, to help support the family with my carpenter apprentice wages and selling drawings.

This matter of someday having a family - well, that was a mystery to me. It looked like some women got children and some did not. I couldn't figure out how that was. Maybe if a man wanted a wife to give him children, he looked for certain traits in the history of her family. If the grandparents and great grandparents had large families, chances would be that his wife might end up giving birth to quite a few children. It was like apple trees. Some trees gave lots of apples. Some did not. However, I wasn't entirely convinced that I was right, so one day

I decided to ask Mom. It was the shortest conversation we ever had together.

"Mom, can you tell me where babies come from?"

"Don't worry, Visti, you'll find out."

I got the impression that for some reason or other she didn't want to talk about it, so I dropped the matter. A few days later I did figure it out. It happened when a man kissed a woman after they were married. A germ or something from the kiss probably ended up in her stomach and then she got fatter and fatter until, lo and behold, a child was born. Having solved that problem, I didn't concern myself anymore about the matter.

The day finally came when I no longer had to work in the carpentry shop or in the lumberyard. I found it remarkable that I hadn't suffocated from sawdust or become completely deaf during that year. My first field job was to help a carpenter build a new roof over an entrance door to a house.

It wasn't long before I noticed a very pretty girl who, on Thursday and Friday afternoons passed by on the other side of the street. She was pushing a baby buggy and went into a portal entrance of a building where there were stores. After about twenty minutes she came out and walked away, pushing the buggy. I presumed she was caring for someone's child and out for a walk.

We were only on the job a week, but that was long enough for me to again fall in love. Saturday afternoon we quit work early and so I hastened home, washed myself, changed clothes, rushed back downtown to our work location and waited. I figured chances were good that she again would be there. Sure enough, almost right on time she appeared, pushing the buggy. As before, she went through the portal entrance and disappeared from my view. I planned to introduce myself to her when she came out. In my thoughts I had rehearsed the details, time and again. I knew exactly what I was going to say to her. It was important to get it right.

My plan was simply to walk up to her - as if I was passing by and then at that very moment, slow down a wee bit and say very casually, looking at the baby, 'That's a pretty baby you have there.' She would agree and then a moment later I would say, 'Oh, by the way, my name is Visti. Can we be friends?' She would say yes and tell me her name - and who knows, one thing could lead to another and maybe by sundown we might even be holding hands.

The big moment wasn't long in coming. She reappeared in the portal opening and proceeded to walk down the street. I immediately followed her, making sure everything looked casual, and keeping my distance. She had already walked two blocks before I entered, what I considered to be the danger zone. That was anything less than fifty feet. I knew that once I was within the danger zone, I was committed. I could feel butterflies in my stomach and something similar to stage fright. Feeling extremely nervous, I was now along side of the buggy ready to utter the well rehearsed words - when at that instant, I saw bags of groceries in the buggy - but no baby! She turned her head and looked at me. Completely confused, I blurted out,

"Excuse me, could you tell me the way to the post office?"

When I told Ilias about this unfortunate episode, he laughed and said, "Gee, I didn't know you were that desperate. Why don't you go for a walk with my sister?"

"Is she pretty?"

"She's okay. Do you want me to set it up for you?"

"How are you going to do that?"

"I'll just ask her if she wants to go for a walk with a friend of mine."

"Okay"

This might just be the breakthrough I was looking for. No longer would I have to rely on hopes and dreams. This would be the real thing - planned and expected by both sides. In other words, a date with a girl.

Two days later, Ilias said that his sister agreed to go for a short walk with me. Would Wednesday evening be okay? I told him any time of day or night was okay. I could hardly imagine a situation where a girl would actually respond to an invitation of mine. For the next few days leading up to the Wednesday, I could hardly think of anything else. I would take her to the woods, where I so frequently walked alone and we would walk around the pond, just as I had imagined and dreamed about so often - and then who knows, we might sit down on a bench together, real close. All the things that were just fantasy were about to come true. I could hardly believe it. It was as though doors were being opened and sunshine was coming in. I had never felt so good before.

Wednesday evening, promptly at seven-thirty, I was at Ilias's house. Ten minutes later he came down the front steps with his sister and introduced us. She wasn't quite what I expected. I had envisioned a raving beauty with flowing hair, descending the front steps and who, merely by breathing, created an aura of romantic bliss and sensuality all around. This girl was shaped like a barrel and seemed to have the hiccups. Ilias introduced her as Erna. I asked her if she would like to go for a walk. It was a silly request, because she knew that beforehand. She said yes. Would a walk in the woods be okay? Maybe, she replied. I assured her there would be no problem in the woods, because it didn't get dark until ten o'clock and I knew all the trails.

As we walked down the street, I could feel that she was very much on the defensive. We seemed to be walking about two feet apart all the way. The beech trees in the woods were turning yellow. Autumn had arrived. The evening breeze sprinkled leaves along the trails, creating a perfect carpet for a romantic stroll. I told her about things I did - about my work, my drawings, the music; and then I switched to the topic to what was supposed to make girls melt - Junction City. However, after ten minutes of this, I got the feeling that it didn't work.

We came to the pond and looked at the ducks and swans for awhile. I then suggested that perhaps we could go on a trail deeper into the woods, but she said she would rather just walk around the pond. I could feel she didn't want to take chances. Did she really think we would get lost? She didn't talk very much and still kept her distance of two feet. We came to a bench. I asked her if she would like to sit down for awhile. She said no. So we continued walking. I was running dry of things to talk about and she didn't bring up any topics. This was not quite the way I envisioned things to be. She seemed a bit more relaxed when we left the woods and were again on city streets. I found that strange, because the woods never bothered me or anyone else I had seen walking there. Arriving at her house, she thanked me for the walk and I did likewise, and that was it. No fluttering of hearts.

On the way home, I began to realize that I was forever living in a fantasy world, believing that girls would be responsive and interested in me. This girl, Erna didn't make my day and she probably thought the same about me. It was probably my accent. My Danish was now pretty good, but one could hear I was a 'foreigner.' And then the 'preacher son problem.' That seemed to scare everybody. Only Lisbeth was an exception, but that was because Lisbeth was a child. Children don't concern themselves with details. I couldn't understand why I allowed myself to get so fired up over girls and go to so much trouble, when the chance of winning was so remote.

The final straw came the next day, when I met Jens Holm on the street. He said, if I noticed him sneaking girls into his basement room, not to tell anybody. Just keep it to myself. His success with girls was in sharp contrast to my feeble effort and the emptiness I felt so often.

Yes, through my basement room window, I did see him take girls to his room on the other side of our street now and then. All this girl stuff was becoming too complicated. I decided to totally forget girls for awhile, since it only resulted in unhappiness and melancholy thoughts. From now on, I would try to concentrate on my drawings and music.

The following week I was told to report to a new construction site. It turned out to be the Latin School - the very school that used to be my daily nightmare. The project here involved adding a copper clad tower to the roof of the school and installing a new floor in the gymnasium. It was a strange feeling to see the place again from the inside. From the roof location, I could look down and see the schoolyard where I used to be subject to humiliation by the hundreds of kids milling around during recess. I clearly remembered the embarrassment I had to endure when lining up for class. And then there was 'Mad' Mikkelsen, the horrible arithmetic teacher - probably now preparing for a new class of unsuspecting victims. I wondered how he was standing up to the stress of it all.

The carpenter crew I worked with, plus other tradesmen on the job, were a rough bunch. One of my assignments was to go to a nearby grocery store each morning and buy beer for them. Drinking on the job was normal and they each drank about three bottles a day. Coarse language and almost continuous swearing went on all the time. During lunch breaks, the talk and things I heard, quickly made me realize that I had been living a very sheltered life.

There were only three subjects: women, beer and sex and they all seemed to flow together. In less than three working days, I knew what my parents were unable to tell me. Not only did I suddenly know where babies came from, which in itself was a shock to me when I first heard it, but I also got to know lots of details. Fortunately, I was able to conceal my ignorance by giving the impression that I was the quiet type. But listening to the crude jokes and raunchy conversations on the job, I felt somewhat embarrassed and somewhat out of place - especially when they jestingly dragged me into their conversations, asking me questions about my sexual exploits. When I expressed reluctance in talking about it, jokes were made in my presence, implying that my silence was just a cover-up, because usually preachers' sons were the worst of them all. This created a lot of laughter.

The first few evenings, as I cycled home from work, my thoughts were somewhat confused. Understanding my sexual feelings and purpose certainly seemed to be a little more in focus. Ever since I was fourteen I had felt sexually frustrated, but it wasn't until I was over sixteen that, apart from romantic feelings, I began to feel a physical attraction to girls as well. And now, after starting this job at Latin school I understood how everything came together. However, this didn't quite harmonize with the information and advise from Daddy, who condemned lust and said that my first interest in a girl should be spiritual, followed by love with marriage. The way these carpenters were carrying on, girls were for the good times and you could have fun being with them, without having to be spiritual in any way. Now I also understood what Jens Holm was up to. I had a lot of thinking to do.

A couple of days later, our work location at the school shifted to the gymnasium, where we were to install the new floor. It was here I noticed the girl who had, what I thought was the Danish sickness. She was one of the prostitutes, who hung around construction sites. By now, I knew quite well what services they provided. This particular girl appeared with another girl at our site during late afternoons when the day was over, and often, both of them went with construction workers into the gym dressing room. They would send me to the grocery store to get beer for the sex parties they had in the dressing room after work, and a number of times I was asked to stand guard at a nearby stairwell, while the hanky panky was going on. As an apprentice I did not have much say, even although it didn't have much to do with carpentry.

When I came home after work I didn't feel right. I had to explain to Mom that the reason I was late, was on account of overtime on the job. I had the feeling I was becoming slightly jaded and that I was part of an underground activity. I was sure Daddy had been misled, when he said that carpentry, as a trade, had biblical significance.

After two weeks of floor laying plus the hanky panky overtime, I was transferred to another job site, making wooden forms for concrete foundations. Since there was no building on the new site, there was no hanky panky stuff going on. It was also a different work crew made up of older men who, during lunch breaks talked only about politics and mortgages. I didn't understand much of either subject. Their discussions were really boring and in sharp contrast to that of the previous job.

It was amazing how much I learned during those two weeks at the Latin School - not only how to lay gymnasium floors, but about life in general. It was certainly a lot more than those classroom nightmares of the past.

CHAPTER TWENTY-ONE

With a lot of good jazz music coming from the United States on radio and in films, a number of Danish bands appeared on the scene, but they were in Copenhagen. I had become fairly good on the piano and thought of starting a band. I knew six tunes. With great difficulty, I was able to play a new brand new tune called 'A Fine Romance,' but others went well, such as 'Tea for Two' and 'Some of these Days.'

Through Ilias, I happened to meet a bass player named Erik. He worked downtown in a basement helping a man repair typewriters. Actually he had never played a bass, but he said he knew all about it. There was reason to believe he was right, because he could make bass sounds with his mouth - almost like the real thing. I told him about my idea of starting a band. He thought that was great. In fact, he even knew a kid who played the sax. I contacted the kid who had a drum from the Kolding Fire Department. Yes, he was also interested and he now had a snare drum - just the thing for brushwork.

A couple of days later, I met the sax player. He wore a long jacket with big outside pockets, pants with narrow legs and big cuffs, shoes with thick soles and a felt hat like one of the Al Capone gang. This was considered the latest fashion if you were with it in the new world of improvised jazz. He played a mean sax and constantly reminded everybody in English that *It don't mean a thing if you ain't got that swing.* His name was Preben.

With this talented group, I got Mom's permission to have practice sessions on Saturday afternoons at our house. Xenia and Vita also liked the idea. Vita, in particular, was enthusiastic, because she liked to sing. She had a pleasant, soft voice and liked to sing 'In my Solitude.' Hopefully the band would some day support her in this effort.

During the winter our musical careers came into focus. We now had a rhythm guitar player by the name of Henrik, instead of the drummer. This change came about, because the big drum had to be returned to the fire department and in the process, the drummer gave up his musical career.

Convinced that we were talented musicians, we felt it was time to let the world know about it. For months we had practised and now had a repertoire of eight tunes. I decided to call our group 'Visti's Swing Band.' It was deplorable music, but being very naive at the time, we were overwhelmed with our potential.

We decided to hold a concert. Xenia would appear as a piano soloist and play the original piano score of Gershwin's 'Rhapsody in Blue' - 28 pages in all. Vita, who now could sing dreamy ballads flawlessly, would be featured with the band. Her numbers would be 'In my Solitude' and 'Stormy Weather.' The band, being piano, tenor sax, bass and rhythm guitar, apart from accompanying Vita, would play 'Mood Indigo,' 'Sweet Sue' and 'Darktown Strutter's Ball.' If there was a likelihood of an encore we would repeat 'Stormy Weather.'

The location selected for this major event, was the small ballroom at Hotel Kolding - a classy place. The owner of the town's only music store supported us in our efforts and made the arrangements, not only with the hotel, but also with a local newspaper reporter. It was agreed that the reporter would do a good write-up about the concert, in exchange for a lavish dinner with drinks in the hotel's dining room, prior to the concert. The music store owner was pretty smart because, holding the concert would indicate to the general public that he supported and encouraged local young talent. He would get some free advertising and promotion for his store.

There were many things to do in preparation for this major event - probably the greatest happening in this small town of Kolding since some invading Spanish soldiers burnt down the castle in 1808. We were all extremely busy. Xenia practised 'Rhapsody in Blue' on the piano every day for hours at a time, so that we almost wished Gershwin had never been born. Vita was singing night and day to get in shape. I wrote out the musical scores for the guitar, and for the sax, which was a full note lower than the piano. We also had to have music stands. These were made of plywood which we painted white, and with the band's name on each one for visual impact. White band jackets were the final touch. We bought some cheap ones at a used clothing store and intended to have necessary changes made by a tailor, but the cost was too great. I made promotional posters, which we managed to display in various downtown store windows.

Erik, our bass player had made arrangement to rent an acoustic bass for the evening. One would think that the music store owner would have let us borrow the bass free of charge since he was running the show, but no - he was out to milk this concert for all it was worth. I was somewhat concerned about Erik never having played bass before, but as he said he knew all about it. At our rehearsals he made bass sounds with his mouth.

After the many months of hard work, the gala evening arrived, and much to our surprise, about a hundred people showed up - enough to pay for the rental of the hotel ballroom. It was very seldom anything happened in Kolding and anything was better than nothing. The reporter, who had spent the last two hours in the hotel dining room, finished his lavish dinner and staggered into the ballroom. We helped him to a seat at the back of the room. He seemed to be drunk.

Promptly at eight the lights were dimmed, and the music store owner, being master of ceremonies, mounted the four-foot high stage in one leap. He introduced himself, gave his store a plug at the same time and thanked the audience for turning up. He then announced the first highlight of the evening, and with a sweeping flourish of his arm and 'Let's give her a big hand,' Xenia appeared on stage. Skinny and frail-looking as always, she sat down at the black grand piano and spread out her sheet music.

There was a hush in the ballroom. Then the dramatic opening of 'Rhapsody in Blue' filled the air. Her nimble fingers, running over the keys, immediately put the audience at ease. As she turned to the second page, her music fell on the floor, but undaunted, she continued as if nothing had happened. Her ability to play delicately with feeling and sensitivity as well as dramatic passages, that seemingly would require more energy and force than her small figure conveyed, was evident in her performance. She mastered the piano and went through the 27 pages of Gershwin without a flaw. The audience was enthralled and clapped enthusiastically. We were at the back of the ballroom during Xenia's perform-ance and applauded vigorously with the rest, to make it sound like a very large audience. Unfortunately, the reporter sitting next to us was fast asleep. Preben, the sax player, tried to wake him up but he was too far gone.

There was a brief intermission, to allow us time to set up. We arranged the music stands side by side and a chair behind each. Erik brought the rented string bass up on the stage. It was the first time I had seen one at such close range. It looked very expensive. There was a microphone on a stand for Vita. I placed the sheet music on the three music stands and piano, and Preben tuned his sax to B flat. Erik thumped a few strings on the bass and said it sounded okay. Henrik really held things up with his guitar tuning, but eventually he got it right and we left the stage. Standing behind the curtains, we signaled that we were ready. The music store owner, who had a stake in this event in as much as he might sell more sheet music at his store, again came up on stage, grabbed the microphone and clearing his throat, announced that *The Whiskey Swing Band* was about to play, featuring the newest singer in the world of entertainment - *Miss Vita*. I wondered if he had been drinking during intermission. And then with an arm flourish and 'Let's give them a big hand,' we entered and took our places.

Everything was planned in great detail. First, Vita would sing 'In my Solitude' with band back-up, then we would play three numbers and finally she would, with our accompaniment, sing 'Stormy Weather.' Our moment in history had come.

Erik stood a bit off to the side of his music stand, so that the audience could get a full view of the bass. It was a beautiful bass and brand new. He even had to pay insurance to rent it. I felt quite exposed, sitting on the piano bench. We were all nervous and experiencing some stage fright. Fortunately, Preben and Henrik were both able to hide behind their music stands. A miscalculation in the design of these stands was apparent to the audience, if not to us. They were too high and being up on a four-foot high stage didn't help. From the floor, the sax player and the guitar player were only heard, but never seen.

I started the intro to 'Solitude.' Vita, backed up by Preben were to fall in after four bars. We had rehearsed this time and again. They fell in alright, but Preben played in the wrong key! Instant cold sweat engulfed the band. After two bars of utter chaos, during which we all wanted to sink through floor, Preben realized something was wrong and stopped playing completely. I must have given him the wrong score. With twenty-five percent of the band out of commission, we struggled on. Vita displayed great courage and composure. The bass didn't sound right. Erik was not in tune at all. I always thought a bass had to be tuned just like other string instruments. Henrik, concealed behind his stand, plodded along, and together with me finally reached the end of the tune, with Vita definitely in a state of solitude.

There was good applause for her. She did well in the face of pending disaster and I think the applause was for that reason. They wanted to cheer her up. She wandered off the stage, feeling greatly relieved. The next tune, instrumental only and being the tune 'Mood Indigo,' practically put the audience to sleep. I became aware of this when we were half way through. It seemed to slow down. I think Erik was finding that thumping strings was heavy work. The bass was very much out of tune and made 'Mood Indigo' sound like a funeral march. I thought it would never end. It was a torture - and it definitely made the audience moody. Afterwards, the light applause was sporadic, but there was lots of coughing. I also noticed a couple of people yawning in the front row. Looking at all those white, silent faces out there in the darkness, I knew it was up to us get our act together. It was obvious that something more upbeat was necessary, so it was very fortunate that our next number, 'Sweet Sue' was just that. It seemed to go all right. Preben even managed to throw in a little improvisation on his sax solo, that almost sounded professional - and living up to his motto 'It don't mean a thing if you ain't got that swing.' The clapping was a little better on this one, because more of the audience had been awakened by the noise.

Following that, our last instrumental tune, 'Darktown Strutter's Ball,' was supposed to have the place jumping, but somehow we failed to achieve our objective. The embarrassing thing was that Erik continued thumping the bass, long after the rest of us were finished. I think some of the audience probably thought it was a bass solo. However, Erik quickly realized that he was out in left field all by himself, so he used the fade-out technique - which in those days, was practically unknown. He was way ahead of his time. This 'musical first' also made the audience fade out. They just sat there, hoping something better might happen.

Anticipating that a situation like this might occur, we kept the best to the last. 'Stormy Weather' was our big number - featuring 'Miss Vita.' As we each sorted out our sheet music, Henrik leaned over and whispered to me that he didn't have his guitar score! I couldn't believe this was happening! We all scrambled around searching, keeping behind the music stands as much as possible, to conceal the calamity that now engulfed us. A few seconds later, I had to face the public and begin the intro - with or without the guitar. We couldn't keep the audience waiting and in a continuous state of suspense.

Vita came in on cue with the piano and the out-of-tune string bass. Preben and Henrik continued the search behind the music stands, which resulted in Preben missing his entrance on the sax by a whole bar. Vita and I suddenly had to backtrack a bar to harmonize with the delayed sax, which was also far too loud. However, this had no effect on the string bass score, as Erik thumped away without any association with the music. He didn't need sheet music, he said, because he knew everything by heart.

The arrangement then called for the sax to take the second chorus to the middle, and remarkable as it may seem, it sounded pretty good - even without guitar background. But with Vita coming in at this point, he played a couple of wrong notes that threw me off momentarily. Vita forged ahead, holding the melody line intact in the face of the turmoil all around her and somehow, we all got back on track and weathered the storm.

The audience applauded out of sympathy. I think many clapped, because they were glad the ordeal was over. We all stood up and took a bow. At this moment the audience saw the sax player and the guitar player for the first time - including their instruments. This generated additional clapping, but not enough for an encore. The music store owner really let us down. He was supposed to have announced the numbers we played and concluded the evening with the 'let's give them a big hand' routine. But everything just petered out and the audience got up from their chairs and drifted slowly out of the hotel as if in a daze. It was so quiet in the ballroom.

Fortunately, nobody asked for their money back. When we left a while later, I noticed the music store owner sitting in the hotel bar with a girl. He had probably been there most of the evening - and really, I didn't blame him. Why suffer when you don't have to?

Erik returned the rented bass to the store the next day and when I saw him, he had bandages on three of his fingers. It was with mixed feelings that we waited for the day's paper to arrive. I wasn't sure whether our musical careers were shattered, or if we were on our way to greater fame. A few hours later, it looked as though we had lost. There was not one single word about the concert in the newspaper. I was about to phone the reporter, when suddenly, he appeared at our front door. He apologized for sleeping through the concert, but he said a friend of his who was also there and was awake, said we were very good. However, he did intend to write something and felt a personal interview about our talents might help make an article about the concert more interesting. So he took notes for about an hour and then left.

Twenty-four hours later, there it was, in print under a three-column heading that read *Talented Preacher Children*. Very positive! I could hardly wait to read it all. Xenia's performance was praised and cited as being outstanding - and rightfully so. Vita's soft voice was mentioned as being mellow and sentimental with good control. I think the reporter's friend, who must have come up with this information, was referring to the good control Vita showed, in holding the band together through all the stormy weather. There was no mention of the leader of the band, except to say that I had talent in drawing and did it all with my left hand. The only reference to the band itself or our music, was a short paragraph about the young, promising bass player who, according to the article, showed great talent and potential. No mention at all about the music of the quartet. This was devastating to our musical careers. Henrik decided to sell his guitar. I decided to concentrate on drawing but a week later we changed our minds. We would give up playing concerts in town and instead concentrate on playing music for farmers' dances out in the surrounding countryside. There we would not be faced with criticism. Farmers couldn't tell the difference between the sound of lower C on a piano and a cow's moo.

For the next year not much happened. I had my work which kept me busy six days a week. The rest of the children were always busy with school and homework, and Mom had enough to do as always, but financially, she was having a hard time. The money I received in apprenticeship wages plus the money I had saved up in my cookie jar were not enough to make ends meet, but now and then I managed to sell a few illustrations and cartoons. The pay was not much, but it all helped.

As far as girls were concerned, I had almost given up completely. None ever seemed to come my way and I was at a loss of what to do or where to go to meet a girl. It was on my mind all the time. A friend at work said it was not enough to take a cold shower in the morning to cool off, but it had to be done also in the evening. It didn't seem to help much. To make myself look more handsome, I spent some of my free time, usually during my lunchbreak, getting a suntan. I thought I was beginning to look pretty good, but there were no girls around to appreciate the result.

I no longer received letters from Harold and it seemed that my letter writing had also stopped completely. So much time had passed and there was nothing more to say. Our lives were totally different. Junction City was still a clear image in my mind and someday I hoped to see the town again, but it was no longer the place of refuge or salvation.

CHAPTER TWENTY-TWO

It was in the early summer, about a month before my nineteenth birthday, that I received a call from a fellow by the name of Borge Ring. He had noticed a cartoon strip of mine in a local publication and was interested in meeting me. Being a cartoonist himself, he felt that we could perhaps share ideas and assist each other in cartooning techniques. He was particularly interested in animated film cartooning. I told him I had the same interest. We agreed to meet, so one weekend I made the trip to his parents' home, which was in a town called Svendborg.

It turned out that we had many similarities in drawing, but I could see that Borge was further advanced than I was. He had actually made a one minute filmstrip, using simple lines, showing a dentist pulling a tooth out of a man in the dentist's chair. The film showed the movement very well. The dentist pulled the whole skeleton out of the body and what was left crumbled in the chair like an empty sack. I thought it was great, and we ran the thing over and over again to analyze the movement from one frame to the next.

After a lot of discussion, we decided that it might be a good idea to visit Copenhagen together. He said there were studios there, specializing in this type of cartooning. Maybe we could visit some of these places and study the latest techniques. Borge suggested that we could stay there a week at his uncle's apartment. I liked the idea and said that the timing was right, because I could do this during my summer holiday.

Borge phoned me a few days later and said that everything looked good. We decided on a Friday as the day of departure. I booked my train ticket and he did likewise. Since we were not going on the same train, we decided that we would meet at five o'clock that Friday afternoon in front of the train station entrance in Copenhagen.

Mom was happy to hear that I was going to Copenhagen. It would be good for me to get away for a few days and see things.

"But while you are there," she said, "you should give the two Falcke girls a call. I'll give you the telephone number. They are such nice girls."

"Who are they?" I had never heard of them.

"Many years ago Auntie Annie visited Denmark, met the family and took care of the girls, while the parents were on holiday."

"I don't think I'll have any time for that. Borge and I got enough to do."

"Visti, they are such nice girls and they know of our family. You only have to make a phone call. That won't interfere with your schedule, I'm sure."

It was clear to me that Mom was becoming concerned that her son never was with a girl. Here I was, at the age of nineteen, still without a single acquaintance. As far as she had observed, I had never had a girl friend or been out with a girl. She was right. Apart from the brief conversations with Lisbeth, the one with Ellen and that uncomfortable walk with that strange girl, Erna and her hiccups, there had been nothing. Mom didn't even know about those episodes, nor did she know about my feelings and frustration over the years.

I had actually got to the stage where I regarded girls as the cause of all kinds of unhappiness and problems, and found it better to forget them completely and concentrate on drawing, which provided me with hours of joy and the satisfaction of being creative.

It was understandable in those days, that a mother was interested in her son falling in love with a nice girl and getting married. Everyone got married. If you didn't, there was probably something physically wrong, requiring the attention of a doctor or a church minister. Very seldom, did one hear of a person over thirty being a bachelor or spinster. Also, divorce was quite uncommon - almost like a disease.

The purpose of life was to have a happy childhood with father and mother, grow up, get an education, court a girl, marry her, have many children and live happily ever after. Therefore, Mom was relieved when I agreed to make the phone call. I decided to make the return trip by boat. This would be the first extended trip away from home since the Haderslev days.

I arrived in Copenhagen about three in the afternoon and spent the next couple of hours looking at the city life near the station. Promptly at five, I stood at the entrance doors and waited for Borge Ring to show up. I heard the chimes of the nearby City Hall tower every quarter hour, By the time it was quarter passed seven, I gave up waiting. Obviously Borge didn't make it. Our plans to meet were down the drain. I wondered what to do then. I knew no one in this big city.

After sitting on a bench for a while, I suddenly remembered that Daddy had once mentioned the name, Bodholt, a man he once knew, who returned to Copenhagen after living many years in North America. It was not much to go on, but going through the telephone book in a booth at the railway station, I found a couple of dozen Bodholts. I picked one at random.

Upon hearing a man's voice on the phone, I gave my name and asked if he knew the Favrholdt family. Almost immediately the answer was yes. I explained the situation I was in and that I had no place to stay in this big city. Could he perhaps help? Immediately, he said it was no problem. I could stay at his villa, which was not too far from city center. He gave me the details how to get there by streetcar number 21.

I arrived an hour later. It was a nice house in a quiet residential area away from the bustling traffic. I met Bodholt's aging parents who lived in the same house. It appeared he was a bachelor who, in his younger days worked at a mountain lodge in western Canada. I was given something to eat and a nice room. They told me I was welcome to stay there for the whole week I was in Copenhagen. I thanked them and felt I was very fortunate indeed.

The next day I went into the city to look around. I did not have any information as to what Borge would have us do together in Copenhagen, so I decided to forget the whole matter and enjoy a week of sightseeing. About eleven o'clock in the morning it occurred to me that I had better phone the girls Mom talked about, and get it over with.

I took the crumpled piece of paper out of my pocket and, standing in a telephone booth near the train station, I dialed the number. Apart from the number, I noticed that Mom had written down the names of the two girls. They were Gerda and Clara. As I waited for someone to answer at the other end, I wondered what I should talk about.

"Hello." It was a girl's voice.

"Oh, hello. My name is Visti Favrholdt. I would like to speak to Gerda or Clara Falcke."

"This is Clara."

"Well, I'm from Kolding and I was told to give you a call."

"Did you say your name was Favrholdt?"

"Yes."

There was a brief pause. Then she said,

"Well, then I believe that our family knows your family. Where are you phoning from? It sounds so clear."

"I'm right here in Copenhagen - just for a week. I'm staying with some friends."

There was a longer pause.

"Are you still there?" I asked.

"Yes, I was just thinking it would be nice to meet you. I've heard so much about your family. Would that be all right?" Her voice sounded very pleasant.

"Yes, that would be fine."

"Have you been to Tivoli?"

"No, not yet."

"Oh, you will like that. I could meet you this evening and we could there. Do you think that would be all right?"

Would I ever! This was a date in the making. I was totally unprepared for something like this. We talked at length and decided to meet each other at the train station entrance at seven o'clock that evening.

I put the receiver down. Well, this was a surprise. A girl actually wanted to see me! I wondered what she looked like. Then suddenly I realized I forgot to tell her what I looked like and she forgot to tell me.

I spent the rest of the day sightseeing. I went to the main city square, which in itself, seemed almost as large as Junction City. The city hall, with the tall clock tower, dominated the whole square. Funny little, yellow streetcars moved along the streets bordering the square and thousands of cyclists were going in all directions. Flower pots, kiosks, benches, hot dog venders, pigeons, people, plus the sounds of traffic, bicycle bells and the city hall chimes - all created the atmosphere of a very busy metropolis. Towering above it all, next to the city hall, was a granite column supporting two Vikings, carved in stone, holding large trumpets to their lips - ready to blow when the first virgin girl passed by, down below. The city scenery was much the same as when I saw it for the first time at the age of thirteen, but it was now much more alive and I looked at it differently.

The important moment finally arrived. Feeling somewhat apprehensive, not knowing exactly what to expect, I stood at the train station entrance and waited. It was a busy place. Not only was the station the main terminal for national and international trains, but also for the local subway system. People were moving about everywhere, and I found I had to be quite alert, if I was going to see her. But then, I noticed a girl about fifty feet away, walking towards the station entrance. She was slim, about five foot seven, had brown shoulder length hair and looked very pretty. I thought to myself, this must be the Falcke girl. I walked towards her. We looked at each other and I said,

"Are you Clara?"

"Yes - and you must be Visti?" She smiled.

We shook hands. I could feel very much I was in the presence of a girl. It was an unaccustomed, but desirable sensation to be so close. In the case of Ellen and Erna, the distance was never less than two feet. And then there was Gertie Gerslund. That was closer, but it didn't count.

We walked down the street together. It was a totally new experience for me. I was very bashful and hardly knew what to say. We exchanged a few words about the weather - which was something we had in common and I made every effort to be as polite and correct as possible. This was my first real date and I was very conscious of its fragility. My two past experiences clearly indicated how difficult it was to be accepted. I had actually entered a state of mind, where I didn't actually reject girls, but had completely given up on them. However, in the presence of this new girl, and on this special day, there was a reawakening. It was encouraging that she was interested in what I had to say. She spoke English very well and so we did away with the Danish. The conversation between us was mostly about what was happening at the moment.

Tivoli was a large garden, equal to about four city blocks, right in the center of Copenhagen. With a history, dating back a hundred years, it was of great sentimental value to all Danes. From the train station, it was only five minutes walk. Clara bought two admission tickets at the entrance and we went through the turnstiles. I could feel that she was a Copenhagen girl, experienced in the ways and activities of the big city. In contrast, I felt like a little country boy, tagging along on a sightseeing tour, but extremely happy and very fortunate.

A walkway, lined with overshadowing trees and hanging lanterns, formed the entrance within the gardens. To the left of us was a pantomime show for children, on a small stage. Further down on the other side, was an orchestra playing Strauss waltzes in a bandstand shaped like a seashell, and beyond that an open area with fountains in lily pad covered ponds. There were many small restaurants with outside terraces, tucked away, here and there in between trees and behind hedges. Winding pathways, surrounded by fragrant flower gardens, led to quiet secluded places where one could rest on a bench and feed ducks and swans. Other parts of the gardens featured entertainment such as high wire aerobatic acts, a ferris wheel, the house of mirrors, boat rides, merry-go-round and a place where you could throw wooden balls at real chinaware plates and win prizes.

A colorful, marching band, called the Tivoli Guard, suddenly came in to view through the main entrance, to the music of flutes and drums. Led by an 'officer' sitting very erect on a horse, a little 'army' of boy soldiers with small wooden toy rifles and dressed in red and white uniforms followed behind, Their presence attracted a lot of attention as they marched through the gardens - a daily tradition for the entertainment of the public.

As evening darkness approached, thousands of colored lights appeared, transforming the gardens into a make-believe fairyland - but for me, it was very real. Not only was I feeling like a boy in a toy shop, but I was with this lovely girl. It was a beautiful evening and there was a full moon.

We went on the ferris wheel, tried our luck throwing the wooden balls at plates, went into the house of mirrors, watched a balancing act and listened to classical music being played. Clara then asked if I would like to go to a place in the gardens called Glassalen, where we could get refreshments and perhaps dance. Being totally in heaven, I readily agreed.

It was a very large building with a roof like a botanical garden conservatory, made entirely of glass. Inside a jazz band was playing, and flanking the beautiful large dance floor on both sides were tables, chairs and a forest of large ferns in pots. Very few were dancing as it was early in the evening. We sat at a candlelit table and ordered ice cream and coffee. We talked about many things. I refrained from dwelling to much on the subject of Junction City being paradise and the cure-all for all unhappiness, because it was no longer the case. Happiness and paradise was right here this very evening.

Clara told me about her family. She was one of five children. Her father was a sales representative for a distinguished millinery firm in Copenhagen, traveling frequently to Sweden. She herself, worked as an office girl for another company in the city and had been in England and in France. We talked for a little while about many things and then she asked me if I would like to dance. I said I would like to. Emerging from a sheltered, deprived environment for the first time, I knew nothing about proper etiquette, gentleman ways or how to escort a girl. But if this was apparent to her, she didn't show it. At a moment like this,

I wished I had stuck with Gertie Gerslund at the dance studio a little longer and learned more about dancing. But Clara didn't seem to notice my faltering steps and neither did I, as the delightful sensation of being so close to her, overwhelmed me - to the point that I seemed to be floating. I didn't know if she experienced anything herself, - being the object of all this dreamy, sensual excitement, but it should be remembered that this was the first time I had really ever held a girl in my arms and it was the first time I ever had been to a restaurant and danced.

The low lighting, the candlelit tables, the glass roof with the moon above and the thousands of colored lights visible outside all around us in the gardens, created and environment and atmosphere that I had never before encountered.

Clara ordered two glasses of wine. The twelve piece band, all dressed in black suits and white shirts, played a tune called 'Lambeth Walk.' We raised our wine glasses and toasted.

"Thanks so much for giving me a perfect evening," I said, looking at her.

"Yes and I say the same, Visti."

She looked very pretty, sitting there. I couldn't really imagine why a girl would do all this for me.

When Tivoli closed, reality returned. Out on the busy street it was time to depart. I gave her my phone number at the Bodholt residence. We stood at a streetcar stop and waited. There were crowds everywhere as everyone looked for transportation to get home. I wished my streetcar would never show up, so that I could be with her a while longer, but that hope turned into a pumpkin, as streetcar number 21 came to our stop. It was all over so quickly. We shook hands. I thanked her for everything and said I hoped to see her again sometime. She said likewise and as the streetcar moved away, I waved to her through the window.

All the way home to Bodholt's place I felt happy. It had been such a perfect evening, but then I started wondering if my manners had been correct and whether I had said the right things at the right moment. I was very much aware of my shyness and total lack of experience in going out with a girl. I suddenly remembered, I forgot to help her with her chair when we returned to our table after a dance. I also neglected to open the door for her when we entered the restaurant, and the fact that I was unable to pay for the evening, was certainly the most embarrassing thing of all.

Also, I should have waited to see her get on the right streetcar instead of the other way around. I should have shown a bit of leadership. And when we said goodbye, did I do the right thing, shaking hands? I couldn't very well have kissed her. I hardly knew her and certainly one could not do this on a first date. All these thoughts went through my mind and it took me a while to forget my concerns. Still, it had been a perfect evening.

For the next three days, I wandered around Copenhagen looking at the castles, the canals, churches and museums and even tried to find something in the phone book about film cartoon animation, but saw nothing. Although I enjoyed walking around, my thoughts were still about Clara and Tivoli -

wondering where she was, what she was doing and what she thought of me. In the evening of the third last day, I decided to call and thank her for the wonderful evening I had. It took some courage on my part to make the call.

Much to my surprise, when I heard her voice on the phone, I knew she was happy I called. She said she was just about to call me. Her parents, she said, would very much like to meet me, because they knew my father. He met them, when he was in Denmark looking for a position as minister. Would I be able to come to her house tomorrow evening? She would be there. Would I ever! I could hardly contain myself, but I tried to act calm and natural on the telephone. She gave me the address and details.

Sitting in the streetcar on the way out there the next day, I felt that I looked somewhat shabby. I didn't expect my visit to Copenhagen to involve meeting a girl and her parents. I certainly wasn't properly dressed for this sort of thing. They lived in a villa on the outskirts of Copenhagen. Clara met me at the door and introduced me to her father and mother. Her brother and her sister, Gerda were also present. They were all very nice and seemed glad to meet me. Clara's parents said I looked very much like my father. During the evening, they served coffee and the conversation was mostly questions about my family. Although I conducted myself well, and politely conversed with them, my eyes were on Clara - not directly, but her presence had a great effect on me. So much, in fact, that when the evening was over, I couldn't remember much of what we had talked about. After shaking hands and thanking them for a lovely evening, Clara surprised me by saying she would come down to the boat tomorrow to see me off.

The next morning I thanked the Bodholt family for allowing me to stay at their house, said goodbye and took the streetcar to the harbor. The small boat was being load with freight when I arrived. Quite a few people were gathering on the wharf, and after waiting a while, Clara appeared on her bicycle. Together we went up the gangplank and we stood at the railing on deck of the boat, watching all the activity on the wharf. We talked about little things and the beautiful evening at Tivoli. She said she enjoyed very much seeing me. I told her I felt the same. As we stood there, I wondered how we would say goodbye.

Far too quickly, a blast from the boat's whistle told us that it was time to go. I was about to take her hand, but then suddenly she kissed me on the cheek! That was the first kiss I had ever experienced from a girl and unfortunately, there was no time to respond. Immediately she turned around and hurried down the gangplank. As the ropes were hauled in and the gangplank removed, we looked at each other. She was very pretty, standing there on the wharf. A few more lingering moments, and the boat moved away. I waved goodbye to this Copenhagen girl who gave me so much joy.

One of the first things I did when I returned to Kolding, was to phone Borge Ring and find out what went wrong. It turned out that he was in Copenhagen at the correct time and stood for two hours waiting outside the train station entrance doors - just like I did. I said that was impossible, because I looked all around and he was nowhere in sight. He said the same. So we had to get more specific. After a lot of discussion, it turned out that he was standing at another main entrance, on the west side of the building.

It didn't take Mom very long before she wanted to know more about my trip than just generalities.

"How were the Falcke girls?" she asked.

"They were nice. I met them both. I went to Tivoli one evening with Clara and saw Gerda at their house. Her parents invited me there."

"So you had a good time?"

"I sure did. I had a real good time."

Back at work, life once again became almost normal - just plain hard work on the construction sites and quiet evenings at home. But the memories of the wonderful holiday were foremost in my mind. Imagine being kissed by a girl! I wanted to tell everyone at work what I had experienced. They were always boasting about their fantastic experiences with girls - and now I could say the same. However, I decided to keep this beautiful happening private for a while. I felt that somehow I must figure out how to get back to Copenhagen. If it wasn't for this apprenticeship contract, I would move there straight away. Mom was also thinking about Copenhagen. She somehow felt that I failed to become sufficiently interested in the Falcke girls to be awakened. This was evident two days later.

"Visti, I really think you should write a letter and thank the Falckes for their hospitality. They would like that."

"I thanked them when I was there."

"Yes, I know. But you know how it is. People always like to receive a letter of thanks. Maybe you could write to one of the girls."

It suddenly dawned upon me that her suggestion was perhaps a good idea. I would write to Clara. Mom was hopeful when I mailed the letter. So was I.

Two weeks passed and a letter arrived from Clara. She said she was happy I wrote to her and she would again like to thank me for the good time we had together. Well, her letter was a real surprise and definitely called for a reply from me. So I wrote her a second letter, saying that I really didn't expected a reply to my first letter and I was really grateful that she wrote to me. Then she wrote back, saying that she really didn't expect another letter from me, but it made her very happy. Again, I felt I absolutely must reply to this latest letter. This went on for a while and I could feel that maybe we were in love - or at least I was, so I decided to take the plunge and I wrote her a letter, saying I was in love with her.

The next few days were almost unbearable. I found it hard to work properly or sleep well at night. I almost got to the point where I wished I hadn't done such a risky thing. It would probably spoil our friendship. I had never gone so far out on a limb before. I didn't feel good at all.

Back at work I found it difficult to concentrate on the carpentry I was given. I had received my first independent assignment of my apprenticeship. It was to measure for a straight run of stairs to go from the main floor up to an open mezzanine level in the front room of a downtown tavern. Under the guidance of a carpenter in our shop I was to construct the stair, which we then would take to the tavern and install in one piece. All went well in the shop.

Out on the job it was a different story. It seemed that somehow I had one step too many in the stair run. When the carpenter and I attempted to place it in position, the top step was seven inches above the mezzanine floor. Instead of getting angry, the carpenter suggested that we sit down at one of the tables, have a drink and think a little bit. The owner, who was busy serving beer to his customers, was unaware of the problem looming up in his tavern.

It was very obvious that a mistake had been made. That was clear. Since the carpenter was responsible for checking my work, he didn't want to experience the embarrassing situation of taking the stairs back to the shop, where it would have to be taken apart and corrected. To saw off the top step was no solution as the railings were made for the full run with main posts at the top and bottom. I was surprised how calm the carpenter was in this situation. Maybe he was one of these carpenters who chose this profession for its biblical significance and simply trusted God to get us out of this dilemma.

The owner came over and joined us at our table. He called a waitress to bring a round of beer for his guests. He told us he was very happy to get the stairs after having waited so long. Now he would be able to put chairs and tables up on the mezzanine level for more customers. He turned and looked at the stair laying on the floor ready to be lifted in place. A drunk man staggered passed our table.

"Nice work," the owner said, "you've done a good job."

Neither one of us wanted to take credit for it. As he left our table, I suddenly got a brainwave.

"Listen to this," I said eagerly to the carpenter, "all we got to do is line up the top tread flush with the mezzanine floor and let the bottom of the stair run rest on the floor below - be that where it may. It will probably give the treads a downward slant in towards the risers but nobody will notice it in this place. Most of the customers are drunk all the time."

The carpenter thought I was pretty smart and said he would recommend me for promotion if an opportunity ever came about. So we went ahead with the work and an hour later it was in position complete with railings - which unfortunately were not vertical. I tried going up the stairs and discovered I had to hold on to the railing all the way to keep my balance. There was a sensation of falling forward when going up the stairs and of falling backward when going down. This wasn't good at all. But the carpenter took the whole matter very lightly and said he would have a short talk with the owner who was behind the bar. We went over there together.

"Well, your stair is now ready for use."

The owner bent forward over the bar counter to look at the creation. "Thanks ever so much, fellas. It looks real good."

"Oh, there's just one thing I wish to point out," said the carpenter - almost as if it was an afterthought, "this is a new design with a slight slant inward on the stair treads. We make these especially for taverns. What it does is help customers who might have had a little too much to drink, from falling forward when coming down the stairs. The slant keeps them upright."

"Wonderful, wonderful, the clever things they think of these days!" The owner was delighted. "You've done a real good job, fellas. Thanks ever so much. Anytime you're here in the neighborhood, drop in for a drink. You're always welcome."

We quickly packed our tools and left.

I continued to regret having mailed the last fatal letter to Clara. I was unable to concentrate on my work or anything else. It was ten days when the world stood still. It was a gamble and I was beginning to regret having proposed to her at all. Being friends was okay, but this was irresponsible. To go through all my teenage years without having a single girl friend and then to suddenly muddle the waters when I finally got one, was not very clever.

The answer finally arrived. Mom received it from the postman and handed it to me.

"Here's another letter from Clara Falcke."

Well, it wasn't just another letter. It was THE letter - probably the most important letter of my life. In the privacy of my room I opened the envelope and prepared myself for the shock that might take place.

Everything melted away when I read the first line, which said 'Dearest Visti'- and what followed was sheer joy. She said she was also in love with me and had been so for quite awhile - since I left Copenhagen. I finally had a girl friend and much more than that.

Not being able to be with Clara, the letter writing went into high gear. There was so much to write about, telling about ourselves, planning for the future and how we might someday be able to be together. Getting to know each other by mail was exciting, but nothing like the real thing. But for now I was very happy. I had a place in this world and a purpose.

One day, as I was writing at the dining room table, I heard Vita in the kitchen, ask Mom,

"Why is Visti always writing letters? He never stops."

Mom whispered, "That's because he's in love."

CHAPTER TWENTY-THREE

The tower of the castle, called *Koldinghus,* was the most dominating structure in the town of Kolding. Part of this thirteenth century fortress lay in ruins, but the square tower with its interior spiral staircase was intact. From the top platform of the ten storey tower one could see in all directions right to the horizon. The surrounding city below, with the narrow winding streets and the two nearby church steeples, seemed to embrace the castle, asking for protection. On the south side of the castle immediately below the tower, was a military garrison. It was rather small - just three one-storey buildings accommodating about fifty soldiers with small arms only, plus four military trucks. At one time the purpose of the garrison with its soldiers was to protect the castle. Now their presence was purely symbolic. The castle no longer needed protection, but the country did.

On the ninth of April, 1940 at quarter to seven in the morning, I was standing together with a carpenter on top of the castle tower. We were installing a wooden frame for the mounting of an air raid siren. World War Two had started, but so far, Denmark was still neutral and relatively peaceful. Nevertheless, throughout the country, precautions were being taken. Bomb proof shelters were being built in city parks and in public buildings. Air raid sirens were being installed to cover the entire country.

At five minutes to seven, I faintly heard a distant hum and mentioned it to the carpenter I was working with. He heard it also. We stopped our work and gazed out over the city. Noticing nothing in particular, we looked south over the country side. Suddenly, there it was, three small specks in the sky just above the horizon. The carpenter saw three more. Then I saw four more groups of three. They were planes. A moment later they were all over the horizon and coming right towards us! It didn't take us very long to realize that this was it - we were being invaded.

Before we were able to do anything at all, we had Messerschmitt fighters flying past us on both sides of the tower. They were so low and close that we could see the pilots' faces. Thousands of leaflets showered over the city like confetti. A few leaflets landed in the castle courtyard. I ran down the spiral staircase to pick one up. It was a message printed in Norwegian which said in effect, that our king had agreed to occupation by the German armed forces to protect us from a possible British invasion of our country. The leaflet was designed to apply both to Denmark and Norway, as this 'protective measure' covered both countries. It was all over in seconds.

Almost immediately we saw the garrison below us come to life with excited soldiers running all over the place, loading trucks with equipment, rifles and boxes of ammunition. In a matter of minutes, they were on their way, racing southward, to meet the enemy. From the tower we followed them through the streets out of town until the four trucks appeared as little dots far, far away.

For the balance of the morning everything was quiet and peaceful. It was hard to comprehend why Hitler would want to invade Denmark when we were considered to be the breadbasket for Europe and most certainly the most tranquil of all European countries. We wondered whether we should quit work and go home, but then it occurred to us that the installation of the air raid siren was suddenly very important. Our commanding view above the city allowed us to see in all directions, but during the course of our work we kept looking only to the south. The German border was a mere 80 kilometers away.

About two o'clock in the afternoon we noticed in the distance, the images of tanks and military vehicles coming northward on the main road from Haderslev. We finished the installation at three. On the way home I had to get off my bicycle and stand at the street curb to allow German tanks and troops to pass me by. The civilian population just stood in silence not knowing what to expect.

I wondered what was happening in Copenhagen and how Clara was taking all this. Everything was so sudden and unexpected. It was a week earlier that a reporter for a Copenhagen newspaper, questioned why so many German tourists had booked into the hotels here in April. We never had tourists so early in the year. On the eighth of April two German ships, loaded with coal, docked at the harbor in Copenhagen. Perhaps unexpected, but the harbor authorities were looking into it. Unknown to them, this was the Horse of Troy.

The next morning, the ninth of April, the German tourists came out of the various hotel rooms dressed in military uniforms and with weapons. The coal in the two ships turned out to be only a foot deep. From below the decks appeared thousands of German soldiers who immediately spread throughout the city of Copenhagen. By nightfall all of Denmark was occupied by the Nazi forces and the lights went out for five years.

Overwhelmed and somewhat resigned to our fate, it took a long time before any resistance was organized. Meanwhile on the surface, life went on as usual. With German soldiers everywhere plus food rationing and darkness, there seemed very little to look forward to. There was no link with the outside free world. As far as Junction City was concerned, it was only a faint memory.

My courtship period continued by letter. I wondered what it was like to be with the girl you loved, instead of being apart all the time. I also wondered how long this would go on. I was still an apprentice with all my wages going to support the family. There was technical school in the evenings, and beyond that, construction school and university ahead. I figured I would be an old man before I finished it all and able to marry the girl of my dreams.

Although we were more American than Danish, our family was never subject to suspicion by the Germans during the occupation. It was just a week after the Germans entered our country that I realized that I had lost my American citizenship. I should have made a decision a year earlier, before reaching my eighteenth birthday - whether or not I intended to return to the United States. But there was no doubt in my mind that the family came first - for many reasons, the main one being financial. So the last bond to Junction City was severed.

Mom, in an effort to earn more household money, decided to give English lessons in our home, as her small pension plus my carpenter apprentice wage were not enough. She had no training as a teacher. For many, this sudden interest in learning English was a passive form of defiance against the occupation forces. Our dining room was used as a classroom during the evenings. She had many groups of pupils, including half the local police force and a group of nurses from the hospital. For my part, I managed to sell a few drawings to a local bookstore which then were made into printed postcards, so this added a little to the family income. The only other evening activity, but certainly the most important one, was my letter writing to Clara. She and I felt, that being apart was hardly the way to enjoy a romance.

I eventually complete my carpentry apprenticeship and construction school. A new labour law in the country cut the apprenticeship time down to four years from five, which for me, was almost like receiving a gift. I was now 'ready' for university, except for lack of money and everything else. By that time I had written almost sixteen pounds of love letters to Clara.

I tried my best to gain the respect of her parents. I was probably in their opinion, a promising young man but had an awful long way to go before I could marry and support their precious daughter. I was the one who really needed support. After a lot of discussion, Clara convinced her parents that I was worth supporting and arranged that I could receive free room and board in their home in Copenhagen while attending university.

I was given a little room upstairs in her parent's villa. It was a big change for me but I gradually I adjusted to the new environment and the challenge ahead. In the evenings Clara and I were together at the villa, but also with her parents, brother and sister. There wasn't much privacy. Clara's cousin, Mia, visited us once in awhile. She worked as a surgeon's nurse at a Copenhagen hospital called Bispebjerg. With the general calamity and unrest everywhere we did not go out very often during the dark winter months. Also I found myself once again burdened with homework, but this time around there was a goal to achieve and I had made the decision myself.

It became apparent with the passing of time, that the Jews in Denmark were at risk. Ever since the beginning of the occupation, the Gestapo had been busy checking telephone books and other directories to determine exactly which Danes were Jews. It was no secret that something was afoot. Many Jews, fearing the worst, had already gone into hiding.

Suddenly one day the Gestapo issued orders to arrest all Jews, and that same day the Germans temporarily switched off Copenhagen's telephone service, frustrating last-minute attempts by Danes to warn their Jewish friends. At Bispebjerg hospital, as well as at other hospitals throughout the country, registers were immediately checked by doctors and staff. All patients with Jewish sounding names were discharged, then readmitted under false names. Later as things became more organized, perfectly healthy Jews were admitted to Bispebjerg Hospital as patients and given beds. Together with other hospitals, arrangements were made to transport Jews under the cover of darkness to fishing boats in coastal harbors for the crossing to neutral Sweden. Very often hospital ambulances were used for transportation. As the number of fleeing Jews increased, so did the congestion at Bispebjerg hospital. Jews had to be transferred from the hospital to private homes to await the boat trip to freedom. The operation was not without danger, as the Gestapo was searching everywhere. German patrol boats constantly scanned the waters between Denmark and Sweden.

About twice a week Mia would phone from Bispebjerg Hospital, saying that she had a box of apples for us. This was our message that we could expect Jews to arrive that evening. The arrival was very quiet. Often we did not know an ambulance had stopped at the villa until there was a knock on the door. The Jews, usually a family, were ushered in quickly and the door closed. We led them up to the attic to a room which was directly above my bedroom. There they stayed in isolation until it was time for them to be smuggled to a fishing boat - usually about twenty-four hours later. Normally, everything was quiet upstairs, but often as I lay in bed, I would hear footsteps above me, pacing back and forth, hour after hour. The waiting and the fear of being discovered by the Gestapo made them very restless.

One evening a Jewish couple arrived, and as we were going upstairs to the attic I spoke to them briefly. The man asked me if they were safe here. I assured him that they could trust us all. Later in the evening he came down the stairs from the attic and knocked on my bedroom door.

"I'm sorry to bother you, but could I ask you to mail this letter for me tomorrow?" he said, looking quite apologetic.

"Certainly," I replied, "I'll put it a mail box on the way to university."

"Oh, do you go to university?"

"I go to Husbygnings Teknikum."

"Oh yes, I know where that is. The Forum building is almost next door."

"That's right."

"I worked on the engineering design of the Forum many years ago."

"Really. Well, I must take a closer look at it. It's too bad that the Germans have taken over the building."

"Yes, I know. I think they are installing bunks for soldiers. It's going to be an army barrack. Well, I guess I better get some sleep. Thanks for your help."

The following morning was an important day. Finally, we university students would be making a decision that would take up all our time, imagination and thoughts for the next one and a half years. It was the selection of a project. They were written on the blackboard the day before - major glamorous projects such as the design of a concert hall, an Olympic size swimming pool complex, a train station, a town hall, a hotel complex and so on. There was much involved - everything from site surveying, planning, structural and mechanical calculations, architectural design and landscaping. This was the final home stretch of my never-ending education and I had serious doubts that I would succeed, given my past record.

As I cycled through streets on the way to university I thought about what I would like to design. Maybe a stadium or a sports complex or maybe an exhibition hall like the glass-enclosed Forum building. Then I remembered I had to mail the letter given to me. I stopped, looked around and spotted a red mailbox on the wall of a building down a side street. I had barely got half way there, when around the far corner appeared two trucks loaded with armed German soldiers who jumped off and immediately formed a roadblock. Turning around and looking back, I saw the same thing happening at the other end of the street. At this time of the day there were many Danes on the street, going to work on their bicycles, who suddenly wondered what to do and where to flee - including myself.

Surprise raids against the Danish population happened often - especially in Copenhagen. There were four types of raids. It could be for the sake of general harassment, a popular pastime. Weapon search in a blocked off area was also common. The search for Jews was another reason for a raid, and then there was the reprisal raids where seventeen Danes were taken at random in reprisal for the killing of one German soldier. The ratio used to be twelve.

I dashed into an apartment building, ran up the stairs to the sixth floor landing and waited. I could hear a lot of shouting down on the street below. A whole hour past. Then suddenly the entrance door opened and the Germans poured in, running up the stairs, banging doors and making a lot of noise. All I could do was sit on the top landing and wait. As they worked their way up, searching all the floors, I figured they were looking for Jews. The letter I was given to mail was of immediate concern - being from a Jew. I slipped the letter into a sack of briquettes that was on the landing outside an apartment door. Moments later I was spotted, went through a body search and ordered down on the street. Eventually the excitement died down. The Germans got into the trucks and drove off. I was glad nothing happened. When I again went into the apartment building to retrieve the letter, it was gone but the sack with the briquettes was still there.

All this caused quite a delay. I arrived at school an hour late and entered the classroom during a recess period. Looking at the blackboard, I noticed that all the projects had been taken except one. I had missed out on all those exciting projects, any of which would have elevated me to a level of architectural respect and admiration among my friends. Looking at the blackboard, it was hard to accept the description of the project that now was mine: *A laundry complex capable of washing and ironing 60,000 sheets and 20,000 shirts daily.*

A few days later each student was asked to submit an outline of how they intended to embark on their project - in other words, a time table with reference to research, site selection, structural engineering, design and other things. I had no idea where to begin, so when my turn came to stand in front of the class at the blackboard, I felt somewhat embarrassed due to the nature of my project. Addressing the teacher and class, I said that I assumed I would have to go out and visit a laundry to see how things are done. One of the students interrupted, saying,

"Why don't you just go home and see how your mom washes your shirt?"

At that instant there was a deafening explosion and the whole school trembled. There was a moment of stunned silence and then we all ran out of the building onto the street. It was the Forum! It had exploded. The street was littered with glass and debris.We knew this was sabotage. It happened everyday somewhere. What made it astounding, was that this happened in broad daylight, and in spite of the building being guarded at all entrances by armed German soldiers. As I looked at the ruins, my thoughts went to the Jewish engineer. Oh well, he was in Sweden by now.

One day a young man turn up at the university, looking around. I met him in the school cafeteria and he told me he just dropped in to see his old class room. He had graduated a couple of years earlier in the same courses we had. He asked me what project I was working on. When I told him it was the laundry, he exclaimed,

"Well, well, arn't you lucky!"

"How's that?" I was sure he was joking.

"The laundry always gets the highest marks"

"Really."

"Yes, for the past six years - maybe more. You just got to make sure you keep it simple. Make sure you have a sawtooth roof design over the factory area with all overhead windows facing north, and all service piping accessible in covered trenches - no fancy stuff anywhere."

One day Clara's parents decided to move to an apartment in downtown Copenhagen. They managed to sell the villa to a Danish policeman. Although it was a major change, it was a good for Clara and myself, as the apartment was closer to Clara's workplace and also to my school.

About a month later we heard from friends where they had previously lived, that the Gestapo suddenly came to the villa one night and took the man away. From what we were told, the Danish policeman knew nothing about the activities that had taken place in the villa. It was just his bad luck that he happened to buy a house that was under suspicion. Certainly it was something we did not know. It could have been us.

After what seemed like a lifetime, I finally reached the end of the road. Two full years had past. Spring had come and the final exams. This was it. The war was still on and there were times when we wondered if it was even worthwhile studying for anything. Why bother if there was no future. The oral and written exams took two weeks and for me was a real torture. No matter how hard I tried, I found everything so difficult. Even after all these years I still felt I was in a foreign country. It became apparent very quickly that the marks I was getting signaled doom ahead, but then on the last day came the marks for our big two-year class projects - and lo and behold, in the late afternoon on the last day I was saved by the laundry! It received the highest marks of all projects in the class, much to the amazement of everybody, including myself. When I added this to all my other marks and worked out the average, I barely passed. I graduated with a diploma and felt quite proud, happy and free.

Clara was proud of me, as well as her parents. For my mother it was a great relief as well as a time of joy, for she knew the struggle I experienced over the years. My future father-in-law felt that I had been a good gamble and looked forward to success in my career for the sake of his daughter.

Clara and I decided to get married immediately. The majority of the churches in Copenhagen were occupied by German troops. Sporadic shooting on the streets and unexpected raids here and there, made us feel that a church wedding was to risky - so it was arranged that we be married in the apartment living room. The modest marriage ceremony was attended by the immediate family on both sides and celebrated afterwards with a dinner in the dining room, complete with candlelight, wine and speeches. Now we could live happily ever after.

We found a place to live on the second floor of a six-storey apartment building in Copenhagen. We shared this place with a dentist by the name of Vermehren. He occupied the two front rooms facing the street and we had the two back rooms. One of the front rooms, with an entrance door to the stairwell, was used for his dental practise. A second entrance door led down a dark narrow corridor to the two back rooms that now was our home. We shared the dark kitchen and a dinky bathroom with only a toilet and a sink, which often had patients' denture molds in it. There were also dentures in the kitchen on a shelf above the kitchen sink. Our only furniture consisted of two chairs, a table and our bed. A pair of obscure glazed french doors separated our rooms from the dentist's living quarters. This was sufficient for privacy, but not for sound. After pulling teeth all day, the dentist would spend his evenings playing music on a saw with a violin bow. The wailing sound could go on for hours.

After a little searching, I managed to find a job. It was at an animation studio, a relative new company endeavoring to make an animated film of H.C. Andersen's fairytale, *The Emperor's New Clothes*. The pay was modest. My work consisted of making intermediate drawings of a red rooster perched on a fence squawking his head off to greet a new day. This was a disappointment for my father-in-law who had higher hopes for our future. But that didn't prevent us from buying a large, beautiful, black grand piano called *Ibach* on credit, with Clara making the monthly payments out of her office paycheck. I was deemed very irresponsible and obviously had my priorities all wrong.

With music in the apartment we now were in competition with the wailing saw. It was an unbearable combination, but with the heavy investment we had made in the piano, we were not giving up. Then just when we thought we couldn't stand it any longer, the saw music stopped. Maybe the dentist was sick or had dropped dead. We didn't know. We seldom saw him anyways. I decided to ask the manager of the building, who had a grocery store on the ground floor, if he would kindly check the two front rooms to see what happened. We were told that was unnecessary as the dentist had been picked up by the Gestapo. The rumor circulated in the apartment building that it was because he stole gold fillings from his patients' teeth, replacing them with lead fillings. I couldn't see what this had to do with the Gestapo - unless some of his patients were Germans.

Having completed the red rooster sequence for the animation company, I found myself unemployed for a few days, but then landed a job as a piano player in a sleazy basement tavern in a harbor area called Nyhavn. This place was so rough that the three-piece band played behind a chicken wire screen as protection from flying beer bottles. After less than two weeks on the job, Clara's brother-in-law came to the rescue, offering me a job at his marble construction firm, designing gravestones.

This was considered a very respectable profession, almost with religious significance, as it touched on peoples' lives at a time when there was much sadness and emotion. Very quickly I learned the tricks of the trade. Sympathy and understanding were paramount when discussing the design or sale of a stone to a client. I was told to always make sure that the client bought the most expensive stone possible. There was a relationship with regards to the stature of the deceased and the size of the stone that would be placed on his grave. It was when emotions were running high that make-believe compassion on the part of our company, provided comfort for the relatives of the deceased, so that they in turn could be lulled into looking only at the expensive stones. In other words, nothing but the best for a grieving family and relatives. Financially, it was also best for the company. Quick emotionally charged sales were important, I was told. If they came around to buy something six months after the deceased was in the ground, chances were that they would settle for a small cheap stone. The more I got into the swing of things, the more obvious it became that this was the 'ordained' destiny of a preacher's son. Selling gravestones almost seemed like a continuation of my father's mission in life. But there were moments when I wondered why I bothered to go to university.

About this time we became a family with a son we named Ken. Other things happened. I won a local gravestone design competition and the company decided to spread the news around in hope of more business. The company policy was 'there's life in the dead.' The company was in good shape even before I came along, employing 50 stone cutters and marble polishers. I was given my own office where I could design gravestones in peace. In the beginning there was no problem coming up with innovative, attractive designs for stones, but after awhile I seemed to run dry of ideas. I thought of making a sawtooth design similar to the roof profile of my university laundry project, but it did not go over well with the boss. He said I should not allow myself to be influenced by my university education, but rather by the tranquility of a graveyard. He suggested I go for a walk in a cemetery to become 'recharged' and enlightened.

Just when I started to feel downhearted about it all, a real challenge presented itself. I was ask my management to submit a design for a marble casket to contain a zinc coffin. This was a very prestigious assignment as the deceased person in the sealed zinc coffin was a baron by the name of Rosenkrantz. The marble casket project included a floor mounted pedestal and it would all be installed in a mausoleum at the cemetery by our company - providing I could come up with a satisfactory design. My last major project, apart from the laundry, was the clubhouse and tower in Junction City. Although there were no similarities, both involved positive thinking and dedication. I was told the baron lay in estate in Holmens church near one of the canals. I was instructed to go there to measure the zinc coffin. To eliminate any possibility of an error, I decided to use a long stick to mark off the length of the zinc coffin, rather than a tape measure. So with the stick I cycled through the streets of Copenhagen to the church.

Inside the empty church it was very still. I walked quietly up to the altar at the far end where, surrounded by wreaths and flowers, the sealed coffin with the baron inside was on display. I could sense the importance of my assignment. Kneeling at the side of the coffin, I marked off the length on the wooden stick - leaving absolute no chance for an error whatsoever. I even double-checked it to make sure.

During the next few days I put my heart into the project, making drawing after drawing. It was decided that Greenland imported marble would be used. I designed the marble casket so that the two inch thick sides and ends were held together with inside angle iron brackets and with connecting bronze bolts with three inch rosettes - in all eight of them. A beautiful rose design entwined a sword on the tapered marble lid - all to be chisled out by our expert stonecutters - experts who spent a lifetime chisling away at stones with no end in sight. The final presentation drawing was, in my opinion, worth serious consideration, as one could not go beyond perfection. After biting fingernails for twenty-four hours, I was informed that the client liked the design and we could proceed with the work. Great news! I immediately started preparing working drawings for the shop.

Cutting a large marble block into slabs is no easy task. Day after day the row of long saw blades mounted in a wooden frame went back and forth, dripping with water spray. Unlike working with wood, what one did to marble was final. The phrase 'cast in stone' was what this profession was all about. Following the two-week cutting period, came the polishing. Big machines with rotating disks that the operators could move around on the flat marble surface, went on for many days. After that there was more to come - the sizing and cutting of the elements, not to mention the delicate work of the stonecutters. After a period of about six weeks the masterpiece, weighing well over a ton, was assembled in the yard for review and approval. It was then dismantled and crated in wooden frames to be sent to the cemetery. There, within the mausoleum, the casket was assembled by four of our stonecutters. It was a great day.

Arrangements were then made by the deceased baron's relatives to have a formal burial ceremony take place at the mausoleum. The four stone cutters would be there to lower the coffin in the marble casket, and to lift the lid into place at the conclusion of the solemn occasion.

It just so happened on the day of the ceremony, after the four stone cutters left the plant for the cemetery, dressed in their Sunday best, that I suddenly realized I just might be experiencing a major crisis. The bolts with bronze rosettes had nuts on the inside of the angle iron corners, that projected inward. I had allowed one extra inch in length to make sure that the baron could fit in the casket, but discovered now, breaking out in a cold sweat as I checked the drawings, that the nuts combined, one at each end, took up two inches - leaving me short one inch! This was a disaster! In desperation I quickly made a full scale cut-out of the zinc coffin and another of the inside dimensions of the casket, and tried to lower the coffin cut-out into the casket. Sure enough, it rested on the bolts and couldn't go in! At that moment I realized that my career was over with. Again and again I checked the dimensions, but nothing changed. The baron simply could not go in. After studying the whole situation for awhile, I discovered that if one end of the coffin went in at a 30 degree angle downward, the other end would just clear the bolts. However, the baron would have to go in head first. My only hope now was that the stone cutters had brains enough to figure this out. All I could do was wait and wait.

I had visions of all the baron's relatives in the mausoleum, gathered around in a circle staring at the coffin resting on the four bolts. One couldn't expect any of them to solve the problem, and certainly not the preacher. Church preachers are not known for logical solutions. If you cannot refer to the Bible for answers, then you are lost. I know they say that prayers can move mountains, but in this case I decided to rely on the stonecutters' common sense. It was a most difficult day to get through. Time passed slowly and I was unable to do other work.

At four o'clock in the afternoon the company truck pulled into the yard and the four stonecutters got out. Through the window I looked at their faces to see if there was any sign of trouble. It was hard to see. They all went into the yard office to sign off for the shift. Moments later, they came out, got on their bicycles and went home. I was convinced there must have been a problem, but it just seemed like another day.

A week later I heard via the grapevine that the baron's wife had died. I was sure it was from shock, from seeing her husband resting on those bolts. Or maybe it was the thought of her husband going head first into the casket. It didn't take long, before a relative of the Rosenkrantz family turned up at our office, requesting that a second casket be made, similar to the first. The job was turned over to me to prepare the work order. Now was my chance to make things right. I would give her at least three inches more space. On the other hand, women tend to be shorter than their husbands so maybe her coffin would go in like a dream. The best would be if I didn't change anything, because then it wouldn't arouse suspicion. Then again, she might be taller than her husband. Or maybe fatter. I never thought of checking the width of the casket, but surely two feet was enough. What did I know? Well, all these imaginary problems and solutions were resolved in a flash when one of the stonecutters came in to talk to me.

"I hear we are going to start on a second casket," he remarked.

"That's right."

"Well, just make sure the coffin fits into the casket with room to spare. I suggest you check it at Holmens church. That's where old lady Rosenkrantz's coffin is right now. We sure had trouble with the baron. If it hadn't been for my quick thinking, they would have had to cancel the funeral."

I didn't dare ask him about details.

CHAPTER TWENTY-FOUR

The war years of total darkness, rationing, curfews, sabotage, raids, street disturbances and harassment seemed to go on forever. Particularly during the icy cold winters when there was little daylight, a feeling of hopelessness was everywhere. Fuel was hard to get. A weekly ration of briquettes was only enough to heat an apartment for one evening. Many people simply stayed in bed to keep warm. Schools conducted classes in the city electric trains, riding back and forth all day long. The trains were heated. The schools were not. When ever Danes showed a bit of ingenuity to eliminate suffering and hardship, the Germans immediately took measures to stop it. Orders were given to remove all the seats from the trains so that students would have to stand up. At one stage, after the Germans troops rounded up all the Danish police under the pretence of an air raid and sent them to concentration camps, all Copenhagen went on strike against the occupation forces. In retaliation the Germans sealed off the city and turned off all electricity and gas. After three days they found that they were themselves without these services, so things returned to 'normal.' One thing seemed to lead to another. There seemed to be no end to the tension and turmoil. The Germans then forbid assembly of more than five people in public places and also imposed a curfew from seven in the evening until six in the morning. As the inevitable day of the freedom drew nearer, so did the suspense. Although it was forbidden, the Danes listened daily to the evening radio news from BBC in London. For the underground movement the broadcasts were vital. Messages like 'Greetings to John, Grandma is sick, The canary is yellow,' etc. were coded orders for the underground movement and activities. It was during the evening news broadcast in May, 1945 that the BBC announcer, while reading the coded messages, suddenly stopped, saying 'Just a moment, please.' A pause and then, *'It has just been announced from Field Marshal Montgomery's headquarters that the German Command has agreed to the surrender of all German armed forces in Holland, in northwest Germany including all islands and in Denmark.'*

Suddenly we were free! Everyone dashed out of apartment buildings and houses on to the street, cheering and shouting. Blackout window blinds were torn down, lights were turned on, Danish and British flags appeared everywhere with complete disregarded for the curfew. Everybody headed for the main city square in Copenhagen on their bicycles and by streetcar. It was a glorious night of joy and celebration.

The liberation of Denmark brought English soldiers to all major towns in Denmark, including Kolding - hundreds of soldiers, who quickly settled in barracks that were previously occupied by the Germans. Everyone was glad to see them after so many years of hope and darkness.

My gravestone job continued without any highlights. I hardly knew what to call myself. But my father-in-law had no problem introducing me to his friends as *the architect*. If this led to the question as to what I had designed as an architect, it was said that I had done design work for the late Baron Rosenkrantz. This really made an impression. We avoided going into details. Although I had never designed a building or structure, other than the laundry , he still kept me elevated on that prestigious architectural level as far as his friends were concerned. There was no way that the Falcke family were going to have any bad apples to account for. Titles meant an awful lot.

My father-in-law, Mr. G. Falcke was a salesman in ladies hats for a Copenhagen firm. With the war now over, his sales territory was in Sweden, - a short ferry trip from Copenhagen where he spent two weeks at a time traveling by train from one town to another, working on commission. But the title of 'salesman' was definitely too demeaning for his ego. He always introduced himself as *Marketing Manager of Overseas Sales*. The only 'overseas' activity the hat company had going was his ability to sell ladies' hats in Sweden.

His return from Sweden after a sale trip was always like major earthquake as far as the family and relatives were concerned, for it was the time to celebrate his homecoming. Two weeks on the road, sleeping in hotel rooms and eating meals alone was tough going for Mr. Falcke who was a social party type. It wasn't bad for his wife, however, because she couldn't stand his nightly snoring, and with him on the road, she could relax, get many good nights of sleep and not be his servant.

The celebration of a homecoming meant that all family members and relatives had to make themselves ready for an invitation - or to use a better word, for an obligation. After slaving away in the kitchen for eight hours or more, and often with additional hired help, Mrs. Falcke managed to present a dinner for the gathering of the clan, complete with all the trimmings, wine and desserts. At the head of the long table Mr. G. Falcke, Marketing Manager of Overseas Sales would raise his glass and propose a toast to the good health of everyone, and we would do likewise with all eyes looking towards him at the end of the table out of respect and gratitude for inviting us to such a festive occasion. The only loser in the toast for good health, was his wife who was as thin as a rake.

Whenever there was an opportunity to upgrade the party, such as for a birthday or anniversary, candlelight and speeches were added and one was expected to linger around for a few hours after the meal was over, to be sociable in an atmosphere of fine liqueurs and cigar smoke.

Much to the surprise of everyone, the H.C. Andersen animated film *The Emperor's New Clothes* was finally completed after suffering financial difficulties for two years, temporary lost of interest by shareholders and near bankruptcy. It was now ready to be shown in theaters throughout the country - and maybe even the whole world. My father-in-law immediately saw another opportunity to elevate the family status by telling his friends that his son-in-law was an artist who worked on the well publicized H.C. Andersen film. Now that the family was associated with the film industry, there might even be the possibility of expanding the social circle.

The film premiere took place in Copenhagen's finest film theater called Palladium, where all performances started off with a man playing a huge diamond-studded Wurlitzer organ which came rotating up out of the floor. If nothing else, you got your money's worth with his ten minute introductory performance. We were unable to go to the premiere showing, because Mr. Falcke was in Sweden at the time, and insisted on joining us when we were to see the film. It was important to him to be publicly noticed in the presence of the artist who made the film *The Emperor's New Clothes*. Perhaps a reporter might happen to be there and take a picture of us. I tried to point out to him that I only made drawings that accounted for six seconds of the two hour long film and that these we not even key drawings, but just intermediate lines for movement that even a child could do - a very, very minor role in film animation. But no, he would not listen to that. The extended Falcke family image definitely could not be tarnished.

The evening we went to the theater, Mr. Falcke insisted we arrived at the entrance by taxi, although it would have been a simple matter to arrive by streetcar and a lot cheaper, - but no, things must be done properly. As we sat there in the theater waiting for the film to begin, I pointed out to Mr. and Mrs. Falcke what to watch for, if they wanted to catch the golden moment - the red rooster on the fence going cock-a-doodle-doo. When they saw the fence, that's when they were to sit on the edge of their seats, with their eyes glued to the screen. Actually, the film wasn't bad. A bit boring, perhaps, but the rooster would change all that. Just as we were getting close to the critical sequence, Mrs. Falcke discovered that she didn't have her glasses. She whispered that maybe they were on the floor. Mr. Falcke turned around and waved to an usher who came to our row with a flashlight. As the three of them were searching the floor area under her seat, the red rooster went cock-a-doodle-doo and it was all over.

However, Clara and I witnessed the golden moment and the brief flicker of fame and glory.

CHAPTER TWENTY-FIVE

During the following years I still found it difficult to live in Denmark. I frequently mentioned to Clara, the longing to return to the American way of life and to see Junction City again. She understood my feelings. Many people were leaving Europe after the war, emigrating to the United States and Canada. There was a trend. Also, designing and selling gravestones was becoming quite depressing. I couldn't see any future in it. After much debate, we decided to make our application. In due course, we received the reply from the U.S. Embassy that our application was accepted, but due to quota restrictions, we would have to wait at least two years before we could enter the United States. We felt that was much too long to wait, and decided to go to Canada instead where there were no restrictions on immigration.

It was a major task to burn all bridges and prepare to leave. The financing of our trip looked like a problem. But then we made the discovery that the Royal Air Force, during the war, had demolished the factory in Germany that made Ibach grand pianos - with the result that our Ibach piano became one of a kind. Consequently, we managed to sell it for a very high price, which turned out to be enough to pay for the trip to Canada. With this clever move, I had completely regained the respect of Clara's father.

The exodus out of war-ravaged Europe to North America during the years 1950 - 1951 was overwhelming. Every departing ship was full of immigrants. Air travel had not yet come about. At the time of our move to leave Denmark, only one vessel from Scandinavia still had room. It was a Liberty ship. It certainly wasn't a luxury liner, but judging from the photo I was shown at the travel agency of the sleeping accommodation, it wasn't bad. The picture was a close-up view of a bunk, nicely made with white sheets and pillow case. The blanket looked like a military blanket, but I couldn't say for sure. For the high price we had to pay, one could have expected something better. However, both Clara and I agreed that we had little choice if we wanted to leave that fall.

What the photo failed to reveal, whether it was intentional or not, was that there were 800 other bunks in the same room - three tiers high! If the photographer had just backed up a bit, he would have got them all. Having lived in darkness and isolation for five years, we did not know that a Liberty ship was a troop ship. The design of this 10,000 ton, 11 knot vessel was down to bare basics. At the peak of American wartime production they were churning out Liberty ships, one every five days. They were made of welded steel plate. All stairways, partitions walls and ceilings were steel plate, spot-welded here and there - just enough to hold everything together for about a dozen trips across the Atlantic with troops and equipment, before being torpedoed by German submarines. There wasn't a stick of wood on board, no carpets, no curtains, no dining room, no recreation area, no lounge area, no deck chairs - nothing at all to provide comfort.

When the war was over, Liberty ships were for sale - real cheap. An enterprising Italian company bought one of them, and headed north to Copenhagen to make money on the exodus of immigrants and displaced persons leaving Europe. So in the early fall of 1951 we waved goodbye to our families and little Denmark from the deck of the Liberty ship *Castlebianco*.

After our departure we went below to acquaint ourselves with the luxuries of ocean travel. Our first discovery was that men and women had separate sleeping quarters. Also women with children were kept apart. My bunk was number 782 in a huge cavernous auditorium area with eight hundred beds. It was below deck level and was accessed by a wide landing with a descending steel staircase twenty feet wide. Clara's and Ken's bunks were in a large room at the bow of the ship reserved for women with children. I was not permitted to go there. On each made-up bed was a small towel and a bar of soap. The most overpowering thing on board the *Castlebianco* was the air conditioning. It was noisy and never stopped. The constant draft it created throughout the ship assured that we constantly breathed fresh ocean air.

For the first couple of hours, as we sailed southward toward the Kiel Canal, everyone was busy arranging the luggage under the beds, hanging up clothes on the bed rails and checking the layout of the ship. The loudspeakers, which could be heard throughout the drafty ship, started bellowing out information and instructions the moment we left Copenhagen - first in English, then in Danish, then in German, followed by French, Italian, Spanish and Polish. This went on nonstop all day. The message was simple:

The towel and the bar of soap on your bed must last the whole voyage. Hot water is only available in the washroom taps between five and seven o'clock in the morning. After that it is cold salt water. Washroom showers have only cold salt water. Three meals a day will be served in the cafeteria - breakfast from seven to nine, lunch from eleven to one and dinner from five to seven. All lights will be dimmed at eleven pm.

It didn't take much imagination to picture ourselves as troops on the way to the front to do battle. As we passed through the Kiel Canal, the ship stopped to let five Finnish men on board. They obviously missed the boat in Copenhagen. We gradually became aware that there were many nationalities on board- a total of fourteen hundred immigrants, refugees and displaced persons from all over Europe. There should only have been a thousand in all, but it was the last boat to leave northern Europe that autumn and many Scandinavians wanted to get out. Lost and found items quickly became a major function in the purser's office, requiring an announcement to be made over the loudspeaker system regarding each item - and in seven different languages. If nobody turned up to claim the item, they would start all over again. It never stopped.

The only place where families could mingle was on deck, in corridors or in the cafeteria. At meal time passengers had to line up along the cafeteria counter to be served meals on tin plates. All dinners had spaghetti as the main ingredient. Everyone got an apple a day as dessert. The lineups for meals started an hour before the doors opened. The lineups for the men's washroom started at four o'clock in the morning - an hour before hot water was in the taps - and for good reason; shaving later on with cold salt water would be a torture. The washroom, serving the eight hundred bed 'auditorium' had 20 toilets 15 sinks, 4 showers and 10 urinals. A definite design mistake was apparent in the washroom. The toilet stalls were built lengthwise with the ship, resulting in that toilet doors flew open when the ship listed in heavy seas, catapulting the occupants out of the stalls and across the floor with their pants down. It was also hard to shave properly when, looking on the mirror, you saw twenty others behind you waiting impatiently for their turn. Furthermore, bars of soap were stolen from those who forgot their soap at the wash basin.

Although the facilities were the same, things were probably worse in women's washrooms, because the lineups outside their washroom door were quite long. The ship's crew, engaged in washing floors and the like, always seemed to be cleaning floors and basins in the women's section. Never did I see the crew clean anything where the men were located.

We were two days out in the Atlantic when we went headlong into a storm. No longer were we allowed on deck. Hatches were bolted down, all portholes were closed with bolted steel plate covers. Half the passengers became seasick The twenty-bed hospital filled up immediately with unfortunate passengers who became victims of the storm - with broken limbs, bruises and sprained ankles. The ship's only nurse was out of commission due to a broken arm.

For some reason or other, the ship's first officer decided this was a good time to get drunk. During the night the storm built up strength, and the roll of the ship had everyone gripping the side rails of their bunks to avoid being thrown to the floor. It was amazing how far the slow roll could go. It was easily thirty degrees. Every now and then a big wave landed on the deck above like a ton of rocks, making the whole ship shudder. The noise level of the storm was a constant roar like a passing freight train.

At the top of one of the steel stairways leading to the deck was a door with a small porthole that was not covered. Looking out the next morning I saw seamen uncovering the lifeboats. They had ropes around their waists tied to railings to avoid being washed overboard. The waves were now as high as a five-storey building - huge rolling mountains of water with white streaks of foam running all the way down into the deep valleys. The ship's propeller seemed to be out of the water now and then, because there was a marked difference in the rhythmic sound when we were on top of a watery mountain as to when we were in a deep valley. The pile of anchor chains in the bow of the ship, adjacent to the women's sleeping quarters, made an infernal noise as the heavy chains slid across the floor and crashed against the steel walls every time the ship rolled from one side to the other.

It was about ten o'clock in the morning of the second day of the storm that we heard that a Liberty boat similar to ours, went down about forty miles away. It was carrying freight. Three hours later rumors had it that a second Liberty boat was lost in the storm. This had everyone most concerned. Many who were not seasick, started assembling in the cafeteria, where various groups, hanging on to railings and tables, were conducting ad hoc prayer services. During all this time the loudspeakers were silent. There seemed to be little to say, although personally, I could think of a whole pile of things to say. Maybe the purser was seasick.

The nights were the worst. A shudder vibrated through the whole creaking ship every time a huge wave crashed on the deck above. All we could do was to hold on to the side rails of our bunks as we looked up at the ceiling and listened to the screaming wind. Sleeping was completely out of the question.

After three days of torment, the storm subsided. A feeling of relief spread throughout the ship and again everyone could concentrate on their future. As things started to settle down, I felt it just might be appropriate to register a complaint about the lack of communication and instructions during the storm - such as the location of boat stations for passengers, the whereabouts of lifebelts and who was supposed to be in charge. And while I was at it, I might as well mention all the other unsatisfactory thing about this miserable trip - such as the dinky towels, the single bar of soap that had to last fourteen days, the salt water in the taps, the drafty air conditioning, the long lineups at the cafeteria counter, the tin plates and tin mugs with tea that tasted like dishwater, the three-tier bunks, the separation of men and women in sleeping areas, the daily spaghetti for dinner, the booming loudspeakers that never stopped, (except during the storm), the lack of a recreation room, no chairs, etc., etc. There was so much to complain about.

But all of this was forgotten, when I suddenly saw land far away across the water as a thin dark blue streak in the afternoon sun. Others saw it also. As it was thirteen days since we left Scandinavia, this must be Canada. The whole ship seemed to come alive with excitement. Hundreds of passengers now stood along the deck railing looking at their destiny, some in silence, others expressing joy.

Everyone was up early the next morning as we sailed up the St. Lawrence River to our destination, Quebec City. While we were busy packing our few belongings, the loudspeaker system went into high gear telling us what to do and not what to do. We could keep the bar of soap we had received, but the towel was to be left behind on the bunk. No more meals would be served after we docked. And then over the speaker system came a long list of lost and found articles that had to be accounted for, so it was a noisy morning. We docked at ten o'clock.

All passengers with their suitcases and luggage were on deck eager to leave the ship. Down below us on the dock were customs officers and the Royal Canadian Mounted Police. They were standing in doorways of a large shed looking up at us. We looked down at them. Beyond the shed were railroad tracks and a long passenger train with a steam locomotive. The dock was at the foot of a large plateau, the cliffs forming a backdrop behind the train.

With the ship secured and the gangway in place we all expected to disembark. But nothing happened. Instead, a number of police officers boarded the ship and the gangplank was roped off. Where they went we did not know but they were searching for something. Maybe they were going to arrest the captain and crew for charging so much for such a lousy trip. The passengers sat down on their suitcases and luggage. By noon many started to get hungry and decided to hurry down to the cafeteria to get a meal, but were quickly stopped by crew members blocking doorways with outstretched arms, saying with agitated Italian emotion 'No more meals. Trip is over.'

By one o'clock it started raining ever so slightly and some of the passengers decided to go inside. Again the crew jumped into action blocking doors, reminding us that the trip was over, kaput, finished. To avoid getting wet, many stood under lifeboats and overhangs. By two o'clock in the afternoon, due to increasing frustration and anger, the ship's crew allowed passengers to use the washrooms on board.

At quarter past three, five passengers suddenly appeared on deck from somewhere, escorted by the Royal Canadian Mounted Police and were hustled down the gangway. Rumors immediately circulated that these were the men who boarded the ship in Kiel. We wondered why they had been hiding on board. Someone mentioned that they were Finnish students who flew to Kiel in a stolen airplane. We watched them being escorted away to a waiting police vehicle.

Half an hour later the rest of us, thirteen hundred and ninety-five in all, walked down the gangplank onto Canadian soil, wet and hungry. We lined up in long queues inside the shed for custom formalities. There were a number of tables with two officers at each table, checking passports and asking questions. A young man in front of us was asked where he was going. He understood nothing. So they showed him a map and he lightened up, saying 'Canada.' They asked him how much money he had. He understood nothing. So they showed him money and pointed to his pocket. He pulled out a couple of strange looking coins from Poland. One of the officers shook his head in dismay and waved him on.

We were much better prepared. First of all we were a young family and we both spoke English. Also we had forty Canadian dollars and we knew our destination.

"Where are you going?" one of the officers asked.

"To Vancouver," I replied.

"And why are you going to Vancouver?"

"To be close to Junction City."

There was a pause. The officer leaned over to the other officer and together they scanned a map on the table in search of Junction City. A bit of mumbling took place and one of the officers looked up.

"And where exactly is Junction City?"

"It's in Oregon," I replied with a feeling of patriotism.

"I'm afraid you are a bit mixed up. You are in Canada and Oregon is in the U.S.A."

"Yes, I know, but some day I want to go there and look around."

When it came to accommodation on the train, we were also well prepared, having assured ourselves sleeper reservations as well as meals for the five day trip. This could not be said for hundreds of others who had to sit upright on wooden seats and somehow supply themselves with food. After many hours delay, the long train, loaded with immigrants and all their baggage, left Quebec City at midnight for the five day trip across Canada.

The following day was like a holiday for everyone as the train passed through Ontario. It was warm and sunny. The blazing red and orange autumn color of maple trees had us all leaning out of the windows. There was so much beauty surrounding us and everything we looked at made us feel that we had indeed made a wise move in leaving dismal Europe. But gradually the maple trees were behind us, and a slight feeling of concern took over as a choice had to made where to get off and start a new life. We passed through a number of towns without stopping. It became obvious that we were being 'transported' to areas where immigrants might find work.

The train made stops at certain stations to allow passengers to buy food and beverages, but it was after we passed Winnipeg that the moment of decision had to be made one way or the other, for now the train seemed to stop at almost every station. And at every station immigrants leaned out of the open train windows to see if paradise was here, but there was always hesitation. Maybe a little farther on things would be better. We noticed farmers waiting at some stations with their horse wagons looking for able bodies to work in their fields.

Often, the Royal Canadian Mounted Police appeared at a number of stations, encouraging some to get off the train. They came on board, and going through the cars, warned us not to stretch our luck too far. It was better to work as a farm laborer on the prairies than end up with no work at all in the Rockies. But looking beyond the little wooden stations to fields of grain that went right out to the horizon, it didn't take much imagination to figure out what the winters must be like on the prairies.

The train engineer, way up front in his huffing and puffing steam engine was very cooperative, making longer stops than necessary at some stations to allow hundreds of passengers to spill out of the train and storm up the main street to the one and only grocery store in sight. Like locusts they pounced on the store, buying everything inside that resembled food. For a grocery store owner near the railroad line out on the prairies, it was like hitting the jackpot. Two blasts from the train whistle was the call to return to the train, but often it was hard to know if everyone made it in time.

A lady, with four children, pulled the emergency brake, bringing the train to a screeching halt a mile out of a town. She was quite hysterical, saying that her husband was not on board! One of the Negro porters got off and ran down the railroad track back toward the station - and from the station came the husband running towards the train, loaded down with bags of food. It is possible that others, who didn't make back to the train in time at various stations, now are employed in prairie grocery stores. We will never know.

As we approached the Rockies, it was much quieter on the train. Many had left the train in Toronto, Winnipeg and Calgary. At least seven hundred immigrants had been lulled into becoming farmers. For the two hundred still on the train there was one consolation. They would not suffer the same fate. The scenery now became majestic with green carpets of forest sweeping up mountain slopes, the sun creating shadows between jagged peaks and deep valleys, and with sparkling streams of crystal clear mountain water cascading over rocks and stones. This panorama of beauty lasted throughout the day without interruption, but in the evening sixty passengers were ordered off the train in a place called Revelstoke, and the next morning a hundred or so got off in a town called Kamloops, to be sent northward to mining and logging camps.

The rest of us, approximately thirty-five in all, arrived at the Vancouver train station in British Columbia at midnight. This was the end of the line and the end of a journey. After all the commotion, excitement and decisions for so many over the last nineteen days we were now all across Canada like a sprinkling of seeds - hopefully for new growth in this vast country. A feeling of freedom and peace, but also of emptiness seem to take over as we got off the train and stood on the platform with our baggage. Everything was so quiet.

CHAPTER TWENTY-SIX

In the beginning we found a single room upstairs in a two storey wooden rooming house. There was a hotplate on the dresser, a small table and the bed. Down the narrow hall was the toilet and a sink in a little room shared by other tenants - seventeen in all. Being so many, the toilet seat was never cold. The rent for our accommodation was ten dollars a month. With a roof over our heads, the next step was to find a job.

After walking the pavement in vain for six weeks, telling people how clever I was and why they should hire me - being university trained and all, I finally got a job pounding eight inch spikes into a plank deck with a sledgehammer on a road gang for the Canadian Pacific Railway.

As time wore on, I decided that swinging a sledge hammer in Canada wasn't really my goal, so I switched to making pen drawings of peoples' homes on Christmas cards. This worked very well - at least up until Christmas. Then I got a job playing piano with a sax player and a drummer six nights a week at a night club called the Smilin' Buddha, a third rate place where the customers were served pigeon dinners, although the menu said 'chicken.' After a few drinks they didn't know the difference. For the club owner and his Chinese workers in the kitchen they had a good thing going.

THE RETURN

A block away at a place called Pigeon Square, drunks and derelicts got money for their booze by grabbing pigeons, hiding them under their coats, going down the dark alley to the kitchen door of the Smilin' Buddha and then selling them for twenty-five cents each to the waiting staff. During our music break we usually stood in the kitchen area and watched the action. None of us ever saw a real chicken.

Although the owner did not have a liquor license, there was no shortage of drinks. The vice squad at the police department knew this very well and conducted raids on the place about twice a week. However, they always phoned in advance, giving the owner ample time to tell the guests to remove liquor bottles from the tables and place them out of sight until the raid was over. With much fanfare and flashing lights on their police vehicles, the cops, usually about four of them, stormed into the place, found nothing, and then at the invitation of the owner, sat down to a lavish 'chicken' dinner with all the trimmings - including girls who somehow just seemed to appear at the right time to join them. The bottles returned to the tables after the vice squad left. On the way out they hinted that they might be compelled to conduct another raid in a few days - and the owner, shaking hands, said that was quite alright.

Throughout the evening we provided what we thought was good music for listening pleasure, but there was a customer who came up to the bandstand and said to the sax player,

"You guys play lousy music and the chicken dinners here don't taste like chicken."

It didn't bother the sax player.

"Your problem is that you're not reading the menu properly. It says 'Smilin' Buddha Chicken Dinner.' It's oriental. Chinese chickens with slanted eyes taste different. As far as our music goes, one lousy thing deserves another."

Turning to us, he said,

"If they called this dump 'Pigeon Palace' and let us have a bass player, there wouldn't be any problems."

We told the owner how important a bass player was in a band to provide better sound and more depth, but he said the sound was okay as it was now and he couldn't afford any more. We were already being paid forty dollars each per week and that was a lot of money. However, the job did have one benefit. It was at night, allowing me to use the daytime hours to find something better.

After many months of searching, I finally landed a job as an architectural draftsman in a large company, and my worries were over. All the frustration and struggles I had with schooling and education over the many years finally paid off. I considered it more luck than anything else. I certainly was not a shining example of anything in particular.

My interest now turned toward the possibility of seeing Junction City again. We worked hard, saved all we could, had another child, David, and bought a Volkswagen Beetle. Five years later we were ready for the glorious return visit to paradise. Clara almost felt she knew the place by heart, having heard so much about paradise for the last ten years. Ken and David were also prepared to be enlightened as we headed south in our Volkswagen, loaded down with camping gear. It was going to be a great moment. Every street and every detail was as clear as a bell in my mind. I knew exactly what to expect.

We camped overnight, a bit north of Portland, so that our arrival time in Junction City would be in the morning. It was important to me that we see it all in daylight. Traveling down Highway 99, I said that very soon now we would be coming to Harrisburg. I told them how we used to rollerskate all the way from Junction to Harrisburg on the concrete highway. One year, the Willamette River overflowed its banks and part of the roadway became flooded, including Junction City itself east of the Southern Pacific tracks. My family agreed with me that the Willamette valley was a very beautiful place. The sun was shining and both the Cascades and the Coast Range mountains were quite visible beyond the fields to the left and to the right.

I became slightly disorientated as we approached Harrisburg. It took me a moment to figure things out. Maybe it was because I had never approached Harrisburg from the north. I recognized the red brick building on the main street, which was Highway 99, but other things looked different. I stopped the car, but we didn't bother to get out. Paradise was a mere ten minutes away and Harold Bruce might still be waiting. I had written to his address as I used to know it, which was *Harold Bruce, Junction City, Oregon* but the letter had been returned, stamped *Address unknown*. Shortly after Harrisburg, Highway 99 West merged into our highway. I remembered clearly that roadway being under construction while I lived in Junction.

Suddenly at this point we seemed to have entered the town. It was a strange feeling. Something was not right. All the residential houses were gone. What I saw was all commercial - businesses that now appeared on both sides of the highway - looking like intruders. I drove very slowly, carefully trying to match the old picture in my mind with the new picture before me. There were no clues, except the concrete highway itself. We passed Tenth Avenue where there now was a Dairy Queen and then on to Ninth and Eighth in silence.

We came to Seventh Avenue. I had returned - just like I had promised Harold.

"Is this it, Dad?" Ken asked.

"Yes, this is it." I replied, feeling totally confused.

The parsonage was gone! The church was gone! The meeting house next to the parsonage was gone! The woodshed, the grape arbor, the garden with all the fruit trees were gone! Someone did all this while I was away. It was almost sacrilegious. I looked in silence at the commercial buildings that had trespassed onto the church and parsonage properties. Closing my eyes, I could see in my mind the tranquil image of yesterday - the way it was meant to be.

"Hey, Dad, let's have an ice cream cone."

I blinked, the image disappeared and the call to commercialism brought me back to the real world. I drove the car into a gravel parking lot on the parsonage property and we got out and ordered cones. Sitting on our car bumper, I explained to Clara, Ken and David how things were long ago.

"Right here," I said, "where we are sitting, was the grape arbor. This is the very spot."

They looked at the parking lot gravel. To them it was just gravel. To me the spot was so sacred, that I almost felt that a monument should be erected, commemorating this location as being the place where a boy looked up at the stars, listened to trains and had so many dreams.

"And over here," I said, pointing to another spot in the gravel, " is where the back screen door to the house was."

I remembered the sound of the screen door when it closed. It didn't go 'click.' No, it went 'ca-lick,' and we six children were in and out of that door a hundred times a day.

"And here, this is where our clubhouse was."

Another good spot for a monument, but it would have interfered with access to the parking lot. Strange to think that a wooden tower was once erected here.

Rather quickly, I adjusted to the changes around me, but reluctantly accepted the new images. Some things were still intact. Doctor Roger's house down the street was exactly the way it was when we left and Miller's funeral parlor across the street was still there, but it was now called Murphy's. The large, white Methodist church next to it was gone.

We walked down the street to Junction City Grade School - the place of so many memories. I never thought I would feel sentimental about a school, but it was one thing to be on the inside looking out - and another thing, to be on the outside looking in. Somehow it seemed a little smaller now, and it lacked the new, fresh appearance of the thirties. I showed them the school yard where the flag was raised every morning, and where we had football games. And then there were the back steps, where school kids were assigned turns after school, to clean blackboard erasers. Clouds of chalk dust would fill the air, when two erasers were banged together. Nobody worried about whether chalk dust was good to breathe or not. The wooden play shed on the west side was still there. It was always full of kids on rainy days.

Unfortunately, the school was locked up for the summer, but looking through the windows, I saw my old classroom - where Opal Burgess used to be. It seemed so empty. We went around to the other side and peered through the windows of Old Lady Ballard's classroom. The desks looked different, but at the front of the room I recognized, above the blackboard, the framed picture of George Washington with his white hair. I remembered when Old Lady Ballard was at the blackboard, her white hair was identical to his.

Looking at these silent, empty rooms behind the glass, it was hard to imagine that I really had been in there. It now seemed like only yesterday. I remembered the order and discipline that prevailed throughout the school term, and those nasty report cards, that not only recorded doom and gloom, but also habits and attitudes desirable for 'good citizenship.' There were spaces on the report cards to be ticked off by the teacher - a label we would have to bear until the next report card period. It could be anyone of the following things in the doom and gloom section - if one was unfortunate: *Indolent, Wastes time, Work is carelessly done, Seldom does well, Gives up too easily, Inattentive, Inclined to mischief, Whispers too much, Appears not to try, Annoys others, Comes poorly prepared, Restless, and Promotion in danger.* It was no wonder that we all hated school at the time. However, there was hope if one got good tick marks in the citizen section of the report card. This required virtues such as: *Obedience and willingness to follow directions, Respect for law and order, Honesty and the keeping of promises, Loyalty and self control, Courtesy to associates and to teachers, Respect for the rights of others, Fair play and cheerfulness. Cleanliness of person, of clothes, of behavior and speech, Respect for property, school books, furniture and building, and the Recognition of the value of time.*

These report cards, issued for Lane County, Oregon, were intended in part to *indicate the progress made by the pupil in the formation of the essential traits of character and attitudes of mind that make for good citizenship. Upon these depend the future of democracy and the stability of government. In this training we recognize that the school shares responsibility with the home.*

This was a tall order for someone who would rather play hookey. As I looked at all the empty school desks, I wondered how many of my classmates had achieved such perfection.

We went back to the car and drove down to Washburne Street to see Harold Bruce. Something was wrong here. I completely lost my bearings. The house was gone, the trees were gone, and the outhouse in the back was gone. Even the street name had been changed - from Washburne to Nyssa. Everything had disappeared, including Harold. I couldn't even figure out the exact location anymore, because new houses had replaced the old. Across the street there used to be fields, with the woods beyond where we used to play. It was all gone and in its place was now a subdivision. It took a few minutes to realize that with the passing of time, paradise had evaporated - everything, including the tree on Washburne where Doctor Roger shot the skunk.

From there we drove out to Benton Lane Park outside of town. I told Clara and the kids how Harold and I used to walk out there and swim in the outdoor pool, which was the only one in the whole Lane County as far as we knew. We paid five cents for one hour and twenty-five cents for a whole day. All we could afford was the one hour, but Benton Lane was a nice place to go to and very popular in the summer. It was still there on the old Highway 99 - the concrete swimming pool, the adjacent building with the ticket office and the changing rooms, the picnic tables and the little carousel. But the pool was empty and full of cracks, the building in ruins, and the rest of the park was disappointing.

Back in town, I noticed that Main Street was now called Sixth Avenue. It was a surprise to see that Highway 99, going south, no longer turned down Main Street. It now went straight through. In the thirties, cars also went straight through - especially at night, but in those days they ended up in a field. Once in awhile, a driver would realize his mistake in the last few seconds and attempt to make the turn on to Main, but usually ended up on the front porch of the house on the corner. Although the house was well back from the road, the owner had a visitor at least once a week. He decided to put a stop to this once and for all, and erected a large concrete block in his front yard. Sure enough, it stopped the cars. It also sent people to hospital in Eugene.

Main Street looked different. I only recognized some of the buildings. This town was losing its identity and obviously no one seemed concerned about it, except me. We crossed the tracks at Front Street. The train station was still there, thank goodness. I told the kids how they used to place two detonation caps on the track rails just outside of town when they wanted the train to slow down and pick up the mail. The mailbag would be hanging from an arm at the station right at the track and another projecting arm in the door opening of the train's mailcar would grab it as the train passed by. The sound of exploding detonation caps, triggered by the train wheels, could be heard all over town. We always knew when there was mail to go.

We walked around at the little station, which now appeared quite old, shabby and no longer in use. I stood on the train platform and looked down the tracks. I had now come full circle. I tried to remember that late afternoon in the autumn of 1933, when the eight of us stood here with our suitcases, waiting for the Southern Pacific - and with all our friends, who were here to say goodbye.

That kid, Francis, who practised the trumpet, didn't play very well, but the tune he played would have been an appropriate anthem for dear Junction City; *Tell me the tales that to me were so dear - long, long ago, long, long ago.*

Out on Dane Lane we stopped at one of the farms, and sure enough, a family by the name of Rasmussen, recognized me and welcomed us all. They said that there were many who remembered my family and they could arrange that we meet with some of them. They told about the many things that had happened in Junction City since we left. Harold Bruce was no longer in town. Some of my boyhood friends were killed in the war. Others had moved away. There wasn't much for young people to do in this area, except farming. The older people were still around - those who knew my parents. The church was not demolished, but had been moved to another street. It had been renovated with new panelling, central heating and carpets. The little library and the Rialto show house were gone. Mrs. Ballard had passed away, but Opal Burgess was still around. This was news! I must see her. They told me she lived in a house farther down the road near the bean fields and the river. She didn't teach anymore.

Dane Lane had not changed very much. It was as I had remembered it, except that some of the farm buildings looked like they needed support. Also, the trees along Dane Lane seemed to be larger and provided more shade. Other than that, everything looked much the way it was - the hay barns, the cherry orchards, the cornfields, the apple trees, the fields of wheat and the mailboxes by the roadside. I remembered the beautiful garden the Skovbo family had, Hansen's barn with the mountains of hay inside and the Gripskov farm where we watched chicks coming out of egg shells.

As we drove on the country road towards the river to see Opal Burgess,

I told Clara, Ken and David how she would throw a piece of chalk at a pupil if one failed to pay attention, how she stressed obedience, how I feared her verdict on my report card - and yet, how good I felt to be in her class, even though I hated school. We turned right on to a road, that went past the famous bean fields - the place of yesterday's sweat and toil, but now, part of paradise.

A modest, two storey wooden house with a traditional covered front porch and railing came into view down the road. A few chickens were pecking away in the front yard. I checked the house number as I slowly drove by. This was it.

I parked the car at the roadside and asked Clara and the kids if they wanted to come with me, but they said they might as well wait in the car, since they didn't know her anyway, but if I was invited in, they would join me. I said I would only be there a few minutes. I just wanted to say hello. The chickens scattered as I went up the dirt walkway to the front porch. The place looked very old and rundown. I knocked on the screen door.

After a few moments, a little old lady with a cane came to the door. My first thought was that it was probably Opal's mother or that I had the wrong address. She looked at me through the screen.

"Excuse me," I said, "my name is Visti. I'm looking for Opal Burgess."

"I'm Opal Burgess."

I looked at her in disbelief. This couldn't be. She looked so old. I quickly tried to recover from another shattered dream.

"Well, I am Visti."

She pushed open the screen door, which I then held open for her.

"I remember that name. I once had a pupil by the name of Visti."

She spoke slowly in a quiet, tired voice - nothing like the way it used to be.

"That's me. I'm Visti," I said again.

"Oh .... are you Visti?" She looked at my face.

"Yes, I used to be in your class - in the seventh grade, - remember?"

She stood there silently for a moment, staring at the porch and then went back in the house. I saw her take a small box from the mantelpiece above the stone fireplace in the living room. She brought the box to the door and opened it. Taking out a folded piece of paper, she gave it to me, saying,

"Then this is yours."

I open it and saw that it was a pencil drawing - my drawing! It was the Santa Maria, Columbus's sailing ship.

We were both silent and she looked out across the fields. So many years had passed. We both had the same memories of long ago.

"Thanks, - but I would like you to keep it."

I folded the drawing and put it back in her hand.